Versailles

Versailles

ABSOLUTISM AND HARMONY

Preface by
Jean-Pierre Babelon

Text by
Claire Constans

Photographs by
Jean Mounicq

IMPRIMERIE NATIONALE
Éditions

The Vendome Press

The Fountain
of Neptune.

Contents

VERSAILLES:
A REACH FOR THE ABSOLUTE

"Pass by and tarry a while above Latona." Thus begins the first edition of the *Guide to the Gardens of Versailles,* written by Louis XIV himself in 1689. The authorship alone suggests how important the Grand Monarch thought it was to lead his guests through the royal parterres and groves, drawing attention to the great vistas and signaling which waterworks to activate along the way, just in time so as not to waste even one precious drop. Viewed from the top of the steps, the vast, regimented world below stretches out before us, always, at every point, completely obedient to the desires of the royal set designer. In the depths of this theatrical setting, rows of tall poplars surge up like decorative flats to frame the central allée and conduct the eye along its axis towards the Versailles plain, the "Val de Gally," which spreads gently between the distant hills. On the 25th of August, the Feast of Saint Louis, this is the heavenly gateway through which the sun sets and disappears from view.

The Grand Canal slices through the greensward like a steel blade, its tip aimed at the distant horizon. The ingenious plan drawn up by André Le Nôtre, especially the expansive width of the terminal basin, makes the perspective seem even longer than the generous mile it actually is. To create such dazzling effects, Le Nôtre had exploited every lesson available from geometry and planimetry. Moreover, he did it on terrain characterized by the Duc de Saint-Simon as "the saddest, most ungrateful place on earth, devoid of life, wood, water, or even earth since all is quicksand and marshes." The result is a living witness to Louis XIV's determination to meet the challenge of nature head on, despite universal opposition to the idea of living at Versailles.

The great mirror, blue as the Île-de-France sky it reflects, races into the distance, accompanied by curtain-like rows of meticulously trimmed lime trees, immobile sentinels yet fully alert. Their intersection at the crossing of the canal allows the curtains to part and thus reveal the departure of the waterway's two lateral arms. These lead to paradises well out of view but formerly known to princes and princesses who, day or night, joyously sought them out by boat. To the right or north lies the Grand Trianon, a palace of marble and flowers; to the left or south, the Menagerie, where once stood a pleasure pavilion surrounded by cages filled with wild, exotic animals. Of this, nothing remains except a few fragments.

At either end, the Grand Canal expands into a large oblong basin, shaped like the hilt of a sword. The transverse avenue pierced through the bosky masses, punctuated by star-shaped clearings, is called the *Allée des Matelots*—"Mariners' Way"—because it was here, in "Little Venice," that the sailors in service to the King lived and kept their gondolas, all gifts from the Venetian Doge. The cut in the forest allows a great shaft of light to illuminate the basin from the side. This part of the wooded estate belongs to the "little park," as opposed to the immense hunting domain (16,340 acres) that formed the "great park," ringed about by 26 miles of protective walls, its 25 gates leading north to Marly and Saint-Germain-en-Laye and east to Chaville and Meudon.

Since there was no want of exterior space at Versailles, the King and his court could relax and be supremely at their ease. In addition to the sheer diversity of the area, with its groves, copses, thickets, moors, undergrowths, and ponds, Versailles offered a great abundance of game, feathered or furred, everything from deer to wolves and wild boar. Women as well as men who lived for riding could revel in this world, which provided escape from the constraints of court etiquette. Here they might satisfy their appetite for fast-moving, physical exercise and the pleasures of spectator sport. The Versailles park has now been reduced to some 1,500 acres, today available throughout to random strollers, who are often surprised to come across rustic countryside near the Bailly or Maintenon gates or to discover the Gailly farm whose land has been under cultivation for over 700 years.

At the head of the Grand Canal begin the gardens of Versailles, a realm of formally designed greenery, flowers, fountains, and statues. The first significant feature, at the bottom of and astride the main allée or avenue, is a large oval fountain—a basin—at the center of which reigns Apollo, the Sun God. His chariot appears to surge up from the waters and depart on his race to light the world, from daybreak to sundown. The sculptural group, by Jean-Baptiste Tuby, was installed in 1670, after Louis XIV chose the solar theme for the main east-west vista. By this time the young monarch, in all his glory, had succeeded in winning over the heart of his subjects. In the aftermath of the civil wars of religion, the rebellious Fronde, and the foreign conflicts, which had ended by making Spain all-powerful, seventeenth-century France needed to recover its pride and self-assurance. The process had commenced, thanks to the Treaties of Westphalia and the Pyrenees, which had left the kingdom both enlarged and consolidated, thereby guaranteeing that it would play a crucial role in the new European balance of power.

To meet this challenge, Louis had everything he needed: youth and beauty, intelligence and determination, physical grace and the romantic tendencies so beloved by the French people. He would soon cover himself in glory by emerging victorious from the War of Devolution, which ended in 1668 with the Treaty of Aix-la-Chapelle, and the war against Holland, settled by the Treaty of Nijmegen in 1678. To celebrate these triumphs, the King staged a series of brilliant festivities in the Versailles gardens, all thematically inspired by Classical mythology and the legends of medieval chivalry. Louis, the modern hero, appeared in all his splendor, even performing as an actor/dancer attired in gold. The public did not hold back; indeed, it gave him an ovation as he sat on his podium, the god of the arena.

At Versailles, the great Royal Allée, leading from the Fountain of Apollo, would also be known as the Green Carpet *(Tapis Vert)*, once it had been widened to 150 feet in 1680, becoming a broad stretch of lawn extending down the middle of the long perspective. As a result, the sun chariot became the nexus of the Four Elements—Water behind, Earth below, Air above, and, at the center, Fire, Apollo himself, who illuminates, heats, and purifies. On the sides, beneath the chestnuts—trees that would have to be replaced every hundred years—Louis XIV, like a Roman Cardinal, installed his collection of Classical sculpture, composed of both originals and copies made in Rome by gifted young artists at the French Academy, recently established by royal command.

The Royal Allée begins its ascent to the Château at a broad esplanade embellished with floral parterres or terraces, flanked by bosky masses enclosing small glades, veritable chambers of greenery lending themselves to the most astonishing effects. The gentle slope down to the Fountain of Apollo, the lowest point along the Royal Allée, also launches the ascent of the hill, whose rise Le Nôtre modulated with infinite subtlety. A series of harmoniously arranged ramps, lined with statues and urns, facilitates the passage from one level to another, culminating at the monumental Fountain of Latona at the top of the Royal Allée. Latona figured in an episode from the childhood of Apollo, as told by the Latin poet

The garden façade overlooking the North Parterre. Above the North Wing (right) looms the high roof of the Chapel, the only structure Louis XIV allowed to violate the Château's dominant horizontality.

Ovid. To dramatize the verticality of the sculptural group, by Balthazar and Gaspard Marsy, the royal architect, Jules Hardouin-Mansart, altered Le Nôtre's garden plan, placing the gilt-bronze Latona and her children, Apollo and Diana, on a tiered pedestal, above figures cast in lead representing Lycian peasants transformed into lizards and frogs for having mocked the mother of the two gods.

Throngs of visitors move up and down the Latona ramps, which lead to a brief but broad flight of stone steps, beyond which looms the colossal Château, its 2,250-foot façade pierced by no less than 414 windows. The magisterial simplicity of the large, rectangular pools on the Water Parterre conform to Le Nôtre's plan of 1684. Originally for this site, there was to have been a row of tall statues carved from white marble, but, in the end, preference went to a group of bronze figures personifying the rivers and streams of France, all ranged about the edges of the sheet-like water. The horizontality of the design clears the way for the Château to come fully into view, an experience available only here and from the far end of the Grand Canal. No more than the upper part of the façade can be seen from the Green Carpet or the Latona ramps.

Louis XIV therefore chose to ignore Jean-Baptiste Colbert, his great finance minister, who had deplored the relatively modest height of the garden façade, at least by comparison with the Louvre and its tall pavilions in Paris. At Versailles the King insisted that the Château extend laterally, with its architectural volumes repeated, along a horizontal line, north and south. In such a scheme, only the "basement" or ground floor and the first floor *(étage noble)* matter, and they alone are linked to the parterres, which serve as a platform for the whole. The attic windows light nothing more than inaccessible vaults above the royal apartments and the Hall of Mirrors.

Louis and his Queen made their home at the very center of the great pile, which, on the garden side, was wrapped in blond stone by Le Vau, who thereby concealed the original château built by Louis XIII. In 1678 Hardouin-Mansart added the seventeen bays making up the Hall of Mirrors, their roofs, flat in the Italian manner, hidden behind balustrades. Saint-Simon, critical as usual, had trouble adjusting to this new architecture, so foreign to French traditions, despite the terraces at Saint-Germain-en-Laye: "It's like looking at a place that has caught fire, with the top floor and roofs still missing." Long, uniform wings extend on either side, their symmetry an illusion given that the south wing rises from a terraced garden, as does the central building, whereas the north wing rests on a full-storey sub-basement to compensate for the sloping terrain. The huge palace overlooking the park once housed the royal family and everyone else who, by reason of blood or function, held a place at court. Versailles thus became a gilded cage for the elite of the realm.

The sole departure from absolute horizontality is the royal Chapel, with its tall Gothic gable, steep, lead-plate roof, and once-gilded ornaments, all of which point heavenwards. The house of God, built by the Most Christian King at the pious end of his long reign, stands on a site formerly graced by the Grotto of Thetis, a solar temple that completed the cycle of Apollo. Created by the great sculptor François Girardon and his pupils, the grotto portrayed the Sun God and his horses at the end of their daily race, receiving ministrations from nymphs and tritons. A sign of the times, the Chapel suggests that the aging monarch had abandoned the mythological conceits of his youth and turned to the one God who could grant him true repose.

The north-south axis crosses the east-west axis precisely at the center of the terrace towards which the Château's garden façade is oriented. At the edge of the North Parterre begins the gentle slope down the hill, the path lined with white statuary commissioned in 1674 to present, for purposes of meditation, an encyclopedic vision of all creation. The program includes the Four Elements,

Four Seasons, Four Times of Day, and Four Continents as well as Four Poems and Four Moods. Today, the marble figures are aligned against a background of hedges in a harmonic mélange of themes. They were part of what was known as the "Great Commission."

Water is dominant on the north side, where the first splendid hydraulic effects were created with supplies from Lake Clagny, stored in reservoirs, now recalled in a street in the town, and delivered by pumps. The immense Neptune Fountain, completed only in the reign of Louis XV, the Dragon Fountain with its hideous monster from which Apollo delivered the earth, the Water Allée embellished with a joyous band of bronze children, the Nymphs' Bath, the Pyramid Fountain, the Fountain of the Crowns, and finally, at the top, the now destroyed Grotto of Thetis traced out an ascent that assumed the character of an initiation rite. The informing idea no doubt came from the *Dream of Poliphilus,* an allegorical novel of 1499 by the Dominican monk Francesco Colonna, which had already inspired many a garden in Italy. The story concerns a young hero who, emerging little by little from the aqueous world, overcomes the trials imposed by the forces of evil and gains knowledge thanks to the love of Polia—that is, Minerva, goddess of wisdom.

On the south side, by contrast, tranquillity reigns, along with peace and the pleasures of the senses. Below the sun-bathed Queen's State Apartment, a parterre elaborated into a *broderie,* or embroidery, of flowers extends the Water Parterre until abruptly arrested by a balustrade. Forty-five feet below lies the Orangery, its esplanade studded with orange, palm, and pomegranate trees. From the vantage point of the balustrade, the sudden shift in level makes the landscape beyond the old Normandy road appear all the more grand, embracing as it does the huge Pool of the Swiss Guards, almost a small sea, ringed about by trees masking the Satory plateau, and, next to it, the *Potager du Roi* (Royal Kitchen Garden), which produced fruits and vegetables worthy of being placed on the King's table.

Any one of the passages through the Château leads us to quite a different world, the realm of urban activity. On the east side, the palace, with its longitudinal wings, faces the Place d'Armes and the two *Écuries* or Stables. Here the environment is mineral rather than vegetal, with stone dominating not only on every side but underfoot as well, in the hard and sonorous presence of cobblestone paving. The sequential courtyards, with their telescopic plan, irresistibly draw every eye from the outer gateway towards the holy of holies, the King's balcony and bedchamber in the extreme depth and center of the Marble Courtyard. Here people once thronged, swarming like bees in a hive, all eager to make honey from the much-vaunted marvels of the Sun King's palace.

The cheerful, polychrome masonry chosen by Louis XIII for his small château, or hunting lodge, was retained by Louis XIV, who would have his architects continue it throughout the new façades erected on the east side of the château. Also preserved were the tall curb or pitch roofs invented for the Louvre by Pierre Lescot, even though they were long out of fashion. And this was true whether the buildings were meant to house the King's interior apartments or the lodgings and offices of the royal ministers summoned to work permanently at Versailles, beginning in 1682. The only exception to the "brick and stone" unity was made by Louis XIV himself, who decreed that the Royal Chapel should be built entirely of pale stone. The insolent Voltaire called the results a *colifichet,* meaning a bauble. Be that as it may, Louis XV found himself urged by enlightened minds of the eighteenth century to have the whole ensemble of courtyards rebuilt in stone.

The scale and material of the Gabriel Wing on the north and the counterbalancing Dufour pavilion added on the south in 1814 undermined the earlier chromatic harmony, which reminds one of the phrase Saint-Simon used to characterize Louis XIV's taste: "The good and the ugly, like the majestic and the mean, were all bound together." Other violations of the royal residence's harmonious unity are the pedimental inscription—"To All the Glories of France"—and the equestrian statue of Louis XIV, both of which belong to another world, the world of citizen tourists, those successors to the old courtiers. They deliver a pedagogical message from Louis-Philippe, the Orléans Prince and "Citizen King" who, in the 1830s, had the Bourbons' Château transformed into a museum of French history and national reconciliation.

Facing the Château from the east is the town, laid out, at the sovereign's command, along the lines of a wooded half-star. Into the Place d'Armes, a square as large as the Place de la Concorde in Paris, converge three tree-lined avenues: Saint-Cloud, Paris, and Sceaux. The one at the center, twice as wide as the Champs-Élysées, races away along a straight line for over a mile. The town, which was new and built to serve the royal court, participated fully in the architectural unity established by the Château, thanks to strict rules governing the height of structures and the materials used to erect them. Even today, palace and town are closely linked, not merely because of the former's overwhelming presence but also because the local citizenry frequently visit the royal precinct, especially the gardens, and take part in the cultural events staged there, most particularly the musical ones. The heart of the town is still host to the Château's old service buildings, among them the Stables, the Water Tower *(Château d'Eau)*, technical facilities designed to operate the fountains, and the *Grand Commun* or Large Outbuilding, soon to house the museum offices. Also alive and well is the Hôtel des Menus-Plaisirs (the all-important agency once responsible for organizing royal ceremonies and entertainments), now given over to the Center for Baroque Music.

Versailles is all this, and it has all been preserved—the open spaces, vistas, gardens, buildings, walls, and paneling. Not so the furnishings, which were sold off in 1794, an action that leaves the museum's curators with the never-ending task of scouring the world for dispersed pieces of what had became a gigantic jigsaw puzzle. Everything else survives, ready to take part in the miracle of rediscovering times past. After a long and complex history, the administration of the Château—or châteaux, given the reality of the Grand Trianon and the Petit Trianon, together with the bucolic structures making up Marie-Antoinette's Hamlet—and the former royal domain was consolidated under the aegis of the so-called Public Board, established in 1995 to assure the ongoing process of restoration and preservation.

The patrimony of Versailles can thus be maintained in all its unity, which in turn will guarantee the spirit of the place and its survival. It is a spirit that springs from a desire for beauty on the grandest possible scale. Even the most severe critics never denied the success of Versailles at satisfying such a need, a success that so impressed contemporaries and made the Bourbons' Château a model for every reigning prince in Europe. If they could not match it, they might at least build bigger, as Ludwig II of Bavaria did in his Hall of Mirrors at Heerenchiemsee, which actually measures six feet longer than the Sun King's original.

As André Chastel wrote in his introduction to *The History of French Art,* "Versailles is both a powerful political message and a treasure-trove of formal inventions, rendered almost inexhaustible by their very accumulation." The role played by the best of the innovators taking part in the collective project—architects, gardeners, painters, sculptors, tapestry weavers, bronze casters, cabinetmakers—was informed by a common message of unity and grandeur, a message formulated by the King alone. Originally, artists were asked to follow the example of the Renaissance princes of Italy and France, such as François I, and scan the *Iconology* of Cesare Ripa, Ovid's *Metamorphosis,* and the historians of ancient Rome for a vocabulary capable of celebrating the glory and actions of the monarch, always in the metaphorical language of mythology, allegory, or history. The language was fully available, at least from all those contemporaries who had studied the humanities under the Jesuits.

By the end of the 1670s the tone had changed. Dropping the mask that had both concealed and signified him, Louis XIV began to figure personally in representations of his glory, as in the painting on the great barrel vault over the Hall of Mirrors, where Charles Le Brun portrayed the bewigged monarch in full command, not only of his victorious armies, against the forces of Holland, but also of the French state and its destiny.

The Moderns now prevailed over the Ancients. In 1684 Louis moved his bedchamber from the Planetary Suite, besieged by courtiers, to the Marble Courtyard, where he occupied a space reserved exclusively for himself. Finally, in 1701, the King took up residence in the central room, at the very heart of the Château, which drew its life entirely from him. Louis appeared before his subjects in each of his daily occupations, and when not present, he could be seen everywhere in numerous portraits hung throughout the palace. Meanwhile, an undisguised political argument erupted for the first time in the gardens, over a sculptural group known as *France Triumphant,* which was to be installed in the new Arc de Triomphe grove.

To the end of his days, Louis XIV remained faithful to the grandeur of Versailles, a grandeur now almost unconsciously taken to be a permanent reality whenever we wander through the enfilade of apartments or the Hall of Mirrors, follow the paths criss-crossing the park, or lean on the balustrades at the Grand Trianon to admire the vista along the Grand Canal. The grandeur, however, fell heavily on Louis XV and Louis XVI, who found themselves condemned to live in a world too big for them—and too much an object of ridicule for their own time, the "Age of Enlightenment." By then, the genius of Louis XIV seemed utterly foreign. Yet both of the Grand Monarch's successors on the throne of France respected this grandiose and now inconvenient place, even as they created retreats more to their own taste. Further, Louis XV himself could not resist the lure of the grand when it came to building the great Royal Opéra, designed on a scale befitting the Versailles of Louis XIV. In the park, too, he commissioned the Petit Trianon and its botanical garden. Louis XVI took care to preserve the overall disposition of Louis XIV's gardens when it became necessary to replant the park. In the meantime, he also allowed Marie-Antoinette to indulge herself in current fashion and build a stage-set village or hamlet near the Petit Trianon, an expensive quest for simplicity at the heart of grandeur that became the final episode in the royal tale of Versailles.

Space and time. Versailles remains intact, its monuments and gardens wide open to visitors from the entire world, who come to assure themselves that the mythical name, with its universal renown, still has some basis in reality. But what reality? The pleasure of identifying with historical figures, such as Louis XIV or Marie-Antoinette, has a lot to do with the success of Versailles. It also explains the fascination with the private apartments and even the most obscure rooms. Yet, the Versailles passed on to us is a more eternal place than nostalgic curiosity would suggest. This immense creation of French kings—this masterpiece of art and science—constitutes a universe ready to be discovered as well as admired by each new generation, in all seasons and in every kind of weather. No visit to Versailles is like any other, because the treasure is inexhaustible, and its creators' dialogue with infinity and eternity continues unabated, right over our heads.

Jean-Pierre Babelon

Member of the Institut de France
Honorary Director-General of the Museum and National Domain of Versailles

VERSAILLES: A GRANDIOSE WORK OF ART

The garden façade, completed in 1678-1680.

Fragile yet alive. The Château de Versailles was very much alive because the history unfolding there made the decorative excess seem irrelevant, much to the satisfaction of people preoccupied with the rational function of a building where alterations and worksites were the bane of the inhabitants. The palace was fragile because everything depended upon the royal will to reconcile the irreconcilable—to control the seasons in the kitchen garden, the wild animals in the Menagerie, or even memory and knowledge through the statuary chosen for the park. Versailles was both the seat of power and a family home, a showcase for the monarchy and a warren of private retreats, the scene of dazzling, perfectly orchestrated celebrations and frequent recourse to makeshift solutions.

What would Versailles have been without the flotilla on the Grand Canal, a miniature version of the navy so brilliantly commanded by Duquesne or Suffren? Without a *cabinet* or office where the King would spend at least ten hours every day? Or all the refurbishments, which continued for a century, revealing each monarch's determination to ignore both his architects and the ever-present curious? As for that etiquette, what ridicule it would have brought the King who made an error. Yet, etiquette was one of the iron-clad rules governing life at court. Louis XV, in the event of infractions, tended to remark that it was of little matter, but not Louis XIV, who, furious, would have taken revenge, and then some, as the Chevalier d'Arvieux tells us.

THE KING AND THE MAMAMOUCHI

On 5 December 1669 at Saint-Germain-en-Laye, the court in all its finery played host to the Grand Turk's envoy, Soliman Aga, who had come to deliver in person a letter from his master to the King of France. The setting was entirely Turkish, everything from perfumes to caparisons, from divans to desserts. The King glittered with diamonds sewn into both his clothes and his hat. The Turk stepped forward, conducted by de Lionne, secretary of state for foreign affairs, and handed the letter to the King, who passed it to the Chevalier who spoke Turkish.

The King then commanded him "to have a look at it and check promptly whether the word *Elchi* [Majesty] had been included. It was not to be found." The King, quick to assess the awkwardness of the situation, realized how vain all the pomp now appeared, and how incongruous the welcome extended to this little gentleman. He remained seated and bade him retire, wondering how to save himself from derision. According to de Lionne, "His Majesty ordered me to join Messrs. Molière and de Lully and write a play somehow involving Turkish clothes and manners. I set off for this purpose to the village of Auteuil, where M. de Molière had a very pretty house. It was here that we worked on the drama. *Le Bourgeois Gentilhomme* made it easier to save the King from the mockers, since the Turk was particularly fatuous throughout his stay in Paris. Pirouettes and ballets won out over unreliable Turks!

Were Louis Le Vau, Charles Le Brun, Jules Hardouin-Mansart, André Le Nôtre, Pierre Mignard, François Girardon, and Ange-Jacques Gabriel the true creators of Versailles? Or was it Louis XIV, who quarreled with his architect and could spend a year planning a festivity? Or Louis XV, whose reign brought a new style of life and perfection in the decorative arts? Or Marie-Antoinette, the patroness of musicians? Or yet the ever-present desire to produce a brilliant effect, whatever the cause? At Versailles art was practiced only by the greatest. Once allegory had been mastered by Le Brun and the French Academy, there was a language through which sentiments could be expressed. The Salon of Diana—fraught with the great conquests of antiquity and laced with details (Indian dress, coral, etc.) reminding the world that the King "had begun to establish commerce in the most foreign countries and had sent French colonists to Madagascar"—took the place of a history simply written in French.

This was a moment of opulent fantasy, when solid-silver furniture called for music and magnificence. Then came esteem for artists and a taste for collecting. Le Brun may have been court painter, but Mignard would decorate the private apartments. Veronese and Guido Reni may have enjoyed the greatest prestige, but visitors from abroad admired everything, even the hooks and window locks. To honor a guest, the sovereign or a member of his family took him or her on a tour of his collections, and if the King exhibited a masterpiece in public, he would expect everyone to admire the work and appreciate the privilege. And who could have treated Madame Vigée-Lebrun more kindly than did Marie-Antoinette?

Louis XIV never ceased to embellish Versailles, his work of art; moreover, he remained ever vigilant against theft and depredation, punishing thieves and protecting the groves with fences and thick hedges. Once he had proclaimed the divine right of monarchy, the King felt freer to indulge his personal taste. And there was nothing to stop him, given the golden moment in which he lived. Paris was becoming a superb city, the Benedictines were busy cataloguing the great royal monuments of France, and the Encyclopedists had under discussion virtually everything known to humanity. In addition, French civilization abounded in skilled cabinetmakers, designers, silversmiths, and bronze-casters, the best of them fully equal to any demand the King might make. Louis XV loved his gold plate, but he also adored French porcelain, ordering whole services and beautiful pieces with the idea of dispersing them at an annual sale. The ceramics proved so popular that copies were made by manufacturers from Meissen to Chelsea, all the while that spies persisted in trying to obtain the secrets of how the treasures were produced. If Meissonnier, Slodtz, Verberckt, and Rousseau attempted fantasy or imitated antiquity, they never went too far, because Louis XV had very likely been heard musing about the need to appear logical, thus to avoid all exaggeration.

As for his successor, Louis XVI had absorbed the teachings of Jean-Jacques Rousseau, as had the Queen, and a taste for nature led both sovereigns to turn away from the Château. In love with

Hardouin-Mansart's Orangery.
Painting by Étienne Allegrain.

life out of doors, Louis XVI had the gardens replanted and a farm built near the Petit Trianon, where Marie-Antoinette and her ladies-in-waiting lived out their pastoral fantasies. Never mind, Madame de Maintenon, the morganatic wife of Louis XIV, had founded Saint-Cyr in 1685, a school for the daughters of impoverished noblemen, and it was here that Racine's *Esther* and *Athalie* received their first performances. In 1738, moreover, ninety-six concerts were played before Marie Leszczynska, Louis XV's Queen, in her Versailles apartment.

Of all the arts, music was the best suited to Versailles. Louis XIV played the guitar endlessly, as well as the harpsichord, and his musical memory was such that he once sang through a ballet score not heard in fifty-eight years and long since forgotten by everyone else. Chapel, riding, hunting, supper, ballet, and opera made up the day at Versailles, but the royal family's passion for music bordered on mania, right up to the Revolution in 1789. Every member enjoyed both listening and playing, had thousands of pages copied, and transcriptions made of works by Lully and Vivaldi, Delalande and Bach. Mozart's concert had already been forgotten by the time his father returned and attended a royal Mass in order to enjoy the Grand Motet, which everyone played under the direction of Couperin's daughter or Guignon, the virtuoso violinist.

Mad Versailles! A melting pot from which the avant-garde did not always emerge, but nonetheless a rare, creative workshop where, thanks to the ability of discerning monarchs to attract the finest talents, scarcely any painting, sculpture, play, opera, or ballet failed to yield something new that would long be discussed in Paris and even farther afield.

THE FIRST VERSAILLES

Building a country house and filling it with beauty and delight—that is an enterprise worthy of a King. Before reproaching Louis XIV for his lavish spending at Versailles, one should remember that the tradition of equating prestige or magnificence with power had a long history. In the Middle Ages there was the great hall with its throne on a dais and its walls decked with splendid tapestries, also the habit of treating artists as friends and the never-ending accumulation of precious objects. This sumptuary tradition began with the Carolingians and continued through the treasure-filled châteaux of the Dukes of Berry, Anjou, and Burgundy to the library of Charles V, housed in a corner tower at the old Louvre. The Renaissance abounded in monarchs, as well as Popes and Holy Roman Emperors, who enthusiastically engaged in art patronage as a means of affirming their power on a grand scale. In France, the Valois built Chambord, Fontainebleau, Chenonceau, the new Louvre, and Saint-Germain-en-Laye, all huge châteaux in which galleries and then apartments provided the setting for a dazzling life-style fraught with drama and intrigue, a world the Romantic playwrights of the nineteenth century would find irresistible. The gardens laid out around these royal dwellings were less Italianate than the interiors, but the detail and regularity of their design helped Du Cerceau and Le Nôtre to realize the *jardin à la française*—the French formal garden—in all its perfection.

Why so many royal residences? Political instability, wars requiring the sovereign to appear at the head of his troops, the demands of refurbishment or simple maintenance, and the love of

hunting—any or all encouraged the court to follow a seasonal round of travels, veritable expeditions with linens, crockery, and furniture forming part of the royal procession. Versailles gained favor because of its abundant game and the pleasure Louis XIII took in stopping there longer than a few hours at a time. For such reasons, the royal houses were, from generation to generation, repaired, enlarged, or transformed in keeping with contemporary taste. Richelieu, the colossal château built by the great Cardinal, and its dependent town are said to have given Louis XIV the idea for Versailles. Also important was Vaux-le-Vicomte, set between courtyard and garden and ennobled by a moat, richly embroidered flowerbeds, and a grand perspective. Here Nicolas Fouquet, young Louis XIV's finance minister, had brought to full splendor what Louis XIII had only sketched out at Versailles. Needless to say, the King could not allow himself to be outdone by a mere courtier.

In July 1589, Henri de Navarre spent two days with Loménie de Brienne at Versailles. Shortly thereafter he succeeded to the throne as Henri IV, whereupon the King returned to hunt at Versailles. In 1607 Henri brought with him for the first time his son, the future Louis XIII. The countryside was alive with game, varied, and marked by lakes (Clagny and the *Étang Puant* [Stinking Lake], which would become the Pool of the Swiss Guards), marshes (future site of the Menagerie), and small market towns, soon to be replaced by such royal residences as Trianon, Glatigny, and Marly, as well as the Saint-Cyr school founded by Madame de Maintenon. The royal hunting parties came from as far away as Paris and Saint-Germain, which prompted Louis XIII to build a pied-à-terre or hunting lodge where he could take off his boots and rest a while.

Nicolas huau's château

In 1623, Louis XIII bought the Galie Hill and had its windmill demolished. On 6 September, Jean de Fourcy, superintendent of royal buildings, solicited bids for the construction of a château in stone and stucco. Nicolas Huau, "master mason, domiciled in Paris at the Louvre galleries," won the commission for the initial work, which produced what remains the heart of the château now embracing the Marble Courtyard. The central block consisted of a pitch-roofed, two-storey structure, on the east side of which projected two parallel, single-storey wings linked at their extremity by a gated wall. The little château or hunting lodge boasted rough-cast walls embellished with plaster quoins. The site was protected by a surrounding platform terrace *(fausse-braie)* below which flowed the waters of a moat. On the west side spread a parterre or terrace.

The Versailles of Louis XIII was clearly a country house meant for the King's leisure, but one that already indicated a certain style of life. Proof comes from an inventory prepared in 1630 following the death of the caretaker Mongey. On the ground floor, facing west, the Comte de Soissons occupied space reserved for the captain of the guards. The north wing housed the armory and the fully equipped kitchens, while the south wing contained the latrines and storage rooms stocked with thirty-nine pairs of sheets, eighteen dozen serviettes, and twenty tablecloths, some of them damasked. It was in a southwest corner room that Louis XIII received Cardinal de Richelieu on 11 November 1630 (the "Day of the Dupes") and, in the wake of fierce court intrigues, assured the minister that he enjoyed the King's full confidence. The little château could also accommodate a number of regular visitors, who had their own bedrooms, mainly in the attics. The company included the Comte de Nogent, the Duc d'Angoulême, the Duc de Montbazon (master of the royal hunt), the Marquis de Mortemart (first gentleman of the bedchamber), the Comte de Beringhen, the Baron de Chappes, Messrs. de Souvré and de La Béraudière, and Lucas, *le secrétaire de la main*. The Comte de Praslin and the Marquis d'Aumont shared a room with two bunks. As for furnishings, the château contained only the simplest, except for the odd wall hanging or Bergamot tapestry.

The *étage noble* belonged to the King, and it had now been extended around all three sides of the courtyard. The royal suite comprised a gallery, a study or *cabinet*, a bedchamber, a hall, a wardrobe, and the room of the Duc de Saint-Simon, master of the King's horse. In the gallery hung a picture representing the siege of La Rochelle. The study contained tapestries depicting mythological scenes, a game chest, a table, a wardrobe with two dressing gowns (one in green velvet and grey fur, the other in green damask and taffeta trimmed in gold), silver-gilt candlesticks, a crystal chandelier, and a warming pan. The green-damask room in which the King slept included a bed fringed in silk and gold, chairs, six stools, and tapestries narrating the history of Marcus Aurelius. The hall was furnished with a billiard table. The Mongey inventory, however brief, provides a clear view of the life led by France's hunter King.

Philibert le Roy's château

Not bad, for a start. Soon, however, Louis XIII began to feel a bit cramped at Versailles. By 1631 the King had purchased and assembled the hundred acres that still form the core of the park, whereupon he decided, even before acquiring the Gondi estate for 60,000 *livres* in 1632, to rebuild the original château, a project that lasted until 1634. The task, as planned by the architect Philibert Le Roy, involved enlarging the U-shaped ensemble all around, beginning with the central block. First came the reconstruction of the western façade on a more ample scale and with two projecting, almost free-standing pavilions, one at either corner.

The two eastern wings were extended to their present length and endowed with terminal pavilions like those on the west side. The one on the northeast corner probably housed a chapel. The new east façade still had five windows and each wing a staircase. In place of the wall enclosing the courtyard on the east came an arcaded portico with green and gold railings. After an expenditure of more than 200,000 *livres*—a considerable sum at the time—the château emerged very much like the one known today as seen from the Marble Courtyard, including the pink-brick walls combined with white-stone bands, mouldings, window frames, pilasters, and quoins, all crowned with pitch roofs of blue-grey slate. The gay chromaticism of the scheme was regional as well as royal.

Clearly, the decorative aspect of Louis XIII's second château had been freshly considered. The ceilings still had exposed beams and floors paved in terra-cotta tiles, but the interior corners of the courtyard were now filled with small domed and squinch-supported *cabinets,* turret-like corner projections that Louis XIV would later replace with aviaries. The tall chimneypieces were made of plaster and embellished with mouldings. A first touch of luxury was noted in a 1634 *Gazette,* which describes a gift to Louis XIII from his sister, Christine, Duchesse de Savoie: four suites of furniture, all upholstered in velvet on a silver ground. One suite was blue, another linen grey, a third green, and a fourth orange-red. The taste for pretty and varied colors would long prevail over the dominant monochromy known today at Versailles.

Now more suitably housed, Louis XIII felt confident enough to entertain guests other than his fellow huntsmen, beginning with Queen Anne, who was invited for light meals or fox hunts but never to stay, whatever the circumstance. During the smallpox epidemic of 1641, Louis asked the Queen to send the children to Versailles, but required that "she lodge at Noisy. I know she could very well stay at Versailles with the children, but I fear all those women, who would spoil everything if the Queen came." Madame de La Fayette, the Grande Mademoiselle, and several other ladies of the court were invited on the same occasion but never assigned rooms. To the end of his life, Louis XIII considered Versailles as very much his own private preserve.

Thanks to the raised terrace and moat surrounding the château, Versailles continued to look a bit like a fortress, a quality further enhanced by the projecting corner pavilions. Two bridges spanned the moat, one on the east and one on the west, both with stone balustrades like those on the central balcony and around the outer edge of the terrace. The western bridge led to an enclosed garden, whose initial design would forever mark the Versailles perspective. Along a fairly steep slope came a succession of features, all on axisa: terrace with a broderie garden whose four compartments surrounded a round basin fountain; an allée stretching to a distant basin, which would later be transformed into the Fountain of Apollo; and, halfway there, a "roundel" where both diagonal and orthogonal allées intersected. The whole garden ensemble had been carried out by Jacques de Menours at a cost of over 40,000 *livres*. A source for the scheme was the *Traité de jardinage,* written by Jacques Boyceau, Menours's uncle, who advocated parterres of box-hedge broderies on blue, white, or red gravel, the decorative effect of which recalled designs created by the ornamentalists of Renaissance Italy.

Shortly afterwards, the marshes were landscaped by Claude Mollet, Hilaire Masson, and the fountain-builder Claude Denis. In 1639 Denis repaired a water pump located northeast of the vast enclosure; three years later, in 1642, he was obliged to erect a second pump, this one a little more to the east, on the edge of Lake Clagny and worked by a horse-powered mill directing water to a reservoir. Steep declivities, marshland, and remote water sources posed difficulties that Louis XIII's successor would have to overcome if he was to develop his establishment at Versailles.

The young louis xiv

Cardinal Mazarin, chief minister of state during the minority and early reign of Louis XIV, died on 9 March 1661. On 17 August the twenty-three-year-old monarch accepted an invitation from Nicolas Fouquet, his superintendent of finance, to visit him at Vaux-le-Vicomte. The reception proved as sumptuous as it was inopportune, and there was no denying the evident genius of Le Vau, Le Nôtre, Le Brun, Molière, and Torelli. None of it escaped the King, already somewhat tantalized by the spirit of grandeur and mindful of the example set by Mazarin. The Cardinal—a great patron of the arts (with a gallery decorated by the Italian master Romanelli) as well as a major collector—had bequeathed all his possessions to the King, including precious works from the collection of the executed Charles I of England. The Louvre remained the first among all royal residences in France; already magnificently decorated, it was to be further embellished by François d'Orbay. By 1661 there would be a *cabinet* for books and paintings as well as "medals, shells, and other curiosities," altogether a precursor to a similar study at Versailles, a treasure-trove in which the King took great pride.

Louis XIV hunted at Versailles for the first time in 1651. Though pleased with the experience, he repeated it only sporadically until his marriage in 1660. Then, suddenly, he developed a passion for the site and its château. The attachment became so obvious and the consequences so costly

The Château de Versailles in 1664, viewed from the east towards the entrance façade. By this time Louis XIV had completed his first building campaign, but the Château still remained essentially a hunting lodge, as it had been under Louis XIII, more than a royal palace or seat of government.
Painting by the studio of Adam-François Van der Meulen.

that Colbert, who would not succeed Ratabon as minister of finance until 1664, felt compelled to communicate with the King in 1663: "This house has more to do with Your Majesty's pleasure and entertainment than His glory... Perhaps He would realize that it will be forever clear from the royal building accounts that, while He was spending such huge sums on this home, He was neglecting the Louvre, which is assuredly the most superb palace in the world, and the most worthy of His grandeur... nothing, apart from striking achievements in battle, reflects the grandeur and spirit of princes more than buildings, and posterity judges them according to the superb homes they erect during their lifetimes. Oh! what a pity if the greatest of kings, the most virtuous according to the true virtue that is the hallmark of the greatest princes, were judged after Versailles! Yet such misfortune is to be feared!"

Still, Louis XIV persisted, realizing yet disregarding how much determination, money, and time might be required. The first campaign of building at Versailles would go on for nearly three years and cost almost 1.5 million *livres*. Initially, there were alterations to the interior, which created an apartment for the Queen in the southwest corner of the upper storey, located between the apartments reserved for the Dauphin and the King. After the death of his mother, Anne of Austria, Louis moved to the ground floor, below his wife's apartment, and transformed his first apartment into rooms set aside for other uses. The suite would be decorated by the painters Charles Errard and Noël Coypel.

In 1662-1663 Louis XIV had the former outbuildings or wings demolished and replaced with structures designed by Louis Le Vau. The north wing would house the kitchens and servants' quarters and the south wing (today's Old Wing) the stables. One of the two pavilions flanking the entrance portal was assigned to the gatekeeper and the other to the guards; both posts overlooked an unprotected, horseshoe forecourt. From here could be seen the fan-like trident of three avenues—Paris, Sceaux, and Saint-Cloud (the road to Paris)—all of which were to determine the street plan of the adjacent town.

The exterior of the château had been somewhat modified. The garden side, for example, was now cinctured with a gilded balcony hung from the *étage noble.* Further additions were staircases at all four corners, where pavilions and main blocks joined, so as to allow free access to each of the King's new apartments. The shape of the surrounding terrace and the moat at its base was regularized, shortly after which the latter would be drained.

The park too underwent a major revision, as well as considerable enlargement, owing to the purchase of land at Choisy, Trianon, and Clagny. The great perspective towards the west remained, but next to the château itself Le Nôtre laid out new parterres, after reducing the variations in the terrain, which had declined a full 60 feet over a length of 130 yards. To the north, where the steep slope remained, he installed a four-part, quatrefoil fountain spread over a terrace adjacent a water pump and overlooking a mirror-like pool, which became the Nymphs' Bath. Here began the descent of a waterfall allée in the form of a trapezoid. A later revision would introduce steps leading down to the parterre. For the first time, the desire for theatrical effect had been fully realized, involving surprise, shifting perspective, appearance and disappearance, reflection and illusion. In brief, everything that enchants today's strollers, who soon fall under the magical spell of an artistically mastered environment, discovering as they move forward how the perspectives actually recapture some of nature's own perfections.

Everything required for a self-renewing promenade of discovery was there in this first true Versailles garden. Was its character also owing to a King who loved the outdoor life? In his *Guide to the Gardens of Versailles,* written between 1689 and 1705, Louis XIV cited a number of fixed vantage points, almost as if he possessed the eye of a photographer. Every day the King walked through the gardens or had himself driven in his *roulette,* always on the lookout for necessary changes and generally

The Château de Versailles in 1668, shortly after Louis XIV had completed his first building campaign. The U-shaped core structure remained that of Louis XIII, to which his son added the large *communs* (service buildings) on either side of the Royal Courtyard, the sentry pavilions, the horseshoe vehicle entrance, and the Grotto of Thetis, a small cubic building with a reservoir on its roof. Still, the polychrome ensemble of rose-brick masonry, white-stone quoins, and blue-grey slate roofs continued an aesthetic established under Louis XIII. Painting by Pierre Patel.

The garden façade prior to its reconstruction by Louis Le Vau.
In the background stands the Church of Saint-Julien, which would soon be demolished.
Nearby lived the Récollet friars. Engraving by Pérelle and Poilly.

playing the role of theatre director. Here, as elsewhere, this astonishing monarch repressed his personal feelings and tastes in order to create an image of perfection. A so-called "French garden"—that *jardin à la française*—is, after all, a carefully composed thing, meaning that it is also a bit artificial.

Louis XIII's parterre was redesigned. Using earth removed from the Orangery work-site nearby, Le Nôtre completed the western edge of the terrace as a half-moon facing the château. Farther out, he widened the sloping allée all the way to a circular basin. Thereafter, the path remained relatively narrow and the slope less steep as it cut through groves on either side—the Girandole and the Dauphin—before reaching the large quadrilobate Rondeau destined to become the Swan Lake. Just as on the north side, the perspective narrowed as it continued through the forest. Already, a domain reserved for hunting was being transformed into a garden.

Festive gardens

In 1662 Le Nôtre laid out a parterre immediately in front the south end of the garden façade, subdividing it along diagonal lines and placing at its center a circular fountain, which in 1667 would feature Lerambert's sculpture *Amour*. The royal building accounts record an important order for sculpture intended to decorate and mark off the grillework fence around the enclosure, identified as a "flower garden." This "hard-stone" population consisted of terms carved by Houzeau, Anguier, and Poissant, each of them costing almost as much as the Cupid in the middle of the pool.

Even before Le Nôtre launched his major campaign, the Versailles gardens already displayed considerable variety. North and west, they were compact and almost enclosed, as in the Renaissance, virtually nestling the château within an Italian shelter. On the south, however, they opened wide to the sun, which brightened the side of the château reserved by Louis XIV for his Spanish Queen, Marie-Thérèse of Austria. Forty-five feet below the Cupid Parterre, Le Vau built an eleven-bay Orangery, reached on either side by a descending flight of broad steps. Here lay a simple parterre where orange trees would stand in boxes, along with more than a thousand young trees brought in from Vaux. The space was entirely open, providing an uninterrupted view all the way to the Satory woods beyond the Puant Pond, or, towards the southwest corner of the château, the square, criss-crossed Greenwood Grove.

Scarcely had all these projects got under way when Le Nôtre found himself obliged to draw up new plans. In 1663 the terrace overlooking the North Parterre had to be moved westward and centered upon an allée that Le Nôtre extended along the château's western façade. Once extended, this avenue would serve as the central path leading through a new parterre, its width doubled by the annexation of a wooded area the same size as the symmetrically placed Greenwood Grove to the south. The parterre now consisted of two rectangles each subdivided by two criss-crossing paths with a Crown Fountain at the intersection. The upper fountain had thus been moved westward at right angles to the northeast corner of the château. The mermaid from which the fountain took its name was accompanied by a triton, sea monsters, and putti, all modeled and cast in lead by the Marsy brothers. Having lost its bosky mass, the parterre was now full of air and light, even before the clearing that would make way for the great Neptune Fountain.

Throughout the 1660s Louis XIV grew passionately attached to Versailles. He even went so far as to have the façades repainted in imitation brick and take advantage of his father's tennis court. The King enlarged as well as embellished whatever he could, spending lavishly on a property that would not become his official residence for another twenty years. As discerning eyes could see, a serious love affair was in the making, and it would break into the open with the first of the great festivities.

PLEASURES
OF THE
ENCHANTED ISLE

The Fountain of Flora (1672-1674), designed by Le Brun
and executed by the sculptor Jean-Baptiste Tuby.

Bread and circuses? Louis XIV, advising his son, the Dauphin, wrote: "The people enjoy the theatre, where, after all, the purpose is to please them. They are delighted to see that we like what they like... By this means we sometimes hold onto their minds and hearts more strongly than by rewards and good works. As for foreigners... what is consumed by these expenditures, which could be viewed as superfluous, gives them an advantageous impression of magnificence, power, wealth, and grandeur." At Versailles, the major events were the *fêtes* or festivities sparked by some royal enthusiasm—an artist, a masterpiece, a mistress.

M. - C. Moine has said everything possible on the subject of Louis XIV's festivities, drawing information from the state archives. These tell of the preparations, the need for economy (by mending a decayed *Apollo,* a *Neptune,* or a *Palace of Thetis* after two years in the open air), and the lessons to be learned (the number of firepots filled with "fine and pure" soot increased by half to replace foul-smelling grease). Also evident was the savoir-faire, for in the years since the *Ballet de la nuit* of 1653 the King had learned much. In 1660, for instance, he presented himself to the audience from a position in front of the gold-brocade dais rather than below it. In 1662, the monarch had the program for the *Carrousel* distributed before the celebration, after which he arranged for the event to be described by Charles Perrault with the aid of engravers. Young Louis even found a way to control the collaboration between the Italians Torelli, Vigarani, and Cavalli and such French artists as Gissey, Berain, and Benserade.

The first day of *The Pleasures of the Enchanted Isle* festivities in 1664.
Engraving by Israël Silvestre.

Miraculously, he learned how to turn expedient into breathtaking spectacle, despite the lack of time, workmen, nails, and wax candles, these last often replaced by coarse tallow because of theft. Yet another accomplishment was the training of teams competent enough to make do with few rehearsals: In July 1682 Versailles mounted *Persée* in eight hours.

In 1664 Louis XIV presided over an entertainment titled *Les Plaisirs de l'île enchantée,* a series of events lasting from the 7th to the 14th of May. Officially, it was in honor of two Queens: the King's mother, Anne of Austria, and his wife, Marie-Thérèse of Austria. Clearly, however, the person celebrated in such magnificent fashion was Louise de La Vallière, and everything had to be perfect. By now the King was accustomed to pomp and ceremony, a way of life assured by the collaboration of Carlo Vigarani, Jean-Baptiste Lully, Charles Le Brun, and Jean-Baptiste Molière. Already, the court had thrilled to such productions as the *Carrousel* at the Tuileries (1662) and *L'Impromptu de Versailles* (1663), both of them brilliant outdoor festivities involving comedy and ballet, music and food, art and entertainment. For *The Pleasures of the Enchanted Isle,* Louis wanted each actor to play himself in a setting destined to become that of the court, causing one to wonder whether this trompe-l'œil staging may have been the most important event ever for Versailles and Louis XIV. Perhaps not, given the evidence of Israël Silvestre's engravings or the description that made its splendor known throughout Europe.

For several months leading up to the month of May, the Duc de Saint-Aignan, gentleman of the bedchamber and the King's friend, drove the preparations forward through all manner of

Rupture du Palais et des enchantemens de l'Isle Troisiesme Journée. d'Alcine representeé par vn feu. d'Artifice.

The third day of *The Pleasures of the Enchanted Isle* festivities in 1664.
Engraving by Israël Silvestre.

bustle and turmoil. An experienced master of such affairs, Saint-Aignan chose the general theme from Ariosto's *Orlando Furioso,* with its tale of Roger and his knights bewitched by Alcina and then freed by Melissa. The whole of this elaborate plot would be recounted in ballets, parades, and cavalcades, all made spectacular by means of lavish costumes, trumpet fanfares, enchanting landscapes, and ingenious machinery. Vigarani, from Modena, designed the machinery, while Gissey, who had organized the *Carrousel,* painted the verdant backdrops. Lully wrote the music, Périgny and Benserade the verses. Molière, called in at the last minute, took charge of the staging.

At sundown on Wednesday, 7 May, the court assembled in a leafy theatre at the top of today's Tapis Vert overlooking the big Rondeau. First they witnessed a glittering cavalcade led by d'Artagnan, the King's page dressed *à l'antique.* The Duc de Saint-Aignan, accompanied by twelve trumpeters and ten drummers, preceded the King, got up as Roger, in whose wake came a number of young noblemen in the roles of Alcina's prisoners. Behind them, Milet, the royal coachman, drove Apollo's chariot, flanked by the Hours of the Day and the Signs of the Zodiac. His passengers were none other than the Four Ages (Gold, Silver, Bronze, and Iron), roles taken by members of the Molière troupe.

The audience included all the great names of Old France—Guise, Noailles, Armagnac, Foix, Lude, La Vallière, Humières, and Monsieur le Duc—each of them determined to make the finest impression. The sovereign, all fire, silver, and precious stones, rode a horse dressed to match. Noailles

OPPOSITE:
Louise-Françoise
de La Baume Le Blanc,
Duchesse da La Vallière,
in a portrait by the workshop
of Claude Lefèbvre.
The beauteous La Valière was Louis XIV's
first officially recognized mistress.
It was in her honor
that the thirty-four-year-old King
staged at Versailles the week-long series
of festivities known as
The Pleasures of the Enchanted Isle
(7-14 May 1664).

RIGHT:
The Duc de Saint-Aignan's costume
for the *Carrousel* of 1685.
Drawing by Jean Bérain.
Saint-Aignan was first gentleman
of the bedchamber to Louis XIV
and very much a master of revels
during the early years at Versailles.
This *Carrousel*, staged in the riding school
at the Large Stables in Versailles,
turned into one of the grandest spectacles
of Louis XIV's reign.

Le Duc de Saint Aignan; maréchal de camp général du Carrousel

wore black, diamonds, and silver; Foix, pink, gold, and silver; Marcillac, yellow, white, and black; the Duc de La Vallière, linen grey, white, and silver, and so forth. By now the first festivities of the reign, and even those at Vaux, must have seemed like ancient history. But the evening had hardly begun, for next came a ring race, which may have been fixed, since it was the brother of Louise de la Vallière who received the victor's diamond-studded gold sword from the hands of the Queen Mother.

No less fabulous or theatrical was the banquet which concluded this first day. It began with a procession of four beasts from the King's new Menagerie. A horse bore in a flower-decked Mademoiselle du Parc representing Spring, followed by Summer in the person of Monsieur Du Parc, mounted on an elephant leading a band of reapers. As Autumn, La Thorillière rode a dromedary and commanded a team of grape harvesters, while Winter arrived in the person of Béjart astride a bear accompanied by elderly men carrying basins filled with ice. Everyone, in fact, arrived bearing food and moved in time with the music. Louis XIV, seated with the Queens, his brother, sister-in-law, and thirty-six ladies all about him, was approached by an enormous laurel-sprouting rock atop which sat Molière in the role of Pan and Mademoiselle Béjart playing Diana. The two divinities paid their compliments to the Queen as did the Seasons, all the while that Abundance, Joy, Cleanliness, Good Food, Pleasures, Games, Mirth, and Delight unveiled a semicircular table. To the King's extreme left sat the beloved, Louise de La Vallière.

The next evening the court moved to a theatre a little farther to the west, facing away from the château and furnished with wind breaks. Against the palace of the sorceress Alcina, Molière and his company praised love and paid homage to a passion the King had already decided to make public. The vehicle was *La Princesse d'Élide,* which Molière had not had time to versify throughout, and so the piece was performed to music. An orchestra composed of thirty violins, six harpsichords, and theorbos played Lully symphonies and accompanied faun and shepherd dances, as well as the acrobats and a ballet presented as interludes.

On the third evening the court saw the freeing of Roger and the defeat of Alcina, a drama staged in the middle of the Swan Fountain (today the Fountain of Apollo). The enchanted palace, flanked by violinists on one platform and drummers as well as trumpeters on another, was a true mechanical stage, rigged up by Vigarani. Alcina and her companions moved about on sea monsters, while the defense of the palace became an occasion for ballets featuring giants and dwarves, knights and Moors. Demons leapt to the aid of Alcina, who, alas, recognized the wise Melissa next to Roger and saw her slip a magic ring onto one of the hero's fingers. This gave the signal for the destruction of the palace and its charms, accompanied by thunder, lightning, and fireworks, all to the greater glory of ingenuity and chivalry.

Les Plaisirs de l'île enchantée had concluded, but not the festivities. On the evening of 10 May, the King won a diamond rose at a race, then promptly put it back on offer. Finally, the Queen presented the treasure to Coislin, the true winner. Sunday brought a visit to the Menagerie, where Locatelli counted more than forty species of birds. For the evening there was a performance of *Les Fâcheux,* whose characters so pleased the King that he had Molière add a new one. On Monday the evening began with a lottery at which ladies won gems, silver, and fine pieces of furniture; it was succeeded by a race at the end of which Saint-Aignan came out the winner. However, the star attraction on this occasion was a performance of the first three acts of Molière's *Tartuffe,* which amused the King enormously. Still, bowing to pressure from both the pious and the Queen Mother, Louis banned the play for five years, "lest it be misunderstood by others less capable of discernment."

On 13 May, following a performance of *Le Mariage forcé* in which Molière flattered the amorous temperament of his sovereign, to the tune of a mock serenade by Lully, every one of the

The *Carrousel* staged on 5 June 1662 by Louis XIV in the courtyard of the Tuileries Palace to celebrate the birth of the Dauphin.
The caparisoned color and vivacity of the scene are typical of the early part of a reign whose taste gradually evolved towards solemn grandeur.
Painting after an original work by Henri de Gissey.

600 guests went away dumbstruck by the marvels they had witnessed over the past week. Olivier d'Ormesson reported: "Madame de Sévigné told all about the entertainments at Versailles that continued from Wednesday to Sunday, with a ring race, ballets, plays, fireworks, and other splendid events, and how all the courtiers were furious, as the King paid no attention to any of them, and how Messrs. de Guise and d'Elbœuf were given little more than a hole in the wall to sleep in." Be that as it may, Louis XIV had learned the political importance of a truly royal entertainment.

By 1668 Louis XIV was at it again, this time to celebrate the Treaty of Aix-la-Chapelle, which ratified the French conquest of Flanders, and to pay tribute to a new favorite: Madame de Montespan. These celebrations lasted only a day, 2 May, but they proved so replete that the whole of Europe would understand the extent of the King's attachment to Versailles as well as his passion for spectacle. And the fête may indeed have been the finest of the reign. It resulted from long and careful preparation carried out under the direction of the Duc de Créquy, then first lord of the bedchamber, who spent over 100,000 *livres,* equal to a third of the annual building budget. The 3,000 guests included ambassadors and the papal nuncio, whose presence, like the size of the audience, reflected Louis's determination to assert the importance of Versailles. They were treated to magnificent sideboards groaning with fruit and jams; a theatre, lit by thirty-two chandeliers, in which Molière staged *Georges Dandin* supplemented with a pastoral by Lully; a five-course dinner, with fifty-six dishes per course, served about a waterfall cascading over rocks. Following a ball in a room decorated with shells, the entertainments climaxed in a light show, during which the Latona Parterre, with its vases and statues, and the château itself were illuminated against the surrounding darkness. The painter Charmeton executed contour drawings in Chinese ink on a transparent screen mounted on a stretcher and lit from behind. The party lasted until dawn.

The lightning conquest of Franche-Comté triggered six entertainments given between 4 July and 31 August 1674. With Molière now dead, Lully came into his own, triumphing on the first night when his *Alceste* was performed in the Marble Courtyard as a prologue to dinner in the sparkling new State Apartments. On 11 July there would be *L'Églogue de Versailles* at Trianon. The 18th brought a visit to the Menagerie, after which a concert was given on the Grand Canal prior to a performance of Molière's *Le Malade imaginaire.* Ten days later came *Les Fêtes de l'Amour et de Bacchus.* On 18 August, Racine's *Iphigénie* served as a prelude to an extraordinary fireworks display organized by the court painter Charles Le Brun. For the final night, 31 August, Vigarani had transformed the Grand Canal into an Olympian stage of shimmering unreality where guests in gondolas rowed among gods. The event proved so enchanting that the King asked Perrault and Vigarani to save the fairy-like décor, which would be returned to the Grand Canal for a fête on 20 August 1676.

The court did not actually settle at Versailles until 1682, but the extent and extravagance of the galas already seen there indicate that Louis XIV had been contemplating the move for many years. Thereafter, court etiquette itself grew into a sumptuous daily theatre; yet there would still be festivities of such beauty that the paintings and descriptions of them resemble the stuff of dreams. In 1685 (the year of the extraordinary reception given the Doge of Genoa) the Dauphin and the Duc de Bourbon organized the first *Carrousel* in the riding school at the Great Stable. It turned into a spectacle as magnificent, if not so imaginative, as any mounted at the start of the reign. Already in 1668 the sumptuous revels had shown less originality than those of 1664. It was as if the King, with his State Apartments completed and his gardens nearing perfection, had no further interest in improvised décor—as if all the pomp and glory had come to weigh him down. Having conquered Versailles, Louis XIV appeared no longer to enjoy himself.

LE VAU'S CHÂTEAU

During the festivities of 1664, Le Maistre's gilded balcony, hung from the garden façade, must have glittered prettily throughout the night. An ephemeral belt around an ensemble of perfect elegance, it would soon prove too narrow to hold the royal family, their favorites, and the great of the realm, all of them vying for position. There was nothing for it but to pull down the château and rebuild. After several years of piecemeal construction, the time had come to start afresh. In 1664, following discussions with Colbert, Louis XIV announced a competition to his chief architect Louis Le Vau, Claude Perrault, the contractor Jacques Gabriel IV, and the royal engineer Carlo Vigarani, asking them to submit designs for a courtyard opening into a lower gallery and a pair of lateral vestibules, with a fountain but not a carriage entrance. Two pavilions at the front would house the grand staircase and the chapel. The bathing suite was to be on the ground floor to the right. Upstairs the King's State Apartment required an enfilade of five rooms, while the Queen's State Apartment would overlook the gardens and her private suite the courtyard. In the attic were to be four or as many as six apartments of four rooms each, as well as others of only two rooms. "Be careful," the designers were advised, "to install as many staircases as possible so as to give clear access to these upper apartments. The gallery facing the court-yard should have a salon at the center, if possible."

The solution proposed by Le Vau won out, despite the disparaging remarks made by Colbert on 18 August 1665: "All that is proposed is nothing more than patchwork, which will never be

Detail of the attic
windows on the garden
façade built by Louis
Le Vau in 1668-1671
as the part the stone
"Envelope" designed
to expand the main
block commissioned
by Louis XIII.
The Envelope (actually
a pair of bracketing
wings added to
the Château's north
and south sides) came
with Louis XIV's second
building campaign
at Versailles.

On the park side, Le Vau took a different approach, for here he was not obliged to work within an established format. Moreover, he innovated, offering a combination of a tall, robust basement, projecting blocks faced with Ionic columns, an attic featuring pilasters, ornamental windows, figure sculptures placed as if atop the columns, and balustrades with trophies. Grandeur and magnificence now reigned, displacing the showy, picturesque, and colorful qualities of the old courtyards, which once glittered so merrily during festivities or performances given by the King's musicians. Now the drama was chiaroscuro, solemnly played out over uniformly pale stones dressed, carved, and hewn to catch and reflect light. On the attic wall and atop the balustrade as well as in niches along the *étage-noble* façade lived a stone population of colossal muses and rivers, putti, nymphs, and divinities, all of them available solely to strollers in the gardens. Le Vau had discovered secrets already known to Le Nôtre, allowing him to create a harmony renewable with each step taken either forward or backward along the entire length of the façade. Vaux-le-Vicomte was already out of date.

Designed by Louis Le Vau, the "Envelope" was completed by François d'Orbay after the former's death in 1670. The new construction did not merely enlarge the château; it also made possible a new layout of the apartments in which the quasi-immutable, semi-private, semi-public life of the King, his family, and the court would unfold. On the exterior, the format had been established for good, consisting of stone, tall Ionic columns and pilasters, a balustrade concealing the roof, and a decorative program of statues, trophies, and vases. It would not change even after the arrival of Jules Hardouin-Mansart. On the interior, the enfilades rolled out the full length of the north and south *cornières*, or wings around the "corner," where the State Apartments *(Grands Appartements)* of the King and Queen were now established. The sovereign, after hesitating, finally decided not to demolish the old château. This made it feasible to reserve the monumental suites for ceremonial occasions, while creating on the courtyards smaller rooms for private living or constructing new, more comfortable ones linked together by numerous corridors and stairways.

THE AMBASSADORS' STAIRCASE

Beginning in 1665, the Ambassadors' Staircase was deemed imperative for access to the northern part of the Château (henceforth capitalized), although work did not begin until 1668. Initially, the design called for a single flight of steps, but, after Le Vau's death, the facility was rebuilt as two flights.

Beyond Delobel's three grillework gates leading into the Royal Courtyard lay a richly decorated barrel-vaulted vestibule, its floor paved in black and white marble, arranged in a pattern of alternating squares and stars. The lower walls were revetted in marble with heavy mouldings, while overhead the vault decoration consisted of a rose-like configuration at the center of each section and a surround of suns, lyres, musical as well as military elements, and garlands. In 1752 Louis XV had this ensemble destroyed, but it is known from Jean-Michel Chevotet's drawings commissioned for engravings published by Surugue around 1723. Eleven steps with diagonally cut corners and no railings led to a landing below a wall fountain in a shell niche fashioned of Languedoc marble. Its water cascaded onto three different levels. Above them stood two bronze tritons and then the *Albani Centaur* excavated in Rome in 1702 and brought to Versailles by the Papal Nuncio Cornelio Bentivoglio in 1712. From the landing rose two divergent flights of twenty-one steps, traveling along the wall and protected on the

The Ambassadors' Staircase, designed by Le Vau and Le Brun and built by d'Orbay in 1674-1680. Until its destruction by Louis XV in 1752, the Ambassadors' Staircase was a grander, double-flight version of the Queen's Staircase on the opposite (south) side of the Marble Courtyard (see page 51), complete with polychrome marble revetments and trompe-l'œil painting on both ceiling and walls. Drawing by Jean-Michel Chevotet preparatory to engraving by Surugue (c. 1723).

open side by a gilt-bronze balustrade, the work of Dominico Cucci. As seen from the entrance, this concealed a geometrical pattern of polychrome marbles like that in the vestibule. Seen from the top of the stairs, the décor was of great splendor illuminated by a large skylight.

  The interior wall displayed, between bays marked off by Ionic columns, a superb, alternating arrangement of carved-wood doors by Philippe Caffiéri, trompe-l'œil scenes painted by Charles Le Brun, and the "faux tapestries" of Adam-François Van der Meulen. Each of these bays was illusionistically construed in relation to a central niche above the fountain and filled with Jean-Baptiste Warin's bust of Louis XIV (1666), until it was later replaced by a work from the hands of the sculptor Antoine Coysevox. On the south side of the entrance hung the arms of France and Navarre fashioned of gilt-bronze and flanked by the attributes of Minerva and Hercules, also in bronze.

  According to Nivelon, Le Brun filled the foreground of his perspectival paintings with "figures representing all sorts of nations, from the East and West Indies, Persia, Greece, Armenia, Muscovy, Germany, Italy, Holland, Africa… in short, all that can be known… They seem to come and go in the Prince's apartments, mostly talking to each another or admiring the ceiling, creating a most pleasing and natural impression of variety; and it may be said that when this great King descends this staircase, in the company of, and followed by all these Princes and Princesses, the sight is so great and so superb that one would think that all these peoples are crowding in to honor his passing and admire the finest court in the world, such is the skill with which the fake and the natural are artistically mingled."

  Van der Meulen's four compositions were also important, representing as they did Cambrai, Valenciennes, Saint-Omer, and Cassel, all the great victories of 1677. The first two had been won under Louis XIV's own command and the last under that of his brother, Monsieur. Once more, the sub-

The Different Nations of Asia. A small-scale model of the monumental painting by Charles Le Brun for the Ambassadors' Staircase.
The clever illusionism of the scene, like the gleaming polychrome marbles, would have been brought to life
by illumination from a skylight, one of the first in French architecture.

ject was the King's glory. The only one of these paintings known today is *Cambrai,* which Picault transferred to canvas in 1752. It reveals the importance attached to a decorative scheme composed of the phoenix, Fames, foliage, and trumpets. As for the draperies, they echo the effects achieved by Le Brun.

Overhead, Le Brun decorated the whole area between the cornice and the skylight with allegories, muses, terms, virtues, and stories alluding to the magnificence and military glory of Louis's early reign. The whole was sectioned in a manner to continue the bays established along the walls. Above the fountain niche, Hercules and Minerva leaned against a globe adorned with the fleurs-de-lis, opposite Apollo and Terpsichore, who rested against Apollo's tripod, above the dying serpent Python. On either side—alternating with trompe-l'œil ceiling panels aligned with Le Brun's "different nations" and the real or mock doors—came the Four Continents, female personifications accompanied by symbolic animals such as a horse, a dromedary, an elephant, or an alligator. Le Brun embellished each corner with a splendid ship's prow, supported by a shell and flanked by two naked captives in chains on a pile of weapons. Two Victories entwine themselves about the ship's beak. Altogether, the corner compositions made sumptuous reference to the fierce naval battle in which the French fleet engaged the Dutch and Spanish at Messina, an encounter that cost Admiral Ruyter his life. Terms and atlantes, representing the Months, provided illusionistic support for the ceiling, around the base of which ran garlands and a balustrade.

On the ceiling the royal narrative assumed a more austere tone, with color replaced by trompe-l'œil. Eight large scenes involving military or diplomatic subjects, rendered in wash on a gold ground, stressed the importance of France in Europe: *The Passage of the Rhine, The Reconquest of Franche-Comté, The Order to Attack Four Dutch Strongholds at the Same Time, The Dual Reparation Made to the King by the Pope and by Spain, The Reform of the Code of Justice, The Renewal of the Alliances, Commerce Restored*, and *Honors Rendered to the Great.* Here again, all were interlinked thematically. On the long sides these panels alternated with octagonal medallions in simulated gilt-bronze entitled *Royal Protection Accorded to the Fine Arts and History.* On the short sides appeared *Fame* and *Mercury,* symbols of immortality. Contemporary descriptions by Félibien, Nivelon, and Piganiol de La Force waxed more enthusiastic about the extent and ambition of the staircase's iconographic program than about the splendor of the gilt-bronzes attached to the colored marbles. This alone reveals the fact that no effort had been spared in the decoration of the State Apartments, even though the Château had yet to become the permanent residence of the King and court. Just how far should such artistry go if, as the architect Gabriel wrote in La Martinière's Dictionary, it was merely a matter of refurbishing this part of the Château: "Louis XIV was tempted to change this superb staircase and move it elsewhere in order to enter the apartment at the end, where the large and beautiful salon is," meaning the Salon of Hercules known today.

The King's State Apartment

The King's State Apartment comprised eight rooms, six facing north and two facing west; the latter were never finished and would disappear in 1678 to make way for the Hall of Mirrors. *Appartement* was the name given to the gathering of the whole Court from seven in the evening until ten o'clock. The fitting out of the suite took some ten years to complete. Early in the process, until 1675, Louis's ceremonial enfilade began on the west only with the "salon between the great landing and

The Queen's Staircase,
built in 1679-1781
by Jules Hardouin-
Mansart on the south
side of the Marble
Courtyard opposite its
pendant,
the Ambassadors'
Staircase on the north
side leading to the
King's State Apartment
on the *étage noble.*
In 1701 a loggia was
added (not visible here),
allowing the Queen
and her ladies to take
the air on the balcony
over the Marble
Courtyard. During
this campaign the upper
wall was decorated
with an illusionistic
painting by Meusnier,
Blin de Fontenay,
and Poërson. Overall,
the aesthetic is the same
as that in the
Ambassadors' Staircase:
Classical orders,
polychrome marble
revetments, and
trompe-l'œil painting.

The Salon of Diana, where Bernini's portrait bust of Louis XIV (1665) was installed on either side of two Venuses from the collection of Cardinal Mazarin. Originally this was the first of the "Planetary Salons" that visitors entered after mounting the Ambassadors' Staircase (destroyed in 1752). With its sumptuous combination of polychrome marbles, Italian fireplace, and illusionistic ceiling designed in compartments, the Salon of Diana set a truly royal tone for the whole enfilade of State Apartments on the King's side of the central block at Versailles.

the guardroom." This was the Salon of Diana, begun in 1671 and decorated with a program of marble panels, monumental frames, and robust mouldings. The rich colorism of the geometric paneling was worked out in white, black, red, and greenish Campana marbles combined with mottled red Languedoc marble. The whole was brightened with gilded swags and stuccos applied to the walls and both ceiling and coving by Hutinot. So important was the undertaking that in 1675, three years into the project, twelve million *livres* had to be set aside "in order to finish all these works of marble and stucco." Around Bernini's bust of the King, executed in 1665, was arrayed imagery signifying navigation and the pleasures of the hunt and the sea. Apart from Audran's overdoors, the decorative program focused on the moon as personified by Diana in Blanchard's painting hung over the marble fireplace, on the animal sacrificed in place of Iphigenia, represented in a painting by La Fosse, and the nocturnal encounters of the goddess and the shepherd Endymion, the latter asleep in the arms of Morpheus, as depicted by, again, Blanchard.

In 1675 the room lost its place as first in the planetary series, for what Le Vau had planned as an upper landing for the Ambassadors' Staircase became, under d'Orbay, a salon whose plan and décor were determined by the room immediately below. Here too, polychrome marbles dominated just as in the Salon of Diana, but the original purpose is recalled in trompe-l'œil panels and columns executed by Rousseau, who also painted the illusionistic statues of Meleager and Atalanta. Houasse transformed the room into a Salon of Venus when he took elements from an earlier project, intended for a small study overlooking the western terrace, and created a celebration of love and youth around a Triumph of Venus. Here he assembled famous figures from the antique world depicted in amorous abductions, in marvelous spectacles, such as games in the Circus Augustea, or yet in the Gardens of Babylon, Semiramis, or Nebuchadnezzar. The opulent Salons of Diana and Venus, with their Italianate décor, served as vestibules to the King's State Apartment, the whole arrangement reminiscent of the Planetary Suite in the Palazzo Pitti in Florence.

Next, the enfilade flowed into a guardroom identified as the Salon of Mars by a large ceiling painting dedicated to the deity. An extensive program of sculpture, executed by the Marsy brothers, featured such military symbols as helmets and trophies. As in the Salon of Venus, a ceiling divided into compartments allowed Houasse and Jouvenet to exploit episodes from antiquity for the greater glory of Louis XIV and his military feats. Both here and in the antechamber and bedchamber that followed, marble was adopted only for door and window frames, the wainscoting, and the mantelpiece, a treatment that identified the rooms as part of the monarch's own living quarters. The regularity of the planetary sequence was somewhat modified in the antechamber (today the Salon of Mercury), given that it received more light, thanks to the presence of a third window, this one on the park side and giving onto the balcony then wrapped about the interior courtyard situated between the Envelope and the old château. Here, in fact, stood the King's bed rather than in the adjacent bedchamber, now the Salon of Apollo, which had been converted into a throne room. The marble décor, although restrained, was particularly well considered, in the view of Félibien, who described it as "green-brown and mottled red with veins of emerald green." "The wall panels and embrasures," he continued, "are of white marble filled with compartments of another, more reddish marble from Egypt, another type of marble in black and white, and fine agate marble from Serrancolin and the Pyrenees." No wonder the royal building accounts mention tens of thousands of *livres* spent for the marble inlay used throughout the ceremonial apartments! As for the room's purpose, it is heralded in Charles de La Fosse's ceiling painting entitled *The Triumph of Apollo and the Sun over the Four Continents*.

A turn back towards the west led to three short-lived rooms designed by Le Vau: the

The Queen's Guardroom. "The sentry shall allow neither priest nor unknown monk to enter... nor anyone ill-looking or recently scarred by smallpox." Those who did enter from the outside arrived by way of the Queen's Staircase (see page 51), which leads directly to the Guardroom, a pendant to the Salon of Diana in the King's State Apartment. As the décor of marble and gilded, white-painted boiseries suggest, the Queen's suite was intended to match the splendor of the King's Planetary Suite. Originally a chapel (1672), the room gained its present décor in 1676-1681, when elements designed for the never-built Salon of Jupiter were reused here. This economy of recycled valuables was characteristic of the Bourbon court. The antique bust is said to portray the Roman Emperor Vitellius.

LEFT: *Louis XIV.*
Portrait bust by Antoine Coysevox (1679), displayed on one of the two marble mantelpieces in the King's State Bedchamber.

OPPOSITE: The King's State Bedchamber, fitted out in 1701 and today restored with the winter furnishings used under Louis XV and Louis XVI. By moving his ceremonial bedroom to a position at the bottom of the Marble Courtyard on the *étage noble* and immediately behind the Hall of Mirrors, Louis XIV made a grand, symbolic gesture, for he would now sleep at the very center of his world. Moreover, the Sun King *(le Roi-Soleil)* could henceforth rise with the sun as its first rays penetrated through his tall windows from the eastern horizon running along the Avenue de Paris.

Council Room or Jupiter Cabinet, whose paintings would be moved to the Queen's State Apartment; the Saturn Cabinet, a small bedroom soon to become a hallway; and the Venus Cabinet overlooking the paved terrace and its fountain. These park-side rooms, which Louis XIV referred to as his Small Apartment, appear not to have been very practical, according to remarks made by the King to Colbert in 1673: "I forgot to say, in my last memorandum, that we need to open two doors through to the dressing room of my large apartment, one from the large corner study, the other from the bedroom between the study mentioned above and the one overlooking the terrace. There should also be a door between the large bedroom and the antechamber, and the small study behind." Three years after Le Vau died nothing had been finally determined, even though work was still under way on an apartment whose splendor was soon to disappear.

On the south side of the Royal Courtyard, directly opposite the Ambassadors' Staircase in the north wing, another grand staircase had been built, only to be replaced in 1679 by the one known today. The steps led up to the Queen's State Apartment, which seems to have been based on the King's suite, since it consisted of the same enfilade and a comparable succession of decorative programs suitable for the various rooms. Work on the chambers continued from 1671 to 1680. The first room, which corresponded to the Salon of Diana, served as a chapel during the years 1672-1676, until it was transformed into a billiard room, then a salon, and finally a marble-lined guardroom. It was here that part of Coypel's décor from the Jupiter Cabinet—portraying the god along with ancient wise men performing acts of piety and justice—would be reinstalled following the destruction of that study to make way for the Hall of Mirrors. Farther along came the antechamber, a onetime guardroom, which corresponded to the Salon of Mars in the King's Apartment. Spread over the coving was Vignon and Paillet's decorative narrative, in camaïeux with gold highlights, depicting the courageous deeds of such Classical queens and goddesses as Rodogune, Artemisia, Zenobia, Ipsicrates, Clelia, and Aprelia. Madeleine de Boulogne's overdoor paintings of military musical instruments had been exhibited at the Salon of 1673. The room had also been furnished with armchairs placed in front of the fireplace for the use of Louis and Marie-Thérèse, who thus made themselves available for admiration by their court and subjects.

The Queen's Salon, or Salon des Nobles, was dedicated to Mercury, as revealed in a ceiling painting by Michel Corneille, who represented the deity hovering above a coving where antique women demonstrated their mastery of the arts and sciences. The vignettes were entitled *Cesicena Painting, Sappho Playing the Lyre, Penelope Weaving Her Tapestry,* and *Aspasia with Philosophers.*

For the Queen's Bedchamber, a pendant to the Salon of Apollo, de Sève painted episodes from the lives of ancient queens—Cleopatra, Dido, Rhodope, and Nicotrix—arranged in a circle about the sun. Finally, back towards the garden terrace, there were three *cabinets* decorated by Loire and Nocret, all of which would later be swallowed up by the Salon of Peace and the Hall of Mirrors.

Members of the royal family may have been crowded into the attic, where the same artists cited above were also at work, but two storeys below, Louis XIV made certain that the ground floor of the Envelope would be as opulent as the ceremonial apartments on the *étage noble*. The apartments of Monsieur and Madame lay to the south, each of the suites composed of antechambers, a bedchamber, and a *cabinet*. For Monsieur, "the King's only brother," there was a guardroom as well. The décor, purely ornamental, presented neither narrative nor historical content, with the result that its rich array of garlands, cabochons, and scrolls veered towards overload, quite unlike what had been achieved upstairs.

Louis XIV had a bathing suite installed below his ceremonial apartment, a project that

Decorative motifs
in the Salon of Venus
and the Salon of Diana.
The *Capitoline Venus*
is an antique bust
bequeathed by Cardinal
Mazarin to Louis XIV
in 1661. The
magnificent room it
adorns was an addition
to the State Apartments
made in 1683-1684 to
provide a vestibule
for the Ambassadors'
Staircase. The porphyry
columns suggest that
Hardouin-Mansart
had something to do
with the overall design.
The relief-carved and
gilded door panels
were created by
Philippe Caffiéri
and date to 1681.

continued from 1671 to 1680. The rooms, located in the middle of the north frontage, comprised, on the west side, a Doric vestibule, an Ionic room, an octagonal corner cabinet, a resting room, and a bathroom opening onto the gallery. The decoration must have been sumptuous, given the nearly 250,000 *livres* doled out to marble masons, painters (François and Jean-Baptiste Le Moyne, Houasse, de Sève, Audran, Le Brun, Bon Boulogne, Paillet, and Colonne), sculptors (Tuby, Marsy, Regnaudin, Le Hongre, Le Gros, Girardon, and Anguier), and the *bronzier* Cucci. In 1685 Louis XIV assigned the suite to Madame de Montespan, his current favorite, for whose sons, the Duc du Maine and the Comte de Toulouse, both sired by the King, the rooms would gradually be dismantled. A couple of generations later, they fell to two of Louis XV's unwed daughters, Madame Adélaïde and Madame Victoire. Yet, the original Bathing Suite is known from archival documents and engravings, which have made it possible to identify Clairion's *Venus* copied from the antique and Houasse's painting entitled *Apollo and Daphne*. Meanwhile, drawings by Le Brun in the Louvre appear to represent the gilt-metal Months that once adorned the octagonal cabinet. The comfortable bathroom boasted a handsome marble floor, two tubs, and a bath made from a single block of Rance marble. Even more impressive was the resting room, with its luxurious décor of marble columns crowned by Caffiéri and Temporiti's gilt-bronze capitals, and its relief-carved wooden shutters. The furniture, specially designed for the "pleasures of the bath," included a large Poquelin mirror with a marble frame designed by Le Brun, as well as a bed, armchairs, cushions and stools covered in brocade with inwoven pastoral scenes.

The grotto of thetis

Of all the supplementary buildings at Versailles, the Grotto of Thetis was the one nearest the Château. Here the pleasure of fountains and the intimacy of a retreat had been combined even more perfectly than at the Porcelain Trianon, designed for rest among flowers during strolls in the gardens, or at the Menagerie, a place offering refreshments but very subject to the weather, or yet the Orangery, empty in the summer and filled with precious trees during the winter. The Grotto of Thetis, a picturesque ensemble glorified by beautiful sculptures, marked the apotheosis of those watery shrines or nymphaea so fashionable throughout Renaissance Europe.

The theme of the Versailles grotto, involving an exhausted Apollo at rest with Thetis following his solar tour of the earth, is attributed to Claude Perrault, who may have been inspired by a rockery owned by his mother and today known only from engravings by Lepautre, Chauveau, and Edelinck published in 1679, shortly before its destruction. Just as at the Menagerie or the original Trianon designed by Le Vau, Louis XIV spared no expense in his pursuit of a brilliant, even extravagant effect. It was as if the King wished to continue or even perpetuate the spectacular festivities of 1664 and 1668. Within twenty years, however, the beauty produced by so much effort and ingenuity would be gone, owing not only to the building's complex fragility but also to the sudden decision to enlarge the Château.

On the exterior, only the front of the cubic pavilion was decorated. A three-bay arcade filled with Breton's grillework gates, representing the rays of the sun, gave visual but not physical access to the interior. Interwoven jets of water playing across the front had the same effect. The decorative program on the façade—faux blocks of ice and Van Obstal's reliefs depicting Apollo, nymphs, tritons, and marine putti, applied to the piers, spandrels, and attic—was somewhat spare by comparison

This anonymous painting (c. 1670) depicts Louis XIV, the Grand Dauphin, and Madame de Montespan gathered in splendor before the Grotto of Thetis. Also included, on the far right behind Madame de Montespan, is Madame de Maintenon, still a royal governess, holding in her arms the infant Duc du Maine, the first of the sons born of the love affair between La Montespan and the King. Louis XIV would acknowledge and legitimatize all his bastard children. Clearly visible on the Grotto façade is the brightly gilded "sunray" grillework radiating across the entire arcade.

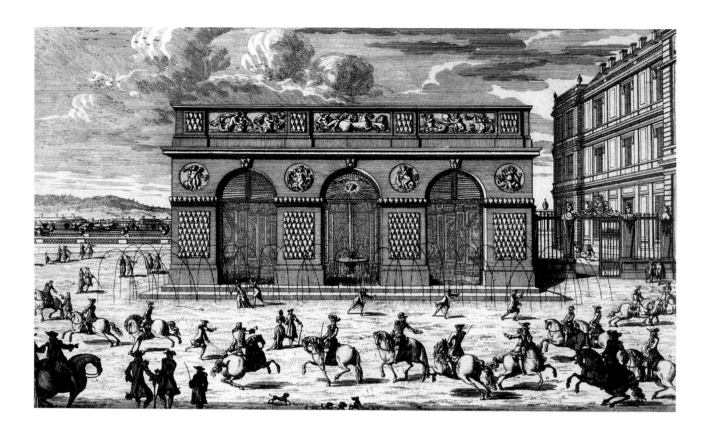

The façade of the Grotto of Thetis, begun in 1664 and destroyed in 1684 to make way for the North Wing. The small jets of water, like the gilded wrought-iron gates, encouraged Louis XIV's courtiers to view the grotto interior from a distance. This made what they saw appear all the more magical: a fantasy of mirrors, shells, and groups of horses and gods carved in white marble (see pages 222-223).
Engraving by Pérelle (1672).

with the plenitude inside. Here the pavement was a riot of rocks, shells, ice blocks, coral, mother-of-pearl, and crystal, all arranged in geometric patterns. Walls and vault alike swarmed with masked figures, sea creatures, fleurs-de-lis, and birds. The pillars all but disappeared under a decorative surfeit centered upon the King's device. Overhead, streams of water, fed by a reservoir on the roof, gushed from giant marble shells carved in Cannes in 1666. Adding to the overall richness were the color of the limestone and pebbles on the floor (laid out like the broderie flowerbeds of the north parterre), the nacreous reflections from the mother-of-pearl, the blue walls and red pillars, and the gold-framed mirrors reflecting everything into infinity. Light radiated from equally *rocailles* candlesticks made of shells. As for the water, it emerged from the floor in sprays while also spilling over the rim of an urn held by a personified river situated deep in the lunette of the central niche. Its flow activated an hydraulic organ purchased from someone in Montmorency. "At the sound of water, the organ joined in with the song of small imitation birds made of shell, perched in the various niches; by an even more surprising trick, you could hear an echo repeating this soft music."

The King, however, wanted his grotto to be more than merely picturesque, and so he supplemented the crashing water and petrified waves with three monumental sculptural groups. In the central niche stood the seven figures carved in white marble by François Girardon and Thomas Regnaudin for *Apollo Attended by the Nymphs of Thetis*. The flanking niches held two groups by Guérin and the Marsy brothers: *Horses of the Sun Watered and Carried by Tritons*. This magnificent, vital ensemble was steeped in both academic tradition and the realistic verve characteristic of the whole Versailles bestiary. Only in the Grotto of Thetis did the sonorous exuberance, decorative imagination, and technical mastery of the sculptors then employed at Versailles come into full play.

Clearly, Louis XIV attached great importance to this project. The royal building accounts reveal six long years of daily expenditure to finish the main part of what was a small pavilion, some forty feet long and just under twenty-five feet high. Petit's reports to Colbert mention the impatience of the King—a constant factor when it concerned his buildings—to see the organ installed and in working order: "We should give the order for the organ at Montmorency to be transported promptly, and lose no time in getting it seen to by Jolly, who is never in much of a hurry" (February 1666). Two months later Petit reported: "His Majesty… wished to see the grotto, which He finds very fine, and said He knows no one who takes longer to complete a job than the said Jolly; this month we received the rest of the organ and machinery from Montmorency, so one hopes that Jolly will soon be with us, as he is sorely needed." When poor Jolly fell ill, it was noted that workmen progressed with the organ "rather slowly."

Equally revealing are the payments made to the artists. For each group of the *Horses of the Sun,* Guérin received 14,000 *livres,* as did the two Marsy brothers. An identical sum went to Tuby for his shepherd, *Acis,* and his nymph, *Galatea,* while Girardon and Regnaudin realized 18,000 *livres* for their work on *Apollo and the Nymphs.* Could Guérin have been treated as a mature and established artist? Is it possible that he received the same amount as the Marsys, both of them younger, because the work undertaken by the three artists demanded greater invention than did the gestural variations found in the other groups? Everyone received final payment in 1677 and 1678, thirteen years after the grotto had been started. The work being artistic rather than mechanical in nature, Louis XIV showed no signs of impatience.

Would Time be the ally of Fame? A close examination of the ewer held by the nymph kneeling before Apollo reveals that a Classical object had been emblazoned with a highly topical theme— "Passage of the Rhine" *(Passage du Rhin)*—an exploit much commented upon by Madame de Sévigné. It was added to the Girardon sculpture after the artist and Regnaudin had already been paid two-thirds of what they were owed, signifying that the work was very likely almost finished. A bit of flattery arranged by an ambitious courtier? Whatever the explanation, the reference exemplifies the manner in which Versailles "appropriated" the Classical world for its own contemporary purposes. Witness the interior of the Château during the same period. After the publication of La Fontaine's *Les Amours de Psyché et Cupidon* (1669), everyone understood that to represent Apollo was to sing the praises of King Louis. Here, a sculptor, in a barely visible place, has accorded the sovereign and his family the same reverential treatment.

In 1684 Louis XIV decided to construct the North Wing of the Château, on the very ground occupied by the Grotto of Thetis. Thus would be lost not just a witness to the dazzling splendor of Louis XIV's first Versailles, but also a major work marking the development of a château that, between 1672 and 1678, ceased to be a country house and became a royal residence.

COMPLETION UNDER HARDOUIN-MANSART

A detail of the Hall of Mirrors.

Under the direction of Jules Hardouin-Mansart, the Château de Versailles would, in essence, assume its final form. The campaign began at the entrance, where the architect had to resolve the discrepancy between the level of the rubble-paved forecourt and that of the Place d'Armes. In 1670-1672 Louis XIV had four large pavilions built for the secretaries of state, one at each corner of the forecourt and linked as pairs by two balustrades, one on the north and the other on the south. In 1678 Mansart was asked to replace the balustrades with two long buildings, today known as the Ministers' Wings. Here, even while erecting the Hall of Mirrors with its pale-stone façade and flat roof, Mansart chose to continue the old red-white-blue combination—brick walls, white trim, and pitch roofs of slate— thereby harmonizing the new structures with the rest of the courtyard and the style prescribed for all buildings in town. Largely free of sculptural embellishment, the new wings had on the courtyard side a basement storey that increased in height towards the Place d'Armes, where the elevation, facing the town, ended up substantially steeper. Monumental stonework and long, nineteen-bay arcades contributed further to the effect of great solidity. This was not mere illusion, inasmuch as the massive constructions helped stabilize the earth moved here from the courtyards.

At the risk of creating the impression of a citadel sealed off by its courtyards, entrance to the Château was fixed at the outer edge of the precinct. Two fast-access ramps were built, again one on the north and the other on the south. The ramps' downward slope towards the Place d'Armes was

managed in two parts. Along each of the new wings a wide paved corridor, reserved for carriages, was edged with a balustrade and given an incline that accelerated only as it curved in towards the gate at the center. The vast space of the forecourt, lying between the two balustrades and their drinking fountains, was laid out in a simple, straightforward manner. Finally, to negotiate the sudden drop from the ramps to the level of the Place d'Armes, Mansart constructed two large guardhouses, one on either side of the forecourt near the entrance and behind massive retaining walls, their height equal to that of the grillework fence ordered from Fordrin and Hasté. The guardhouses, over which the final, descending curve of the ramps passed, were linked to the entrance fence and thus to one another by sentry boxes capped with sculptural groups from the hands of Girardon and the Marsy brothers. Together, the marble figures symbolized victories over Spain and the Holy Roman Empire.

Beyond the forecourt, towards the Château, the Royal Courtyard was also transformed, its area defined by an iron fence, lower than the one facing the Place d'Armes but made by the same artisan, Hasté, who undertook the project in 1679. In 1682 the two sentry boxes would be crowned with Tuby's *Peace* and Coysevox's *Abundance*. Ten years earlier the flat roof terraces of the two lateral wings had been replaced by double-pitch roofs behind balustrades, thereby providing stylistic continuity among the roof lines from the Ministers' Pavilions to the bottom of the Marble Courtyard. The new attics offered space for lodgings, garrets, and furniture storage, all of which proved most useful once Louis XIV moved his court permanently to Versailles in 1682, when the wings would become centers of intense activity. While Bontemps, the governor of Versailles, occupied the Government Wing on the north, the south wing, today known as the Old Wing, housed the Council Chamber and the Ambassadors' Hall.

The Royal Courtyard, compared to the plain forecourt, was fairly ornate. The façades, with their colonnades, would be further elaborated, above the balustrades, by the addition of gilded leadwork, mouldings, and stone vases on both bull's-eye windows and dormers. The presence of a fountain confirmed that few carriages could gain access, other than those arriving from the Louvre.

The Marble Courtyard also came in for further embellishment after Le Vau's death, a campaign that began with the removal of the corner aviaries. Arched windows were opened in the central salon, which would later become Louis XIV's ceremonial bedchamber, and extended down to the floor. However, the installation of Delobel and Goy's balconies had to be delayed, as Madame de Sévigné reported in 1672: "The other day at Versailles, Monsieur de Berny walked through a window, thinking it was a door. He was given medical treatment; his head was split, but his life is not in danger. This is what happens with these casements that go all the way to the ground—one should never forget to put up a railing. This accident caused quite a stir at Versailles…" Even more impressive was the mansard roof, with its fretwork crest, new ornaments, and lead drainpipes all gilded or painted. In 1679 came the crowning splendor: Girardon and Marsy's mighty pediment at the center, carved with Mars and Hercules seated upon heaped trophies around a clock, which was stopped at the precise moment when Louis XIV died in 1715 and Louis XV in 1774—a pious or reverential application of the principle that the court lived in time with the King.

THE SOUTH AND NORTH WINGS

Also in 1679, the budget allowed for a new 465-foot wing to be built immediately east of the Orangery and extending southward from the Château's core quadrangle. Here too, Hardouin-

The Château de Versailles in 1722.
Painting by Jean-Baptiste Martin, executed during the year the court returned to Versailles, after seven years in Paris, where the Regent, Philippe II, Duc d'Orléans, preferred to live. The Versailles in which the twelve-year-old Louis XV would reside was, owing to neglect, the very one Louis XIV left at the time of his death in 1715. And thus it would remain until the third quarter of the eighteenth century, when Louis XV had Ange-Jacques Gabriel build the "Gabriel Wing" along the north side of the Royal Courtyard and the Theatre or Opéra at the far end of the North Wing.

Hardouin-Mansart modified Le Vau's Envelope by adding two enormous lateral extensions: the North Wing and the South Wing (seen here). With their absolute horizontality, they served the original concept admirably, which was to enlarge the Château without increasing its height. The view seen here provides a detailed glimpse of the paired statues on the attic façade and the crowning balustrade serving as a base for stone urns, firepots, and trophies.

Mansart drew up the plans, while Jacques Gabriel IV oversaw construction. As wide as the entire depth of Le Vau's château, the new wing took into account the living needs of the Dauphin and princes of the blood. On the urban side, the façade adhered to the old brick and stone combination. Here, the apartments gave onto long stone galleries that permitted the inhabitants to access the public area. Never-ending special claims forced the architect and builder to insert mezzanines around the interior courtyards. On the south side, the apartments overlooked the magnificent gardens and park

For the garden façade, Mansart took his queue from the Le Vau Envelope, which meant an elevation comprising ground floor, *étage noble,* and attic, thus one less floor than on the urban side. The garden façade was elaborated with three blocks of projecting bays—at either end as well as at the center—atop which stood a series of monumental figures designed by Le Brun à *l'antique*: gods (Mars and Cebele); virtues (Piety, Justice, Vigilance, Foresight, and Fidelity); arts (Melpemone); and sciences (Cosmography and Chorography, Altimetry, Democracy, and Industry). The sculptors participating in the commission were Buirette, Le Comte, Lespingola, Mazière, and Lespagnandel. A colossal project, the new wing was finished in 1682, by which time the monumentality of the façade, as well as perhaps the instability of the landfill at the far end, spelled doom for Le Nôtre's Cupid Parterre. After briefly reconsidering the whole area, Louis and his advisors decided to move the Orangery farther south and to create a large horizontal parterre, its entrance flanked by two sphinxes intended for the Grotto of Thetis but never placed there.

The installation of a new chapel in 1682, the demolition of the Grotto of Thetis, and the imminent decision to erect a proper chapel, and, of course, the ever-pressing need for more space—all made it seem imperative to construct a wing on the north side comparable in every way to the new wing to the south, except for the deep slope of the terrain. It would have the same interior courtyards accessed by stone-built galleries; however, the part near the royal apartments was to be reserved for the needs of the chapel, meaning a sacristy and lodgings for the priest or missionary. The rest was divided into apartments for high-born members of the court, with such illustrious names as Berry, Maine, Noailles, Beauviller, Lorge, Sforza, Antin, and Villars.

Saint-Simon, at a somewhat later date, comments on the unremitting struggle required to find a space in which to live at Versailles. Writing in 1710, the Duke confided to his diary that "the King rose from the head of the table (he willingly sat at one of the ends), and I begged him to think of me for a lodging so I might attend on him more assiduously. He replied that none was vacant." Finally, however, by evicting several occupants, Louis XIV installed his importunate courtier in a fine, spacious apartment with five rooms, an extra storey, studies or *cabinets,* and even back *cabinets* that seem to have satisfied him hugely. "In my rear *cabinet* I had a desk, chairs, books, and everything I required; people who knew it referred to it familiarly as my boutique and, in fact, it looked rather like one."

The hall of mirrors

Once the two State Apartments had been finished, Louis XIV began to think of the Hall of Mirrors *(Galerie des Glaces)* as indispensable. Mansart, after examining the plans drawn up by Le Vau's team, realized that the project would entail major remodeling of the entire garden side of the Château. Again, time was of the essence, and so the job of demolishing the terrace was already well advanced by June 1678, even though several different approaches to the new addition were still being considered. Come the autumn, construction was already in full swing and work had started on the decorative sculpture. For the entire façade, Mansart retained the architectural rhythm already established by Le Vau on the lateral façades, except for the rectangular windows on the *étage noble,* which he replaced with arched ones: monumental ground floor, *piano nobile* with colonnaded avant-corps, statues atop the cornice, and trophies on the roof balustrade. The sculptors Jouvenet, Le Hongre, Houzeau, and Buyster carved the pilasters, capitals, trophies, consoles, and urns. On the interior, however, something new was happening, thanks to the collaboration of Le Brun and Mansart. Already they had Caffiéri and Lespagnandel at work on the great stucco frieze, which would be gilded by La Baronnière in 1686. A project of such complexity needed to be well organized, in the interest of which Prou was paid 619 *livres* for a canvas-covered platform of pine planks, making it possible for the painters to work overhead relatively undisturbed by marble and stucco dust.

Needless to say, the King closely monitored the progress on the great hall. The interior measured five bays long, with each bay comprising a three-unit arcade, separated by niches enclosing tall piers embellished with relief carvings. The series of arcades terminated at either end in a bay with a single arch. In the words of La Martinière, "seventeen tall round-headed casements match a parallel range of seventeen blind arches filled from top to bottom with mirrors that double every object." Mansart had adopted the most economical of all solutions, which was to bond the hall directly onto the original structure by means of the wall of mirrors. A genuine innovation, the sparkling revetments reflecting daylight from the garden must have struck seventeenth-century eyes as wondrous indeed. A few years later, the same solution would again be employed at the Trianon, to improve daytime illumination in a deep corner room, also named for its mirrors.

Now Charles Le Brun entered the scene. In 1681 the *Mercure* noted: "The ornaments, sculpture, and, finally, all the things that contribute to the Hall's embellishment result from the genius of His Majesty's First Painter." Thus, it was Le Brun who made the drawings for the lion skins above each arcade, perhaps vestiges of an earlier project with the story of Hercules as its theme. Girardon prepared the model for the windows' keystones, while Caffiéri executed the metal capitals. These gave Le Brun the opportunity to create a "French composite order" but à *l'antique,* of course. It consisted of two corner cockerels, palm leaves each with a fleur-de-lis at the center, and a head of Apollo in the middle of the abacus.

As for the great barrel vault, Le Brun proposed two different solutions before the program now in place was finally adopted. One of them, about which little is known, would have involved Apollo and produced a ceiling covered with pictorial scenes framed by stucco draperies, opulent mouldings, putti, and medallions—altogether a décor reminiscent of the Ambassadors' Staircase. Reserve passages would have been filled with sky effects. A project drawing dated March 1679 indicates that Le Brun continued working at the Apollo scheme for some time. The artist based his second idea on the life of Hercules, and he pursued it in some depth, for numerous fine drawings still exist. Le Brun knew the subject well, having already developed it in Paris for Cardinal Richelieu's palace (today the oldest part of the Palais-Royal) early in his career and then again at the Hôtel Lambert. Around the central composition—the Apotheosis of Hercules on Mount Olympus—the surface was to be divided into large oval compartments, separated by smaller ones forming bands narrating the exploits of Apollo, Bacchus, Neptune, and Pan. Despite its symbolic relevance to royal history and its advanced state (even partly engraved by Simonneau), Le Brun's second project would also be abandoned. Too allegorical? Perhaps too Italian, with its illusionistic view into the heavens, a device reminiscent of a project the artist longed to complete for the chapel.

The Hall of Mirrors, created
by Jules Hardouin-Mansart
and Charles Le Brun between 1678 and
1686. An arcade of seventeen windows
is reflected in a parallel arcade,
this one glazed with mirror.
Also adding to the luminosity
of the gallery are twenty crystal
chandeliers and twenty-eight
free-standing torchères,
these executed in gilt-bronze
and installed in time
for the celebrations marking
the marriage of the Dauphin
(future Louis XVI)
to Marie-Antoinette,
Archduchess of Austria.
The arcade of tall windows
provides an unobstructed view
onto the full panorama
of the Versailles gardens
and park.

For a century the Hall of Mirrors was the busy center of court life, a place to exhibit the latest additions to the royal collections as well as a place for social encounter and diplomatic receptions. Anonymous eighteenth-century engraving.

Suddenly, in the autumn of 1678, after having settled the first Treaty of Nijmegen, the Secret Council, Nivelon tells us, "found suitable, and resolved, that his history of the conquests should be portrayed. Le Brun shut himself away for two days in the former Hôtel de Grammont and produced the first design for this great work, the central painting of which forms the hub of everything; whereupon he was ordered to continue the rest along the same principles and with the same fine lighting, with Monsieur Colbert's careful proviso that nothing be featured that was not conform to the truth, or too burdensome for the foreign powers who might be concerned."

The central panel set forth the determination of the King to make a show of arms in the face of the age-old arrogance of powers adjacent to or near France. All about this pivotal element, Le Brun alternated scenes and medallions in more or less symmetrical order. The largest vignettes concern the most recent military or diplomatic successes, those dating from 1672 to 1678. The medallions near the cornice (except those towards the Salon of Peace) and the two medallions on either side of the great central composition recall events dating back to the early part of Louis XIV's reign. The other medallions celebrate improvements realized throughout the realm in matters of justice, economy, transport, and police. A curious, zigzag disposition of disparate iconography, Le Brun's vault painting has provided rich fodder for a dozen old guidebooks and a more recent critic, whose explanations are best followed by those skilled at hopscotch.

The first project for the barrel vault over the Hall of Mirrors, its theme the Feats of Hercules.
Drawing by Charles Le Brun, Louis XIV's official court painter and the principal author of the State Apartments.

The Le Brun vault was not the great hall's only ornament. Indeed, babbling courtiers could stand amazed before the wealth of gleaming opulence arranged along the walls. The furnishings included eight Classical statues, such the *Arles Venus* and the *Diana with a Female Deer*, some of the pieces restored by Girardon, porphyry busts of Roman emperors clad in alabaster robes, sixteen large stands supporting crystal girandoles, twelve agate and alabaster tables with carved gilt-wood legs, "vases of porphyry and Oriental alabaster, with different subjects and of extraordinary size, arranged with a number of crystal girandoles, some on tables, others beneath… and in front of the arcades filled with glass mirrors…" Yet, this prodigious hoard, just described by Félibien, had been installed to compensate for the lost solid-silver furniture.

As if Le Brun had not devoted enough of his talent to the ceiling, or provided sufficient guidance to the army of artists busy at Versailles, the King's First Painter was also asked to design and produce the Hall of Mirrors' original, fabulous but short-lived, silver furniture—a vast ensemble of urns and stands, chandeliers and girandoles, basins, incense-burners or braziers, buckets, *scabellons,* ewers, dishes, andirons, candlesticks representing the Labors of Hercules, stools, benches, and a table. The sheer quality of the design and chasing made this exquisite *mobilier* worth a thousand times its weight in metal. In fact, Louis XIV regarded it as a kind of state treasury, which he unhesitatingly consigned to the melting pots in December 1689, so as to finance renewed war against the League of

PAGES 78-79:
The two salons at either
end of the Hall
of Mirrors—the Salon
of War on the north
and the Salon of Peace
on the south—also
played a central role
in the life of the court
at Versailles. Their
décor, realized by
Le Brun and Hardouin-
Mansart in 1678,
consists of vaults
painted with historical
themes, polychrome
marble revetments,
gilt-bronze wall reliefs
depicting mythological
subjects, and antique
statuary sometimes
restored by sculptors
in service to the King.

RIGHT: Detail of
a gilded relief
(*Bound Slave*)
decorating the fireplace
in the Salon of War.
Designed by
Charles Le Brun
and executed
by Antoine Coysevox.

Machine for raising the chandelier in the Salon of War.

Augsburg. However, this did not happen without regrets, as noted by the Grand Provost, the Marquis de Sourches, on 1 December: "We were most surprised when the King announced that he was going to send all his silver to the Mint to be melted down, and we were extremely sorry to see so many admirable works being destroyed overnight. It was an incalculable loss, as making it had cost a fortune; but the King paid no heed to any of these reasons and, believing it essential to melt all these magnificent ornaments from his Château at Versailles for the well-being of his State, he implacably resolved to do so. It is said that, after taking this decision, he sent for Du Metz, who was in charge of his furniture and, after inviting him into his *cabinet* alone, told him: I am going to tell you something that will surprise you a good deal; I am going to send all my silver to the Mint to have it melted down." Du Metz was taken aback and exclaimed: 'Oh, Sire! Where is Monsieur Colbert? If he were still alive, he would never have suffered Your Majesty to melt down all these fine works of art.' And what else could he have done?' retorted the King. 'He would,' answered Du Metz, 'have found a thousand other ways to spare Your Majesty such sorrow.' The King shrugged and replied: 'That's as it may be, but none can be found at present!'."

   The brilliance of the reign may have climaxed in the Hall of Mirrors, but the salons at either end of the great gallery—the Salon of War near the King's State Apartment and the Salon of Peace near the Queen's—proved to be almost as impressive. Large rooms in their own right, they were faced in marble throughout, like the Hall of Mirrors, and their pilasters, too, adorned with metal trophies. Moreover, they had benefited from the attentions of the same team of artists: Coysevox and Prou in the

Salon of War, Legros and Massou in the Salon of Peace, and, of course, Le Brun, who painted the ceilings. In the Salon of War his theme was France's struggle with the Holy Roman Empire, Spain, and Holland, whereas in the Salon of Peace, the subject was twofold: peace magnanimously extended by France to the three defeated powers, and Christian Europe triumphant. Work progressed slowly, and Coysevox's huge relief medallion entitled *Louis XIV Victorious* would never be replaced by Coustou's *Passage of the Rhine,* the work actually commissioned for the site. Similarly, the painting over the mantelpiece in the Salon of Peace—*Louis XV Granting Peace to Europe* by Lemoyne - was installed only in 1729, well after the death of Louis XIV, and its subject served as a clear signal that this room would soon become part of the Queen's Apartment.

THE CHAPEL

In 1689 the King, having grown pious, finally decided to build a great chapel. Hitherto services and prayers had taken place in rooms set aside as oratories, at first in the northeast corner of the Château, and then at the far end of the Queen's Apartment. As for the temporary chapel of 1672, installed in what is now the Queen's Guardroom, little is known beyond a few decorative sketches made by Le Brun. Four years later the chapel migrated next door, to the Great Guardroom, which would never be completed, and so neither would the oratory.

The fourth chapel lasted longer, from 1682 to 1710, occupying the site of what is now the Salon of Hercules and the vestibule below. It was here that Bossuet and Bourdaloue preached and the main religious ceremonies of the reign took place. Still, the décor was relatively sober, despite the contributions of Mazeline and Jouvenet and those of Le Hongre, who prepared the maquette for the pulpit and carved two door reliefs. The interior can be visualized, however, thanks to depictions by artists such as Dieu, in *The Duke of Burgundy's Wedding,* or Pezey, in *Dangeau's Oath of Loyalty to the King,* a picture marking the appointment of the said Dangeau as Grand Master of the Order of Our Lady of Mount Carmel and Saint Lazarus in 1695. On both east and west sides, a three-bay arcade gave onto the courtyard and gardens, while the pedimented high altar stood against the north wall, flanked by two columns and a pair of tall angels. This chapel, too, looks as if it were merely provisional. A number of extant drawings record ideas for a central-plan chapel, a veritable monument, complete with dome and lantern, that was intended for the middle of the North Wing. Nothing came of the grandiose scheme, but it would not be forgotten.

Once construction began, the new Chapel rose at a hectic pace. The nave built abreast the north wing, the fitting out of the vestibule and salon, the wall reliefs—all were under way when suddenly work had to be halted because of war with the League of Augsburg. The year 1698 brought a fresh start, not least in the aesthetic domain, for now polychrome marbles had been abandoned in favor of pale stone, except in the paving. Work continued for several years, although not without delays in payment for the lack of funds, according to the royal buildings accounts.

In 1700 the King had to reduce his provisional budget by a third, just when the sculptors were about to undertake one of the most prestigious projects imaginable. They had no choice but to manage with small wages, sometimes no more than few hundred *livres* for a capital or gargoyle. Underneath, however, the artists seemed determined to keep the project going. Thus, work recommenced on several fronts: the cornice, the altar, and the statues on the exterior balustrade, for which Tonnerre stone had been purchased. On the tall, peaked roof there would be monumental groups of cherubs

The Chapel, built in
1698-1710 from plans
by Hardouin-Mansart,
possibly with ideas
drawn from an earlier
proposal made
by Claude Perrault.
The architect Robert
de Cotte supervised
the decoration of the
beautiful interior, where
color is reserved entirely
for the marble paving
and the vaults overhead,
the latter—God the
Father at the center of
an illusionistic
Heaven—painted by
Antoine Coypel.
Guillaume and Nicolas
Coustou executed the
sculpture, including the
Way of the Cross reliefs
on the piers. The King
sat in the soaring
tribune, its Corinthian
colonnade inspired
perhaps by the Louvre
Colonnade. The whole
is flooded with light
from a tall clearstorey,
which, largely free
of stained glass, is truly
clear, anticipating
the taste of the
eighteenth-century
Enlightenment.

The Fall of the Rebel Angels, a study by Le Brun for the third chapel installed at Versailles.
Although never realized, it would serve as a point of departure for Antoine Coypel when he undertook to paint the ceiling
in Hardouin-Mansart's Chapel, the first at Versailles to be an independent structure.

cast in lead as well as a lacy, fretwork crest. The King, together with Mansart, spent a long time considering the design of the lantern; made by Hardy, it would be removed under Louis XV. Finally, candlestands and urns extended the upward thrust of the flying buttresses, which sprang from an outer range of piers serving as bases for stone figures: Fathers of the Church, around the apse; the Twelve Apostles, along the nave; and the Four Virtues (Faith, Charity, Justice, and Religion), over the lower courtyard.

On the interior, the elevation of the three-storey nave consists of a massive arcade, a deep as well as very high tribune with a Corinthian colonnade soaring aloft from a balustrade base, and a clearstorey above a handsome cornice serving as a white framework for the colorism of the entirely painted vault. The interior was radiant with light flowing through the clear panes of tall windows on either side.

The Versailles Chapel, a true house of prayer, was dedicated to Saint Louis. From the north side projected a tall, narrow structure housing the Chapel of Saint Louis on the ground floor and the Chapel of the Blessed Virgin on the tribune level. Along the side aisles were secondary altars dedicated to the patron saints of the royal family: Carlo Borromeo, Anne, Adelaide, Victoria, and Philip. Behind the high altar stood the Holy Sacrament altar, which was removed in the eighteenth century, at the behest of the Dauphin and the Queen, to make way for an altar consecrated to the Sacred Heart.

Jean Jouvenet, *The Descent of the Holy Spirit upon the Apostles (Pentecost).*
A study for the actual ceiling over the royal tribune in the Chapel, where the Boullogne brothers executed a series dedicated to the Apostles.

Louis XIV in the fourth chapel installed at Versailles, on the site of the present Salon of Hercules.
The scene, painted by Antoine Pesey: "Louis XIV accepting the oath of the Marquis de Dangeau, grand master of the merged orders
of Notre Dame of Mount Carmel and of Saint Lazare, 29 December 1685."

Despite Saint-Simon, who likened the Chapel to a vast tomb, the decorative program devised for the interior was in fact highly sophisticated: God the Father represented on the high vault; the Ascension above the high altar; God the Father in Glory and the Prophets in the nave; and Pentecost around the tribune. Intermingled with all the images were angels bearing trophies or instruments of the Passion and the kneeling figures of Charlemagne and Saint Louis (similar to those in Paris's Church of Saint Paul). Looking down from the tribune ceiling were the Twelve Apostles. When it came to the overhead areas, Charles de La Fosse had hoped to obtain the commission for the whole, but the scale of the project, the time it would require, and the Versailles tradition of team work prompted a division of labor, at a cost of almost 100,000 *livres.* The tribune ceilings were assigned to the Boullognes, the apsidal vault to La Fosse, the nave vault to Coypel, and the royal pew and Saint Louis Chapel to Jouvenet. To integrate and harmonize the various parts and styles, an overall decorative network was developed. Gilded or trompe-l'œil, it consisted of check patterns, fleurs-de-lis, trophies, rosettes, and garlands organized around the windows as well as about the illusionistic composition at the center of the nave vault.

The heroically scaled sculpture program took many years to complete; indeed, it would be finished only during the reign of Louis XV. In all, the decorative stonework cost the royal treasury nearly 800,000 *livres.* On the interior it was just as extensive as outside, encompassing piers, spandrels, pediments, capitals and columns, keystones, cornices, transverse ribs, pilasters, altars, and an organ. Nothing was without its ornamental figure or motif carefully chosen in relation to the overall iconographical scheme and ceiling décor. The themes include the Passion, the Way of the Cross (evoking perhaps the crown of thorns fragment kept in the Sainte-Chapelle in Paris), the two deacons Laurence and Stephen, the first martyrs, the sacraments, and Hebrew law. This extensive program reflected the demands of Louis XIV *(le Roi Très Chrétien)* as well as careful study of Cesare Ripa's *Iconology.*

The team of sculptors assigned to the Versailles Chapel was huge, even though it excluded both Girardon, by then too old, and Coysevox, too busy at Marly. Among the participants were the Coustoux, Van Clève, Le Lorrain, Frémin, Le Pautre, Vassé, Dugoulon, Le Goupil or Taupin, Lemoyne, Tuby, and Raon. It was as if an all-out mobilization had been had been decreed, for the benefit of the aging King's last great building project, perhaps even the one that meant the most to him. After all, he had always been sincerely religious, not merely in the late years following his "conversion" by the pious Madame de Maintenon.

The wide-sweeping recruitment very likely accounted for the Chapel's decorative richness, which extended to the polychrome marble floor designed by Blin de Fontenay. Audrain painted the window frames, while the excellent team managed by Le Goupil carved the organ case.

The splendor of divine service, held several times a day in various forms, and the perfection of the setting, whose every detail was closely supervised by the King, had as well to meet the demands of royal etiquette. Although the monarch did not attend the Chapel's consecration on 5 June 1710, he had arrived from Marly a few days earlier for a close top-to-bottom inspection, even having a motet performed so he could test the acoustics. A few days later Louis attended Mass, whereupon he observed that "the old chapel is now being turned upside down; all that's left is the gallery, which serves as a passage to reach the new one." Work on the Salon of Hercules had already begun.

LE NÔTRE:
THE GARDENS

The Shellwork or Ballroom Grove,
created by Le Nôtre in 1680-1685.

While Le Vau was busy transforming Louis XIII's hunting lodge into a royal residence worthy of Louis XIV, gardeners swarmed over the vast domain, planting and raking, but also installing the King's statues, at least temporarily. These included nymph and satyr figures carved by Lerambert and Buyster and ranged about the Rondeau. Soon to come was the grand, overall design prepared by André Le Nôtre, who would devote twenty-eight years of his life to the Versailles park.

"Leaving the château by the vestibule on the Marble Courtyard, one should go out onto the terrace and pause at the top of the steps to admire the disposition of the parterres, ponds, and fountains." Between 1689 and 1715, Louis XIV published no fewer than six editions of his *Guide to the Gardens of Versailles.* The text is sober and serious, quite unlike the effusive comments of Mademoiselle de Scudéry and La Fontaine in regard to the water spectacle and its magical effect. The Grand Monarch himself wrote little about the masterpieces of sculpture in his collection, but he made a great point of drawing attention to the fountains, which had cost him a fortune. Moreover, the twenty-five directives, all so precisely phrased, seem to insist upon a single, perhaps even static, view of each grove or fountain. Yet, a closer reading of the text leaves the distinct impression that what the King had in mind was a circuit, complete with detours and "pauses to take in" a detail or a whole ensemble. "Turn to the right... descend the ramp on the right... walk along the allées..." This would appear to be less

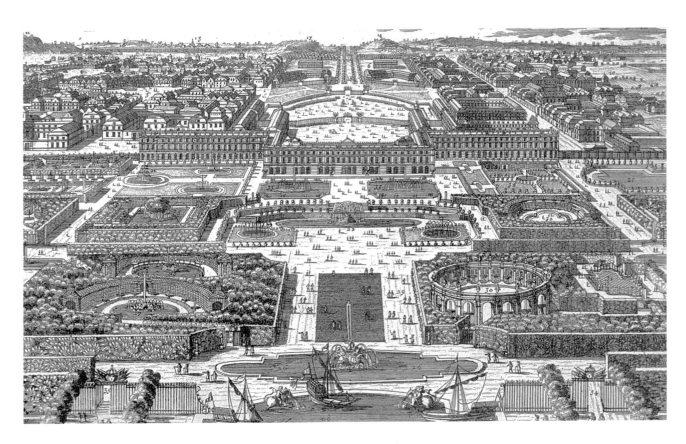

The Versailles gardens around 1705.
The engraving, by Aveline, clearly shows the architectural concept underlying the whole. Each grove stands within its own bower of hedges and hornbeams. The engraving, however, does not take into account the variations in the terrain.

a succession of fixed vantage points than a progression through a decorative environment. It is as if Louis had wished to turn his strolling visitor into a kind of actor who, by his very presence, triggered the play of fountains, which otherwise lay silent and deserted. Is it too much to suggest that the spectacle of Louis XIV's court assumed even greater meaning here than in the Château, where history was made and interpreted within an immutable setting? Even today, some sense of this can easily be gained; one has only to take particular note of the vistas, the articulation of the bosquets, and the formal plantings, with their colorful interplay. It helps as well to use a camera, thus fixing in memory what is seen if not entirely felt.

Le Nôtre had first to master an exceedingly ungrateful terrain, a task at which he succeeded, thanks to his deep knowledge of perspective, acquired in the studio of the painter Simon Vouet. He also benefited from experience acquired at the Tuileries as well as at Vaux-le-Vicomte. At Versailles, Le Nôtre then organized the ensembles, set up the water system, with its complex network of pipes and pumps, and arranged for the placement of hundreds of sculptures evoking an antiquity both severe and elegiac: Time, Mankind, the Universe, and the Elements, the King and Apollo.

Italy still offered the dominant model, for it was from the Italian Renaissance that the builders of France's royal châteaux had learned about terraces, grottoes, and fountains. Also important were the Francine or Francini brothers, celebrated fountain designers *(fontainiers)* recruited in Italy for work in France. Transcending all else, however, was the native genius of Le Nôtre, who understood how to exploit the site creatively, even its vastness (by comparison with the Pitti and Tivoli gardens). It was he who visualized how to overcome or take advantage of the land's variable topography, to respect the old broderie gardens already in place, and to plan the complementary relationship of pools and reservoirs as part of an immense circuit of conduits through which to supply and activate the fountains from a great distance. Finally, Le Nôtre proved no less skilled at trimming and shaping a hierarchy of carefully selected trees and shrubs. The trees may have been imported full-grown all the way from the forests of Normandy, Compiègne, and Tronçais, and the green oaks, chestnuts, and pines may have been both rare and exotic, but the practice of trimming the bowers transformed the very spirit of the gardens. As a realm where hostile nature had been thoroughly conquered, the gardens became a kind of architecture which completed that of the Château itself. The alternating terraces, sheets of water, jetting fountains, and walls of greenery, accented by artfully placed marble, bronze, or lead statuary, functioned like an antiphonal response to the great façade which, with its gilt-bronze balustrades and polychrome marbles, hid the urban world outside.

The gardens also spurred hydraulic research, particularly in the recycling of water for the sake of economy, just as they encouraged botanical experiments, in, for example, the cultivation of exotic as well as overwhelmingly pungent flowers. At Versailles, Jean de La Quintinie even managed to supply the royal table with figs and radishes. The gardens were always undergoing change, to the very end of the *ancien régime,* but the general plan remained constant. Apollo, Latona, the Metamorphoses of the Gods, and the Sun continued to provide the structural spine of the great perspective along the Tapis Vert. This was in part because the gardener was not alone; rather, he had to collaborate with the King, who always wanted to see plans and maquettes, as well as with the King's architects (Le Vau, Perrault, Mansart), the sculptors, and even Le Brun, a painter, who designed the statues for the "Great Commission."

The Versailles gardens were the product of much reflection, but also a place of etiquette. Louis XIV made daily visits to the park, the length of each dependent upon the season, and he might very well board one of the gondolas afloat on the Grand Canal, or stop somewhere for jams and pastries. If there were any foreign visitors, the King made certain they had a tour of the park. Among those so favored was the envoy from the King of Siam, who, in 1686, expressed amazement that the French monarch had built such a marvelous home for his orange trees.

THE PARTERRE OF LATONA, THE WATER PARTERRE, AND THE TAPIS VERT

Le Nôtre was no stranger to Louis XIV, for whom he had already worked at the Tuileries as well as at Saint-Germain. The King had also, fatefully, seen the gardens at Vaux-le-Vicomte. Versailles, however, involved much more than gardening, for here Le Nôtre was obliged to cooperate with both Charles Le Brun, the author of the iconographical program, and the sculptors chosen to complete the new open-air architecture. Right off, the new team set about redesigning the west parterre and its extension: the long axial perspective cut through the dense forest.

After the festivities of 1664, Le Nôtre mitigated the downward slope of the terrain and installed a horseshoe ramp with two curved approaches gentle enough for carriages, at the center of which he built an amphitheatre focused upon an oval basin. This was the first Fountain of Latona, a waterwork completed by two smaller fountains a bit farther down. Now, as if on its own, the half-moon facing the château seemed to pivot 180 degrees, while simultaneously it did an about face, opening a vista towards both the west and the approaches to the Château. This in turn required a transformation

PAGES 94-95: *Lysias* by Dedieu and *Theophrastus* by Hurtrelle, both terms designed by Pierre Mignard after the antique for the Roundel of Philosophers. They stand at the head of one of the long allées or perspectives so characteristic of the formal French garden created by André Le Nôtre.

LEFT AND OPPOSITE: The hemicycle of the Latona Parterre, installed between the Château and the Green Carpet *(Tapis Vert),* is embellished with stone-carved urns, statues, and groups styled in the antique manner. The tiered, circular fountain, designed by Le Nôtre in 1668-1670 and executed in lead by the Marsy brothers, serves as a base for the statue of Latona accompanied by Diana and Apollo, her children by Jupiter. All about are water-spouting frogs, originally Lycian peasants transmogrified by Jupiter after they had mocked Latona during her flight from the jealous Juno. The frogs are typical of the richly inventive bestiary found more or less everywhere in the Versailles park.

The Knife and Scissors Grinder, one of many copies of antique sculptures commissioned for the Versailles park.
This work was cast in bronze by Foggiani in 1684 and then installed on the North Parterre.

tion lasted for at least a short while. By 1672, however, the Water Parterre had been constructed, five steps below grade relative to the Château. The project involved moving earth, building reservoirs, laying in conduits, and commissioning artists (Anguier, Tuby, Cucci, Caffiéri, and, most of all, Sibrayque), who would produce the model for the new terrace, with its complicated clover-leaf plan centered upon a circular basin. Box hedges were to outline the structure, which, it was soon decided, should be further embellished with an important ensemble of sculptures, generally known as the "Great Commission" of 1674. The quartets of personifications or allegories—Abductions, Seasons, Elements, Hours, Temperaments, Poems, Continents—elaborated the solar theme according to the codifications established in Cesare Ripa's *Iconology*. A payment made to Edelinck in 1679 for engraved plates representing several of the sculptures indicates that the project had advanced. Seventeen of the twenty-eight figures were installed in 1682, and by the following year the Water Parterre had assumed its present form, consisting of two white marble pools and sixteen bronzes, all cast by Keller and positioned along the curbs: nymphs, putti, and personifications of rivers. This left the marble statuary to be reinstalled in the vicinity of the horseshoe ramps, the North Parterre, the Colonnade, and the Tuileries gardens in Paris.

Next, the first allée, leading from the Latona Parterre to the Rondeau, was to be widened, which meant cutting down the rows of flanking trees in 1667 and then improving the slope in 1668. The following year, new trees, transferred from the Water Allée, were planted along what hence-

The Chariot of Apollo,
a gilt-lead masterpiece
created in 1667-1672
by Jean-Baptiste Tuby,
who took his inspiration
from Guido Reni's *Aurora.*
At the center of the
former Roundel or *Rondeau,*
the Apollo Fountain
constitutes one of the principal
focal points along the main axis
of the Versailles park,
leading from the Water Terrace
by way of the Latona Fountain,
the Royal Walk, and the *Tapis Vert*
(Green Carpet) to the Apollo Fountain
and, finally, the Grand Canal.

forth would be known as the Royal Allée. Other trees—pine, yew, spruce—were to be added over the next several years. In 1680 came the lawn, laid in straight down the middle, thereby inspiring a more popular name: *Tapis Vert* or Green Carpet. Finally, beginning 1684, twelve statues alternating with twelve vases took their place immediately in front of the hedgerows on either side of the avenue.

The onetime Swan Lake, placed like a period at the west end of the *Tapis Vert,* would now be transformed into the Fountain of Apollo. In 1667 Houseau received an order for marble terms, and in 1668 Tuby agreed to provide "a fountain ornament for the great water jet at the end of the small park, representing the sunrise." Over a four-year period Tuby would be paid 18,800 *livres* for what became an enormous composition of a kind new in France but symptomatic of the artist's Italian roots. At the center of the broad basin, four powerful horses surge up from foaming waters as they draw a chariot bearing Apollo on his daily round of bringing daylight to the world. Contemporaries would have had no difficulty reading the monumental group as an allegory signaling the virtues of the Sun King.

THE GRAND CANAL AND NORTH PARTERRE

Directly west of the Fountain of Apollo lay the Grand Canal, the product of a colossal, lengthy, and expensive undertaking initiated in 1668. Three years later work had progressed only as far as the crossing. It entailed digging, draining, pumping, laying stone, moving earth, constructing paths entirely around the perimeter, building access ramps to the Trianon and the Menagerie, and terracing the banks at the end of each arm. In total, this cruciform lake, with arms measuring 4,920 by 204 feet and 330 by 264 feet, required ten years of titanic effort and cost hundreds of thousands of *livres.* Once filled, the waterway became a showcase for the Royal Navy, particularly on festive occasions when Venetian gondolas, English yachts, launches, galiots, brigantines, galleys, and a great masted vessel set sail for Trianon under the command of Captain Consolin. The royal building accounts for 1669 cite the manufacture and purchase of these vessels, all carved, gilded, and soon to be equipped with awnings of waxed canvas, armchairs, stools, and damask cushions, some fashioned of "gold and silver brocade on a red ground, adorned with gold and silver fringes and tassels, and mock crimson covers."

The stamp of Le Nôtre is probably most evident on the North Parterre. As part of the overall design, the landscape architect installed the Mermaid Fountain near the Château and the Crown Fountains farther down the slope in the middle of boxwood broderies. The latter pair of fountains had been created by the sculptors Tuby and Le Hongre between 1669 and 1672. Le Nôtre then closed this level area with a pyramid fountain cast in lead from a Le Brun design worked up by Girardon, who very likely received the commission in 1670. At the top, water gushed from an urn, before spilling into four shallow bowls held aloft by lobsters, tritons, dolphins, and lion paws. The sheer verve of this work, with its robust realism and expressiveness, its sense of movement, detail, and surface modulation, recalls the treatment of the *Horses of the Sun* as well as the taste for ornamental abundance in the neighboring Grotto of Thetis. From the bottom of the pyramid the cascading water flowed into a wide basin, the shape of which was changed from quadrilobate to circular in 1683. Here it drained into a pool below, where the retaining wall was rebuilt in 1669-1670. Given this complex circuit, one can only imagine what kind of plumbing had to be devised!

Girardon also received the commission for the large lead relief at the Nymphs' Bathing Pool, which had small panels on either side and along the allée made by Le Gros and Le Hongre.

OPPOSITE: The crossbar of the Grand Canal where it terminates at the terrace leading to the Grand Trianon. Louis XIV and his court often arrived here on a flotilla of vessels under the command of a captain in France's Royal Navy.

OPPOSITE: The *Grande Commande* or "Great Commission" of 1674 was planned for the Water Parterre but ended up partially installed on the North Parterre. Designed by Charles Le Brun, it comprised seven quartets of large allegorical figures representing Abductions or Rapes, Seasons, Elements, Hours, Temperaments, Poems, and Continents, each of the groups executed in white marble by such sculptors as Girardon, Le Hongre, Le Gros, the Marsy brothers, Desjardins, Guérin, Sibrayque, and Houseau.

RIGHT: The Water Allée, or Children's Walk, was originally flanked by the Three Fountains Grove and the Arc de Triomphe Grove, both of which have disappeared. At this time (1669), the Allée itself boasted seven matched pairs of fountains composed of groups of children bearing baskets of flowers and fruit, the whole cast in lead and realistically painted. In 1688 the infants would be recast in bronze and the baskets replaced by basins of pink Languedoc marble

PAGES 106-107: The North Parterre, viewed from a position near that enjoyed, for five years, by Madame de Pompadour, who lived, very elegantly, on the attic floor of the Château above the Planetary Suite. Adding to the purity of the design are the decorative elements based on the drawings of Charles Le Brun: the Pyramid Fountain, the statues delivered in response to the *Great Commission,* and firepots.

Cross-section of a "water buffet" in the Marsh Grove (before 1704).
This stepped design allowed water to cascade musically over a series of shallow falls, as well as the display of ornamental vases.

The allée appeared in Le Nôtre's first plan, drawn up in 1666, but it was Claude Perrault, according to his brother Charles, who conceived the overall decorative scheme. In its 1669 state, each of fourteen groups of three small figures—boys and girls, cupids, satyrs (Le Hongre), a Bacchus (Le Gros), musicians, singers, and dancers (Lerambert)—supported a basket of flowers and fruits from which sprang the fountain's waters. This show of plenty had been executed by Masson in lead embellished with gilt and naturalistic colors. In 1678 eight additional groups were placed in the hemicycle around the Dragon Fountain farther down the slope. In 1688 the entire series would be recast in bronze and the floral baskets replaced with bowls carved from Languedoc marble. The square bases, recalling the piers in the Grotto of Thetis, would also give way to circular ones, which, however, retained the picturesque scheme of imitation ice blocks found on the originals.

It was from this allée that Louis XIV, in his *Guide to the Gardens,* urged visitors to admire the Dragon Fountain completed by the Marsy brothers in 1667. Also the vast marvel dedicated to the God of the Sea that closed the perspective on the north. Designed rather late by Le Nôtre (1678), the Neptune Fountain still lacked its famous sculpture, but it could already boast a rich array of vases, shells, and no less than sixty-three jets of water.

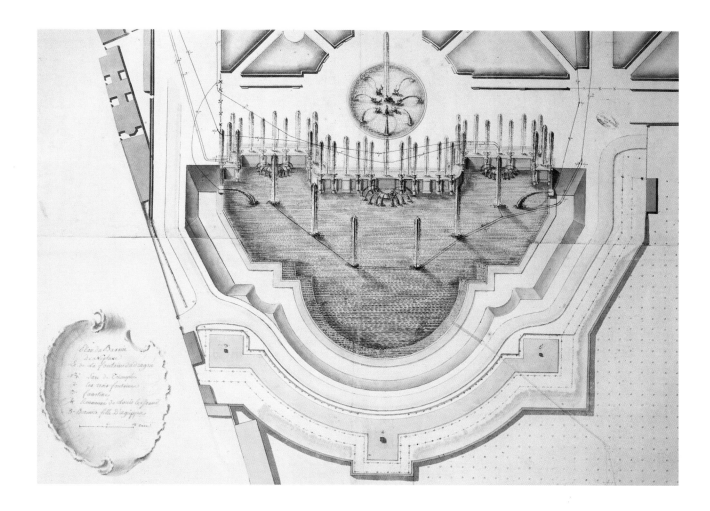

Plan of the Neptune Fountain (detail), created by Le Nôtre in 1678-1682 to close the northern perspective. The colossal waterwork then remained unfinished until 1739-1740, when the architect Gabriel oversaw its completion. The design seen here was carried out between 1702, the year Guidi's *Fame* was installed, and 1740, when the last sculptures were integrated with the whole.

Vanished groves

Of the several important groves designed by Le Nôtre in this northern sector, none exists today. All were cut, like clearings, from the surrounding woods. On the east side of the Water Allée stood the Water Pavilion, a modest grouping of basins set back in the boxwood hedges. In 1677, five years after its creation, Le Nôtre replaced the arrangement with a splendid Arc de Triomphe, built during the golden moment of Louis XIV's early reign. It remained under construction until 1684. This *bosquet*, with its elongated, hourglass shape, always caught visitors by surprise, located as it was at the end of two converging allées. At the entrance to the grove stood an impressive sculptural group—which still exists—overlooking a white marble fountain. Created by Coysevox, Tuby, and Prou in 1682-1683 and cast in lead, the group is entitled *France Triumphant*, a theme brought to life by three personifications: the title player, a cock-helmeted female figure on a chariot, riding high above two male prisoners, one seated upon a lion (Spain) and the other upon an eagle (the Holy Roman Empire). Between the vanquished appears Hydra, symbolizing the defeated Triple Alliance, together with an assemblage of shields and helmets. Higher up in the grove, towards the Château, stood two basin fountains in niches cut from the greenery and, at the foot of five concave steps along a trellis, two more fountains—*Victory* and *Glory*—both complicated sculptural

groups featuring female figures enthroned upon trophies and laurel leaves. Down the center of the narrow section ran two narrow fifteen-step channels. Thereafter the grove opened again into a wider clearing, this one almost square, with two large "buffets," marble fountains flanked by a pair of truly extraordinary obelisks. Sometimes referred to as needles, these triangular forms were made entirely of wrought-iron mounts, each with ten openings and all chased as well as gilded. They stood on recumbent lions, which in turn rested upon marble bases relief-carved with swags and fleurs-de-lis. The water sprang up inside the forms and then tumbled down the outside, making the ensemble look as if it were fabricated of crystal and gilt-bronze. The whole of this intricate splendor served primarily as a prelude to the Arc de Triomphe, a veritable monument of architecture and sculpted marble, made of superimposed blocks supporting a three-bay arch inspired by those of Classical antiquity. It was crowned by a triangular pediment decorated with fleurs-de-lis, horns of plenty, and acanthus leaves. Atop the whole were seven bowls with jets of water, while inside each bay was another water-spouting bowl. This ensemble, with all its complication and abundance, or perhaps overabundance, survived intact until the Napoleonic era, when it was virtually destroyed.

On the opposite side of the allée was a water bower that surged up on either side from grassy borders and banks. Created, as well as dismantled, at the same time as the Water Pavilion, it would be replaced by the sumptuous Three Fountains, the idea for which came from Louis XIV himself.

The Three Fountains constituted a rare site in the Versailles park where sculpture played no role; rather, the entire effect arose from the complementary interplay of cascades, jets, and pools. All of it came into being in the years 1677-1679. Louis XIV, in his *Guide to the Gardens,* recommended approaching the area from above. The *bosquet* spread over three levels, the upper one host to a small bubble fountain. From here two lateral flights of steps separated by a waterfall led to the central clearing with a large square basin emitting numerous jets of water. Next came three stairs separated by two cascades, leading to the lowest level, where the fountain was octagonal, like the three-tiered bubble at its center. The clearing was ringed about by a tall boxwood trellis and a low wall decorated with floral vases, which, together with the waterfalls' rockwork, gave the site its only real touches of fantasy. Piganiol, in his *Guide to Versailles*, writes without hesitation: "This is the most ingenious of the groves, and had to be in order to exploit the unevenness of the land. Its beauties, although entirely rustic and natural, never cease to delight, and its fountains, with their murmuring waters and pools, charm both eyes and ears."

Farther to the east, along the same axis, was the immense Water Theatre, rapidly brought to conclusion in 1671-1673. Measuring some 150 feet across and surrounded by both hedge and trellis, this large circular clearing had a stepped embankment on its north side, opposite which three wide allées sliced into the thick woods, each of them a narrow canal built of shells and lined on either side with topiary trees shaped like obelisks. Along these channels, water coursed through eight successive pools before spilling into the basins on the "stage," where the liquid treasure welled up on every side—jets, bubbles, lances, cascades, and bowers—all thanks to the imagination and virtuosity of the King's hydraulic engineers. The Water Theatre was also a tribute to the team spirit shared by Le Nôtre, the Francine brothers, and Denis, the *fontainier*. Yet, however magical, the water spectacle alone did not suffice. The performances and refreshments frequently offered here demanded a rich and carefully prepared décor. This consisted of two thousand hornbeams, rockeries and shells designed by Berthier and Quesnel, gilt-bronze vases, and, several years later, a gradated amphitheatre with eight small circular basins each with a water jet leaping into an arcade of greenery. Needless to say, it included statuary based on drawings or sketches made by Le Brun: groups of cupids frolicking with animals (Houzeau, Massou, Tuby) or with a lyre (Le Gros); and, most of all, a Jupiter, a Pluto, and a Mars posed above the top fountain. From this important

The Cock and the Fox.
Watercolor by Sébastien Leclerc and Jacques Bailly.

The Parrots and the Monkey.
Watercolor by Sébastien Leclerc and Jacques Bailly.

and extremely theatrical ensemble, only three groups of cupids survive, one of them, by Marsy, still at Versailles, where it once stood at the entrance to the grove.

Even more picturesque may have been the Marsh Grove, composed, built, and decorated between 1670 and 1672. As filled with fantasy as everything else in this sector of the park, the design appears to have brought great delight to the King and Madame de Montespan, who had proposed the idea. The deep placement in the woods was itself spectacular, as noted by Félibien: "There is a large oblong pond, with a large tree in the middle, so ingeniously made that it looks quite natural." The trunk had in fact been fashioned of iron and the leaves of copper, tin, and brass. "Countless jets of water gush from the tips of the branches and fall over the marsh. Apart from these jets, there are a great number of others that gush from the reeds along the sides. At each end are two verdant recesses, like arbors, with grass steps. Each contains a large white marble table with a gilt-bronze basket filled with imitation flowers. A tall spray shoots up from the flowers, and the water falls back into the basket, all without wetting the table. Halfway along the sides of the pond there are more recesses like those at the ends, with grassy steps supporting long white and red marble tables with tiered buffets. Water pours from these tiers through nozzles in ewers, glasses, carafes, and other sorts of vases that seem to be made of rock crystal mounted in silver-gilt." To all this must be added the flower-filled "porcelain vases" placed around the sides; the "natural-seeming" swans, like those at Trianon, nesting in the reeds; and the superb sculptural décor on the buffets with lion-paw feet: Medici vases, dolphins, and faux wickerwork baskets. Animating the whole were all manner of water jets, falls, lances, bubbles, troughs, and channels. The ornamental plenitude of this ensemble would seem almost to have predestined it as a site for the large sculptural groups from the Grotto of Thetis.

"After leaving the orange garden, we passed by the Labyrinth." Here, Mademoiselle de Scudéry, writing in her *Promenade at Versailles* of 1669, cites one of the oldest of the King's *bosquets,* completed in 1677 with the addition of two trellis pavilions. It sprang from a collaboration between Charles Perrault, who generated the idea, and Le Nôtre, who executed it in the southern sector of the park. The deep originality of their work lay in the rich, decorative treatment of both shrubbery and fountains. Thirty-nine groups of animals—sculptures cast in lead and naturalistically painted—were placed at the intersection of allées, in basins or on shallow bowls. The ultimate source of the subject was Aesop, then quite familiar thanks to La Fontaine, who had just published the first six books of his *Fables,* dedicated to the Dauphin. From this very likely came the tradition according to which Bossuet, tutor to the young Prince, regularly brought his charge to this grove, where each fountain was emblazoned with a gold-lettered quatrain by Benserade explaining the relevant fable or its moral.

Fantasy and pedagogy found reinforcement in the colored leads and the abundance of the shell décor. However, everything possible was done to prevent visitors from becoming lost, as Charles Perrault explained: "It is called a labyrinth because it contains countless little paths, all so mixed up that it is almost impossible not to lose one's way; but, to ensure that those who do get lost may do so enjoyably, several fountains can be seen simultaneously at every turn, so that at each step one is surprised by something new." For the Labyrinth, it was again the same artists seen so often before: Massou, Le Gros, Houzeau, Desjardins, and Le Hongre. Today, only a few reliefs remain. The fragility of both the lead sculptures and the trellises, which required frequent repairs, plus the constant need to reletter the inscriptions and deal with costly problems of maintenance, all but ensured that the Labyrinth would not survive once Louis XVI undertook to replant the park in 1774.

The purpose of the Royal Island, installed between 1671 and 1680, was mainly to impose order on a sector of the park besieged by mud and humidity, just as had been done at the short-lived

PAGES 118-119: The Ballroom (1680-1685), the last grove created by Le Nôtre. Designed as an amphitheatre, with tiered or gradated waterfalls at the center flanked by lawn-covered steps for the audience, the Ballroom (also known as the Shellwork Grove) served as an outdoor performance arena for concerts or ballets. The "orchestra" usually played at the top of the waterfalls, fashioned of millstones and exotic seashells.

LEFT: Mansart's Colonnade, a work of 1684, is an arcaded ring of thirty-six unfluted Ionic columns—the inner members circular in plan, the outer ones square—made of polychrome marbles quarried in France rather than Italy. They combine with the white marble of the arches to create one of the most sumptuous installations in the Versailles park.

Springs Grove in 1679. The Royal Island waterwork comprised two large basins, one of them encircled by small fountains whose sprays reflected in the basin's mirror surface like a sparkling hedgerow.

In 1680 Le Nôtre created the Antique Glade, a long, narrow clearing encircled by a small "canal" and accessed by a pair of footbridges. Some twenty Classical statues—copies or antiques restored by Flamand—rose up from the channel amidst lance-like jets of water. Louis XIV appears to have grown tired of the picturesque effect and disparate character of this glade, given that in 1704 he had all the statuary removed. The watercourse was filled in and overplanted with chestnut trees, after which only a few Classical busts remained, positioned along the cincturing palissade of greenery. The results left Versailles with a "dry" grove, one of the few in a park known for its waterworks.

Not far from this site, Le Nôtre laid out the Ballroom in 1680-1685, and it still exists. The terrain, with its steep incline, permitted the installation of five high, parallel waterfalls around a quarter section of amphitheatre. Their eight tiers were fashioned of millstones transported from Gros-Rouvres and exotic seashells brought back from the Red Sea and the Indian Ocean by the Royal Navy. Elsewhere, all about, lawn-covered steps provided seats for spectators come to enjoy ballets performed at the center—at first on a small island and then, a few years later, on the arena floor—or listen to musicians playing at the top of the steps. Indian seashells dangling from copper wires along the entrance walls contributed to improved acoustics. The Ballroom became the scene of not only concerts and ballets but also suppers, which explains the presence of such opulent furnishings as tall, stone-carved candlesticks and gilt-lead urns, works attributed to Mazeline, Jouvenet, Le Hongre, and Fontelle, the authors of many of the park's decorative benches.

In 1684 "the King commissioned a marble colonnade with large fountains at the site of the Springs." The order went to Jules Hardouin-Mansart, who had the ground leveled and paved before erecting a thirty-two-bay arcade, its columns made of breccia-violet and slate-blue marble. Red Languedoc stone served for the buttresses and veined white marble for everything else—urns, frieze, guilloche patterns, spandrels, and basins. By 1687 the ensemble appears to have been far advanced. Initially, Guidi's *Fame* was to have been installed at the center, according to Dangeau, who writes that on 24 April 1689 "the King had ordered that the statue of Fame be placed in the middle of the Colonnade; but in trying to lift it from where it was kept, the crane broke, and it fell to the ground so violently that there will be lots of little pieces to put back." The following day Louis XIV went to inspect the damaged sculpture. Two years later the group was set up near the Colonnade, albeit not for long. In 1699 the central position would be given to Girardon's *Rape of Proserpina,* originally commissioned for the Water Parterre.

By now the Versailles gardens abounded in waterworks of every sort, calm pools and gushing fountains alike, all mingled with a profusion of flowers and architecture. Within this outdoor extravaganza, even the intersection of allées had to play its part. When Colbert, writing in 1672, mentioned "four new fountains" he was referring to the Seasons, with their gods and goddesses set among fruit, flowers, and frolicking cherubs. The Banquet Hall, dating to the same period but transformed into the Obelisk Fountain in 1706, was an island with a wealth of jets and four corners reinforced to support small circular basin fountains. One of the simplest of the intersection waterworks is the monumental Enceladus Fountain, made in 1675-1677 by Gaspard Marsy, who appears, incredibly, to have received only 2,000 *livres* for this masterpiece. The agonized face of the "giant crushed by the rocks he had piled on top of one another to climb to Heaven," the vigor of the head, the awesome scatter of stones, the mighty hand and shoulder, the water welling up, bubbling, and springing from every part—in brief, the art of the sculptor and the *fontainier* at its most complete—come together and, with minimal means, convey a sense of vast despair, a rare phenomenon, especially for these years when the King appeared so sure of himself.

OPPOSITE: The Children's Isle Fountain (1710) by Jean Hardy. This frolicsome composition is one of several such waterworks commissioned for the intersections of Le Nôtre's criss-crossing allées.

RIGHT: In marked contrast to the Children's Isle is the Enceladus Fountain (detail), another intersection waterwork, this one created in 1675-1677 by Gaspard Marsy. One of the Titans who warred against the gods, Enceladus found himself crushed under the tumbling rocks he and his fellow giants had piled up in the hope of reaching the heavens. There is no more powerful work of art in the whole of the Versailles park.

ORANGERY, MENAGERIE, STABLES, HIDEAWAY CHÂTEAUX, AND PAVILIONS

Peristyle of the Grand Trianon.

In 1662 Le Vau started work on the first Orangery immediately below the South Parterre, where a steep drop in the terrain made it impossible to terrace as had been done on the north side. An order was therefore issued allowing earth and stone to be moved so as to make the site usable in the way planned. The task proved long and laborious, carried out by a band of mercilessly driven workers. In January 1663 Le Vau wrote to Colbert: "Our fellows are on the job at last—it's not been easy. They're at the Orangery with the others, who have already made good progress and will work even quicker with these fellows at their heels." The team had to excavate under the South Parterre, where they created a vaulted chamber with an eleven-bay arcade facing an esplanade flanked by two flights of steps leading down from the South Parterre. Planted with fruit trees, the esplanade spread southward in the direction of Satory. It was here that Louis XIV had the orange trees seized at Vaux-le-Vicomte installed. They would be joined by four more trees, these taken from the Hôtel Séguier in 1664, as well as by an additional 177, the latter purchased in 1675. Once replanted in new boxes, freshly painted and reinforced with iron bands, the King's orange grove had to be watered regularly.

ABOVE AND OPPOSITE: Hardouin-Mansart's Orangery (1684), where, as Louis XIV wrote in his visitors' guidebook, one should "descend the steps to the right of the Orangery, go through the orange garden and directly to the fountain for a view of the Orangery."

In 1672 the Green Wood, southwest of the Château, was felled and a decision taken to double the size of the South Parterre, evidently dooming Le Vau's Orangery. Indeed, it was demolished as the new work progressed, which opened the way for Hardouin-Mansart, who, in 1684-1686, would build his own Orangery, much larger and taller, its elevation extending from the Saint-Cyr Road below to the South Parterre above. The thirteen-bay façade was framed by two monumental flights of steps that served as buttresses, while also providing the only direct access between the South Parterre and the Orangery esplanade. Beyond the plain entrance arcade, its piers free of both pilasters and capitals, lay the great vaulted hall under the South Parterre. Entirely functional in purpose, the facility had only one embellishment: a statue of the King by Desjardins, placed there only in 1683 following its presentation by Maréchal de La Feuillade. The interior space stretched into right-angle, projecting wings built under the lateral steps. The vaults were carefully cemented and sealed with oily mastic to prevent leakage, and the rear wall doubled to provide a narrow safety corridor. As for how to approach the Orangery, Louis XIV advised: "One should move straight ahead to the top of the Orangery and admire the garden of orange trees and the Pool of the Swiss Guards. Then descend the steps to the right of the Orangery, go through the orange garden and directly to the fountain for a view of the Orangery; pass through the allées of tall orange trees to reach the Orangery, and leave by the vestibule next to the Labyrinth." Clearly, no one enjoyed these gardens more than Louis XIV, a man not given to baring his soul. He could often be found there, strolling through the trees and forever on the lookout for possible improvements. As the King's guidebook suggested, no one would even have suspected the existence of the Oran-

gery or its garden before arriving at the very end of the South Parterre. And the splendidly simple façade came into view merely at the bottom of the steps. Times had changed since the Grotto of Thetis and so had taste; yet the element of surprise remained a constant throughout the gardens. Although Louis said nothing about the scenographic aspects of his creation—so that visitors could experience their own sense of wonderment—contemporary reports took pains to emphasize them, once the engraver or the King had established the best vantage point. As for the esplanade, Le Nôtre made it a true parterre, complete with lawn compartments and broderies, large marble vases and monumental Abductions, also in marble. There were to have been four of the sculptural groups, but one was never commissioned, while the second, a work by Girardon, would be placed in the Colonnade. Only Regnaudin's *Rape of Cybele by Saturn* and Flamand's *Rape of Orithyia by Boreas* actually came to rest on the Orangery parterre. Finally, there were the two wrought-iron gates facing the Saint-Cyr Road, their flanking posts crowned with monumental groups, each of which cost 20,000 *livres,* at a time when funds were becoming scarce. Still, the sculptures gave the gardens a superb outer boundary, overlooking the Pool of the Swiss Guards and Bernini's *Marcus Curtius.*

Behind the Bernini sculpture lay a complicated story telling much about the aesthetic and emotional character of Louis XIV's taste. Gianlorenzo Bernini had come to France in 1665, responding to a promise from Colbert of a commission for a large statue of the King, to be realized in the Baroque manner of the master's *Constantine* at the Vatican. Back in Rome, Bernini took his time, working on the project from 1670 to 1674. The result was an equestrian portrait in white marble showing the King "in an act of majesty and command," a pose chosen with the idea that the sculpture would stand high upon a plinth representing the Mount of Glory. The colossal figure finally arrived at Le Havre on 2 January 1685, five years after Bernini's death. First, it would be given to Paris for placement on the Pont Rouge—until ice floes carried the bridge away! So, off the great marble went to Versailles, where, as Dangeau wrote, "the King was walking in the Orangery, which he found in magnificent estate, when he noticed the equestrian statue by the cavaliere Bernini that had been placed there, and felt that the man and horse were so badly done that he resolved to have them not only removed, but also smashed to pieces." Still, the sculpture remained inside the Orangery for a good while, then on the parterre, until moved to the far end of the Fountain of Neptune. Finally, someone came up with the notion of having it transformed by Girardon, a development reported by Tessin, the King of Sweden's architect, during his visit to France: "Here was placed the marble equestrian portrait of the King by the cavaliere Bernini, whose great reputation was spoiled by this disaster at the end of his days; it was given a different name and changed into Marcus Curtius rushing towards the abyss: a helmet has been placed on his head, and the rock supporting the horse has been changed into flames, thought better suited to the steed's contortions." In the summer of 1702 Louis XIV ordered the work removed to the far side of the Pool of the Swiss Guards.

The Menagerie and Porcelain Trianon

On the site of La Boissière, a farm southwest of the Château towards Saint-Cyr, the Menagerie was built in 1663-1664. As the goal of excursions and a place to satisfy interest in the exotic, the Menagerie called for a complicated and refined structure, which, over time, would be remodeled on several occasions and endowed with extraordinary ornaments and details. The clever plan, drawn up by Le Vau, was regular but far from simple. A long allée led to a pavilion, which, like the Château itself, had two bracketing wings, one north and the other south, each housing an apartment. A brief gallery led to an octagonal pavilion, entirely belted about by a balcony offering a clear view of all the various courtyards. It stood at the center of a courtyard, also octagonal in plan and closed by high fences on seven sides, which left the eighth side for access to the central pavilion. Each of the monumental wrought-iron fences served as the base of a trapezoid bordered along the bottom by buildings or sheds, everyone of them with its own courtyard kept mostly for birds, eagles, ostriches, pelicans, Numidian cranes, or beautiful hens. In the Numidian courtyard—much admired by La Fontaine in *Les Amours de Psyché et de Cupidon*—was installed a large aviary, composed of three pavilions linked by a gallery, its arches filled with light-transmitting brass mesh. Through the gallery ran a channel of water equipped with jets.

Around this original ensemble the avian population would soon be joined by peacocks, ravens, turkey hens, purple gallinules, and pheasants. Then, in a circle about the inner complex, came a dog kennel (in addition to others in town), gazelles, swine and wild boar, horses (Mansart's two stables opposite the Château had yet to be built), and such wild beasts as tigers, rhinos, and elephants. The Menagerie provided not only court entertainment but also an opportunity for scientific observation, in the interest of which Louis XIV had Nicolas Robert, "ordinary painter to the King for miniatures," produce twenty-four paintings on vellum every year. Be that as it may, the artist appears to have been considerably more involved in turning out albums of engravings, among them a 1676 series illustrating "the rarest birds from the royal menagerie of Versailles." Versailles, a delightful place of escape from the court at Saint-Germain-en-Laye, offered yet other comfortable, well-appointed sites for simple, intimate pleasures. The Menagerie, for example, boasted a dairy and a chapel as well as the two apartments. Louis XIV adored fountains and loved to control their height and flow himself, either from the balcony, where he had an overview of the effect, or from the dairy, where he opened the valves with his own hands. The pictures he commissioned during this period are remarkable for their range, painted by such artists as the Dutchman Nicasius, of course, but also, a bit later, by Stella, Blanchard, Poërson, Coypel, and Boullogne. And this at a time when the Menagerie was being refurbished, prior to its transfer, at the end of the century, to the enchanting Duchesse de Bourgogne, Louis XIV's granddaughter-in-law and the mother of Louis XV. According to Dangeau, writing in 1698, "the King has taken his first resolution thereupon, which is to give her the proper menagerie. To make the gardens we will use some of the yards where there are currently animals." On the interior, two five-room apartments were created by Mansart, together with the brilliant team of sculptors from the Chapel—Dugoulon, Goupil, Jouvenet, and van Clève. Mazeline and Hurtrelle modeled the cornices after drawings prepared by Audran, his iconography suggested by the King himself: games, pastoral scenes, music, and country frolics. As a result, the little château, though quite transformed, remained a place of amusement, both within and without, where Lassurance designed a new garden. In 1700 Louis declared himself "most content with all that has been spent here, which is a great deal and, for the paneling, painting and locks of the most refined taste." The aging monarch continued to import animals from the East, among them ostriches, purple gallinules, and *bellauchans,* and he often arrived to visit his great-grandchildren or indeed Madame de Maintenon. The company would lunch, dine, and perhaps even dance "to songs," for what had been a summer house was now a proper château, luxuriously and comfortably furnished, as the various crown inventories reveal.

The magic of Versailles can, in some respects, never be more than memory. Entirely gone, for instance, is the first Trianon—the Porcelain Trianon—designed by Le Vau and quickly run up in 1670, but with finishing touches supplied by d'Orbay in 1672. Facing west, like the great Château itself,

The Menagerie, a complex refuge for the King's collection of wild beasts and birds,
stood at the south end of the Grand Canal's crossbar. Engraving by Pérelle.

the main one-storey pavilion was preceded by four small service pavilions, each giving onto a courtyard,
all of which indicates that the site was intended merely for relaxation and refreshment. One pavilion, at
the entrance, was "for making jams," another "for sweets," this one with a supplementary shelter "for
roasting." Next came the pavilion reserved for the preparation of starters, hors-d'œuvres, and soups.
Opposite, next to the jam pavilion, stood the pavilion dedicated to desserts, the buffet, and the princes'
and lords' table laden with fruit. The main pavilion included two small suites—the Diana Apartment and
the Cupids Apartment—each with a bedchamber, a cabinet, and two wardrobes, one of them in the attic.
The decoration, both inside and out, was extremely intricate, with cornices carved by Mazeline, ceilings
painted by Francart, and Poquelin mirrors framed by Caffiéri and Lespagnandel. Blue and white prevailed everywhere, on ceilings, floors, and walls alike, making a harmonious color scheme that would
soon become all the rage in Paris. The Trianon decorations were thought to be "in the manner of works
from China, with walls and floors that match, these being made of porcelain [i.e., faïence] tiles," some of
which came from Holland, others from Nevers and Saint-Cloud. Completing this colorful habitat, which
today can only be imagined, were furnishings of great richness and delicacy, the tables, guéridons,
couches, easy chairs, and stools all painted and upholstered mostly in white, blue, or violet. All this sprang
up when Madame de Montespan was in her glory, a favorite for whom the smitten King could not gene-

The Porcelain Trianon, built by Le Vau in 1670, was a folly erected for the delight of Madame de Montespan, the most brilliant and demanding of Louis XIV's official mistresses. Clad in blue and white faïence tiles, the little "château" comprised a main, central pavilion housing two apartments and, on either side of the forecourt, four smaller pavilions, each serving a different kind of refreshment.
Drawing by Swidde

rate enough brilliant effects and lavish embellishments, picturesqueness and accessories offering pleasure, entertainment, or simple repose. To appreciate the extent of all this, one has only to read a description of the fantastic bed in the Cupids Apartment: "Bed with a carved headboard with a large mirror; the top is composed of sixteen sections of cornice and eight sections of frieze, surrounded by linen-grey and silver ribbon, supported by three cardboard cherubs in the air, holding eight cords and various ribbons that serve as their scarves; three large curtains, four small ones, the top, the headboard, the eight sections serving as a frieze, the ceremonial bedspread, the three valances, all in white taffeta with blue-grey, silver, and gold embroidery, with a border of linen-grey taffeta around all the pieces, enriched with the same embroidery. The said bed adorned with large and medium gold and silver lace and fifteen passementerie tassels, also of gold and silver with blue silk rosettes serving as ends, both on the inside and the outside, eleven consoles and eleven sheets of cardboard, with eleven gallands to open the bed curtains, a large strip of the same material as the bed above the mirror, and two other smaller ones surrounding the cherubs on the headboard, a surround of white taffeta for the said bed, adorned with small gold and silver lace." The building's exterior, moreover, was altogether as remarkable and opulent. The walls, clad in the same blue and white tiles as those within, and the upper balustrade concealing the roof served as bases for faïence vases and iron cauldrons painted to look like faïence. With its trompe-l'œil devices and other tricks designed to surprise, the "Porcelain Château" was stage-set architecture, suggesting that what would be viewed as Marie-Antoinette's frivolity in the late eighteenth century had been introduced at Versailles in Louis XIV's projects of the early 1670s. Could the King have already begun to sense the ponderousness of the great Château? One could be persuaded of it, given that Louis soon built the Pavillon des Parfums near the Trianon's main block.

Here, close by orange trees in boxes, the gardens were perhaps even more splendid that those seen elsewhere in the park. Parterres of trimmed boxwood laid out before the pavilion constituted an upper garden, which led, on axis, to a lower garden, always, Félibien tells us, "embellished, in whatever season one visits, with every sort of flower. And the air one breathes here is invariably fragrant with the jasmine and orange trees past which one walks." Further on came a park laid out in a grid pattern. To the west, the ground fell away towards the Grand Canal, while on the right stood the service buildings, ice houses, and kitchen garden. For the comfort and benefit of strollers, in the event of rain, the lower garden was bordered by two long trellis arcades and various leafy bowers within the ambient verdure. Iron cauldron-vases painted to imitate faïence again made their appearance, as did ceramic tiles, this time paving the curbs around the fountains.

The Trianon fairyland, created during the King's youth, emerged from the fantasy of the same team of artists already employed at the Château: Le Hongre, Massou, Houzeau, Sibrayque, Mazeline, and Jouvenet. And this despite the fact that in 1673 and 1674 they were also engaged in restoring deteriorated parts of the area and constructing a new roof for the Porcelain Château, the latter an enormous project carried out in tandem with work on the gardens (the Pavilion des Parfums, a drinking fountain, a landing stage on the Grand Canal, and still more greenhouses needed by the gardener, Le Bouteux, for winter storage of orange and jasmine trees). The process of embellishing and enriching this first Trianon—no doubt for the seduction of Madame de Montespan—went on continuously right up to the moment when Mansart would transform it utterly.

In 1671 Louis XIV decided to change the roofs of all the Trianon pavilions. New roofs were designed and the old ones removed by Yon, leaving the interiors exposed to rain, which loosened the tiles and spoiled both paintings and stuccoed ceilings. The work dragged on, a symptom of royal hesitation.

Mansart's grand trianon

In July 1687 the Trianon roofs had still not been replaced. Yet, a large budget now existed "for the buildings that His Majesty has ordered to be done at Trianon during the present year." Louis XIV had his reasons, among them the disgrace of Madame de Montespan, a loss of interest in the exotic, the fragility of the ceramic décor, which cracked during winter freezes, requiring continual replacement, and the spatial inadequacy of the Porcelain Trianon. The disintegrating pavilion was to be incorporated into a new structure: the Grand Trianon. Work progressed swiftly and efficiently. During the autumn, the secondary pavilions were pulled down and everything possible taken away for preservation, just as at the Château a decade earlier, when the King ordered the Jupiter decorations reinstalled in the Queen's Guardroom. The salvaged bits included the attic ornaments and the vases, the latter refinished with a bronze-like paint. Some of the demolished materials were sold to building contractors. Meanwhile, orders went out for fabrics to cover furniture and walls, and by 22 January 1688 Dangeau

The Grand Trianon under Louis XIV, viewed from the landing at the north end
of the Grand Canal's crossbar. Colored engraving by Guyot after Sergent.

could note in his diary that "the King went to dine for the first time at his new house at Trianon. He took with him in his carriage Monseigneur, Madame de Maintenon, Madame de Mailly, the Comtesse de Guiche, Madame de Noailles, Madame de Montchevreuil, and Madame de Saint-Géran." Clearly, if not altogether finished, the Grand Trianon was ready for more than a simple outing.

Initially, the main pavilion of the Porcelain Château was to have been retained and made to serve as the focus of the new forecourt, again following a precedent set at the Château some twenty years before. The plan called for two oval salons, in oblique alignment, linking the central core to the former soup and dessert pavilions, these flanked by two wings, the left one with a chapel at the front and the right with a music room and small theatre. At the end of the right wing, on the garden side, a long gallery would have led to the old Pavilion des Parfums.

Then came the revisions. A. Marie has brought to light an important payment made on 2 November 1687 to the carpenter Malet "for the wood for the beams he had cut for Trianon, which will not be used because of the change in design." The main pavilion was demolished and its great columns of Languedoc marble salvaged, to be used, much later under Napoleon I, on the Carrousel Arch at the Tuileries in Paris. The general disposition remained, but with a flat or rectilinear main façade overlooking the gardens. Meanwhile, work on the two oval salons was already well advanced, for, in their entry dated November 12-13, the diarists Sourches and Dangeau tell of a visit by Louis XIV to the worksite and His Majesty's eagerness to see the apartment made habitable. The speed of invention acceler-

The Marble or Grand Trianon, built in 1687-1688 by Jules Hardouin-Mansart and Robert de Cotte. On both the façades and the peristyle, Mansart imposed the same kind of regularity created by Le Vau for the Envelope at the Château. He would, however, revert to a polychromy comparable to that in the Marble Courtyard but now executed in richly veined marbles, pink from Languedoc and green from the Pyrenees. The notion of a grand peristyle of paired columns, linking the two main wings, originated with the King, who wanted a full view of the magnificent gardens from every courtyard.

ated, beginning with the King himself, who came up with the notion of a central peristyle, as B. Jestaz has recently disclosed. Louis asked Robert de Cotte to design it and had work started immediately, even before Mansart could review the plans. The project continued throughout 1688—terracing, construction, and, of course, embellishment. Le Gros, van Clève, Magnière, and Goy did the sculptural work, while Mazeline, Jouvenet, and the inevitable Charmeton supplied paneling and cornices. Also ordered were locks and, of course, sumptuous crimson damask with gold brocade.

Louis XIV's haste was matched only by his confidence in his own judgment. Saint-Simon, writing twenty years later, describes a lively argument between the King and Louvois, his finance minister, at the very beginning of what would become the Marble or Grand Trianon: "The King, who had an incomparable eye for detail, noticed that one window was a little narrower than the others. He showed it to Louvois so as to have it redone, which was easy enough. Louvois maintained that the window was all right. The King insisted again the next day, but Louvois—blunt, unbending, full of his authority—refused to give way. Next day, while passing through the Château gallery, Louis ran into Le Nôtre, whose job, of course, was to take care of the gardens, which he did superbly. Still, he often found himself approached by the monarch about his buildings. When asked if he had been to Trianon, Le Nôtre said no, whereupon Louis instructed him to go. The following day the two met again. Same question; same reply. The King saw what he was up against, so much so that, a bit vexed, he ordered the gardener to appear there that afternoon, when he himself would be at Trianon with Louvois. This time Le Nôtre dared not refuse. Once the King had arrived, with Louvois present, the discussion once more turned to the window, which Louvois stubbornly held to be the same width as the others. Louis wanted Le Nôtre to measure it, knowing that he was honest and straightforward, and could be counted on to say precisely what he had found. Louvois, stung, flew into a rage, but the equally furious King let him carry on. Meanwhile, Le Nôtre, though desperate to be elsewhere, made not a move. Finally, Louis told him to get on with it, while Louvois continued his grumbling and loud insistence upon the window's sameness. Le Nôtre, having found the said window, declared that the King was right by a few inches. Louvois shot back, but the exasperated Louis demanded silence and commanded that he have the window removed within the hour. Going further, well beyond his usual moderation, he gave the minister a thorough dressing down. Worst of all, for the outraged Louvois, was that the scene had unfolded not only in front of the buildings people but also in the presence of the royal retinue—the seigneurs, courtiers, guards officers, and others who accompanied the King on his promenades. Even the servants could take it all in, because the structure was only just above ground, so that the whole company was standing fairly close together on the courtyard level, where everything was open and everyone followed wherever things led. The contretemps was intense and lasted some time, with reflections on the consequences of the mistake, which, had it not been noticed until later, would have spoiled the entire façade and caused it to be knocked down." Even allowing for the elaborations of a memoirist not given to charitable opinions, one gains a clear sense of how tenacious Louis XIV could be when it came to his buildings.

Nevertheless, Trianon continued to be a *maison de plaisance,* a place for relaxation and refreshment, but no one seriously thought of living there. The left wing, apart from the chapel and the new mirror salon at the end, still contained numerous service rooms, for washing dishes, cooking, roasting, baking bread, storing wine, preparing jams, and making chocolate or coffee.

In 1691 these would be transformed into an apartment for Louis XIV. Meanwhile, the King had his suite in the right wing on the garden side parallel with the more modest apartment of Madame de Maintenon, whose rooms gave onto the King's garden. Louis's apartment included a vestibule

OPPOSITE: Trianon-sous-Bois. Here, even more than at Versailles, flowers constituted a jewelbox setting for an enchanted palace. To reach these perfumed gardens was the purpose of the final, northern extension of the Grand Trianon.

OPPOSITE: Napoleon I's bedroom at the Grand Trianon, now redecorated and refurnished as it was in 1809.

RIGHT: The Salon of Malachite at the Grand Trianon is so named for the hardstone objets d'art kept there, all carved from blocks of malachite given to the Emperor by Tsar Alexander I at the time of their encounter at Tilsit. Note the malachite slab top on the cabinet supporting the two vases. The furnishings date from 1811, but the décor was created by Lassurance in 1699. Napoleon had Jacob-Desmalter mount the objects made from the original blocks in gilt-bronze.

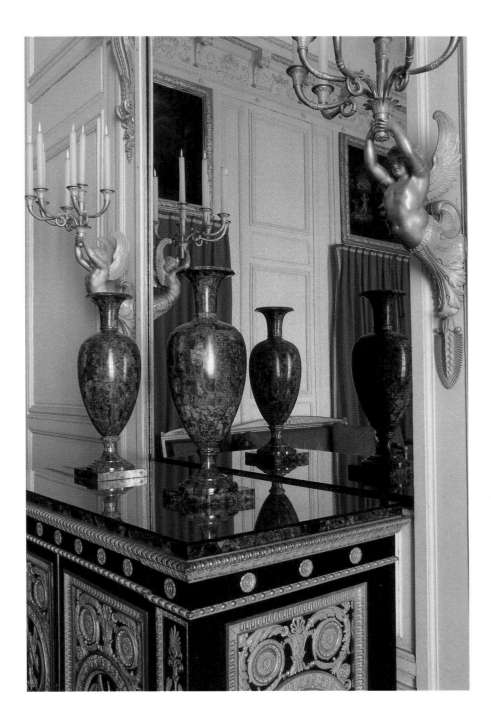

(the Round Salon), an antechamber (the Music Room), where the King ate with the royal family and the ladies of the court (while their husbands took their meals in the other wing, in the Salon des Seigneurs), an antechamber for games, a state bedroom, the *Cabinet du Couchant* (the Sunset Study), and the *Salon Frais* (the Cool Room), which opened onto the gallery. All the rooms were paneled or fabric-covered and generously furnished with armchairs, tables, consoles, stools, and canapés.

The Trianon Gardens

The construction of the Marble Trianon meant that the surrounding gardens had to be completely reorganized, while those around the pavilions would disappear altogether. The upper and lower parterres retained their original form, but the lawn at the end of the western perspective was entirely redesigned. Here the two small box-hedge parterres vanished, as did the large circular fountain and the grassy embankment, all replaced by a lawn leading to a fountain whose complex, split-level design, complete with a double cascade, sprays, and animal figures, exploited the downward slope of the terrain. Beginning in 1694, what would become the Chestnut Garden was created on the side of a hill at the far end of Trianon-sous-Bois. From a double series of four parterres rose a grassy knoll decorated with two parterres and a crowning circular fountain. The ensemble was ringed about by a double range of trees, an innovative feature, like the floral borders replacing the usual hedge of trimmed boxwood.

In 1702 a new château was built slightly apart from the marble Trianon, and the fact that it included an orangery, greenhouses, and dwellings for gardeners, fountain mechanics, and building inspectors suggests the importance the King now attached to the Trianon gardens. Indeed, Louis XIV appeared there more and more often, evidently keeping close tabs on the work in progress. Not only was the project enormous, but it involved the usual delays and changes of plan. In 1701, however, the huge, buffet-like waterfall richly sculpted by Hardy and Lespingola rose from the ground virtually overnight.

The gardens were constantly being expanded, a reality the King may have wanted to make clear, inasmuch as he issued an order, on 27 March 1699, requiring that "gates no longer be erected at the end of the allées, in the boundary wall of the new park at Trianon, but to make bridged moats." Also growing were expenditures and the number of flowers and trees planted, a process involving all manner of equipment—supporting poles, barrows, pitchforks, trowels, twenty-five sets of watering vessels, pots, fencing, and espaliers. Annual plantings numbered in the thousands: 3,460 chestnut trees and 2,000 giant lilies in 1690; 2,500 chestnuts and 90,700 hornbeams in 1697. In 1689 the royal gardeners set out boxwood hedge not by the yard but by thousands of yards. The slope of certain allées had to be modified to allow for the royal carriage bearing a monarch who was now increasingly rheumatic. Not only did the trees and hedges require regular trimming, but benches had to be installed as well as painted green and gold. Yet, despite all these attentions, the process of decay went on, as in the Springs Garden created by Le Nôtre in 1688 near Trianon-sous-Bois, or in the damp gallery, whose old trees the gardener preserved by digging a network of gutters circling about small islands of grass. On either side a gradated channel lined with water jets made this tree-shaded spot a cool and much-favored place of refuge.

Is it possible that the Grand Trianon, with all its royal luxury, built during the heyday of Versailles etiquette, was the Palace of Flora proposed by Le Nôtre? One could be persuaded by the painted décor, especially since this was carefully integrated with the scheme inside the château. Here the

Versailles painters evoked the loves of the gods, with Corneille contributing *Flora and Zephyr,* La Fosse *Clytia* or *Thetis,* and Houasse *Minerva.* Most of all, there was the gallery leading to Trianon-sous-Bois and hung with views of the gardens, a unique ensemble painted by Cotelle, Martin, and Allegrain, together paying homage to a cherished and superbly mastered nature.

STABLES AND SERVICE BUILDINGS

On 28 December 1710, "Monseigneur le Duc de Bourgogne and Madame la Duchesse went to the Menagerie, where there was a great cavalcade of ladies trying to mount horses, one leg here, one leg there, trying to hold on." Outings, rides, and hunting parties demanded serious attention. Le Vau, in the course of making the first extensions, transformed the outbuildings into lodgings, but the horses also had to be lodged. In 1672, the architect built the first stables in brick and stone to the north, not far from the Lake of Clagny, on land, in the Rue de la Pompe, purchased from Mademoiselle de la Vallière. He arranged the structures around a large courtyard, with housing for smithies on the street side, a long coach house hiding a farmyard with a compost heap to the right, and, beyond, the small stables for carriage horses. Opposite the entrance stood the large stables for saddle horses, with a courtyard facing the Rue de la Paroisse.

As visits to Versailles grew ever more common, frequent, and long, a more convenient solution had to be found. It lay immediately opposite the main gates to the Château, where, on two large plots of land, the Duc de Noailles and the Comte de Lauzun had built more or less twin mansions, each with a single storey, an attic, and an octagonal central block with two façades designed as pedimented peristyles approached by flights of steps. Flanking the core pavilion were two short wings, which housed the living quarters, while on the garden side the pavilion contained a domed salon. On the street side were two service wings and a wet moat.

The King would soon lay claim to these properties, placing Mansart in charge of transforming them into stables. At first the architect proposed keeping the two mansions at the center of two courtyards laid out like flat-base, truncated fans unfolded between the three avenues—Saint-Cloud, Paris, and Sceaux—and defined along their three major sides by extended service buildings. In 1680 and 1681, however, Louis bought the mansions and had them promptly demolished. The worksite was enormous, because both stables rose at the same time, between 1679 and 1686. Although impressive, they remained, as *Mercure Gallant* commented in December 1686, "low enough not to obstruct the view of the château: thus, the level of the roof crests corresponds roughly to that of the marble paving of the small courtyard." Composed of huge wings enclosing a vast courtyard, each stable was sealed off, on the side facing the Château, by a wide wrought-iron gate. At the center of each crescent stood a monumental pavilion, its portal designed as a kind of triumphal arch with vigorous sculptural embellishments. Principal among the latter was the semicircular arch over the portal to the Large Stable (*Grande Écurie*), for which Raon modeled three galloping horses. In the triangular pediment above appeared Granier's composition of Fames brandishing the arms of France. The commission for the wood transom went to Briquet and Pallu, who carved an allegory of France. On either side of the portal were embedded tall reliefs composed of military trophies.

For the portal arch at the Small Stable (*Petite Écurie*) Le Comte created three horses in harness and driven a charioteer. Like Raon's high relief seen above, this sculpture was not stone-carved

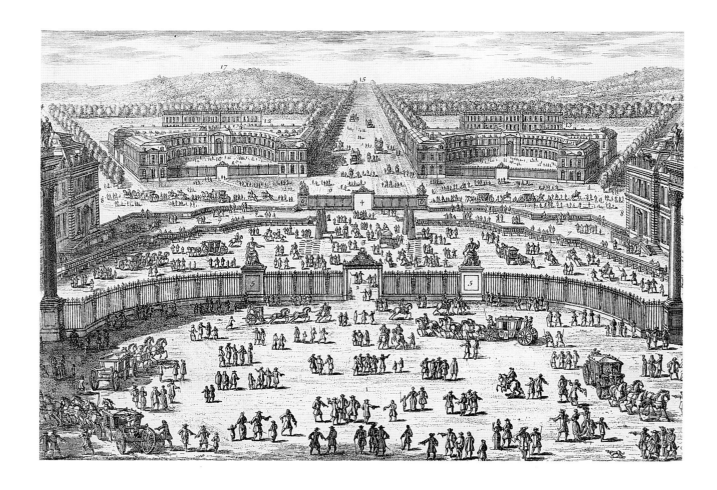

The Stables, built by Jules Hardouin-Mansart in 1679 as a pair of crescent arcades neatly fitted between the three broad avenues (the "crow's foot") fanning away from the Château forecourt. Shown as well in this eighteenth-century engraving is the wrought-iron gate through which only the vehicles of the privileged could pass.

but made of reinforced stucco. The plans for the two stables may have been similar, but they differed at the back, where a pair of small interior courtyards were joined by the intervening presence of a riding school. While this space remained empty or open in the Large Stable, it was apse-like at the Small Stable and contained a sort of semicircular salon, the tympanum of whose door contained Girardon's *Alexandre et Bucephaus* carved from Saint-Leu stone. The interior courtyards were embellished with urns executed by Houzeau, Le Comte, Girard, Meusnier, and Pernaux. The two stables came into their own once the court moved to Versailles in May 1682. In addition to the horses—under Louis XIV, 300 in the Large Stable and 250 in the Small Stable, but under Louis XVI, almost 1,000 in each facility—the stables housed, on one side, the Master of the Horse (*Monsieur le Grand*), Jacques-Louis de Beringhen, famille de Lorraine and, on the other, the First Equerry (*Monsieur le Premier*), not to mention other equerries, pages, coachmen, grooms, a school as well as its instructors, and a chaplain. The stables had to accommodate water and straw, along with ceremonial and everyday harnesses, ribbons, plumes, and embroidered trappings in varying degrees of splendor. The First Equerry was responsible for providing teams of six well-matched horses for the King, also his carriages and those of his retinue. The Master of the Horse housed the ceremonial officers, the Trumpets of the Bedchamber, the heralds, and the "Music of the Large Stable." Each of the stables had its own page-boy choir. In other words, the stables were a world unto themselves, on the margins of the Château, but full of intelligence, efficiently run, and well maintained. (Anyone freshly presented at court could use a royal carriage to join a hunt, but once there he mounted a horse

Today the high vaults and noble galleries of Hardouin-Mansart's Large Stable shelters not horses and grooms but rather major works of sculpture originally made for the Versailles gardens, where, in certain instances, they have been replaced by copies. In the foreground stands Girardon's *Abduction of Proserpina by Pluto.*

from the Large Stable.) For proof of the care taken of these magnificent vessels one has only to consider the payments made to the painter Le Hongre for a redesign of the bricks in the great vaults.

THE CHÂTEAU DE CLAGNY

"It's fine, just right for a girl from the opera." This was all Louis XIV could get out of Madame de Montespan when he took her to see the worksite at Clagny in the spring of 1675. A year earlier the King had decided to provide a château for "My Lords the King's Natural Children," its construction given over to Antoine Le Pautre. Louis and his mistress approved the plans, but those responsible were urged to have "the gardens ready for planting by autumn." The new château—a one-storey affair with an attic—was to be composed of a central domed building and long flanking wings articulated by quoins.

When, subsequently, Mansart rebuilt the château, he retained Le Pautre's ground floor but demolished the attic and replaced it with a proper storey crowned by a high roof behind a balustrade with dies and fire pots. The ground floor featured Tuscan columns, while the Corinthian order prevailed on the upper storey, above which a large, gilt-lead sun added lustre to the dome. Before long, even this enlargement would not suffice, as the King's natural family continued to grow. After the Duc du Maine, born in 1670, came the Comte de Vexin, born in 1672, followed by Mademoiselle de Nantes in 1673. Four years later, the siblings would be joined by Françoise-Marie, future Duchesse de Chartres, and then, in 1678, the Comte de Toulouse. When called to the rescue, Mansart did what had been or would be done at the great Château and erected supplementary wings on either side of the courtyard.

In 1678 Mansart began this new campaign of building with the left wing, which, around the corner on the garden side, would provide for an orangery. On the courtyard side, the wing itself contained apartments and on the garden a gallery running the full length of the structure. At either end, however, the vaulted gallery boasted a salon at the center as well as at either end, each crowned by a flat dome that Le Brun was supposed to have decorated with scenes from the *Aeneid* but never did. The sculptural decoration, however, was carried out, and it is known: a stout cornice between ceiling and walls, Corinthian pilasters, swags and chutes, consoles and shells. The intermediate salon also boasted statues displayed in niches. Properly finished, the gallery would have resembled the Hall of Mirrors. Alas, the fate of "Clagny, house of delights," followed rather closely that of La Montespan herself once she lost the King's favor. In her moment of glory, however, the demanding favorite had been omnipresent at the worksite, prompting Madame de Sévigné to compare her to "Dido building Carthage." As for the King's large apartment, it lay in Le Pautre's original building on either side of the large salon on the ground floor and continued to the very end of the right wing, which terminated in a chapel. Secondary rooms faced the courtyard. On the garden side around the corner, a pendant to the orangery wing opposite contained kitchens and servants' quarters. The dense intermingling of state apartments, which gave onto the gardens only, as at Versailles, and practical rooms, such as the library and Louis's small bedchamber giving access to the gallery, confirms that the King never thought of Clagny as a regular dwelling place. Like Trianon, it served as a complement to Versailles, despite the imposing garden façade, its projecting bays, balustrades, and roofs ornamented with lead fretwork.

The same richness and abundance characterized the gardens, as Madame de Sévigné noted at the time of her Versailles rambles in 1675: "Dangeau wanted to give presents as well as Langlée.

He began with the Menagerie at Clagny, and spent more than two thousand écus to procure all the most passionate doves, all the fattest sows, all the milkiest cows, all the fleeciest sheep, all the most gosling of goslings." Meanwhile, the King never ceased to fuss over his mistress's pleasure: "I am most pleased that you have bought orange trees for Clagny; continue to have the finest if Madame de Montespan so desires." What impressed visitors above all were the ornamental trees. The surrounding park may have been little more than woods pierced by straight allées, but along the garden façade Le Nôtre laid out a terrace overlooking a parterre with broderie compartments ranged about a large central fountain and a clear view of the lake. On either side stood small trellised pavilions, lime trees, yews, and groves crossed by narrow paths. Narcissi, hyacinths, and daffodils were planted in the thousands, much to the consternation of those in charge of the royal buildings, who were called upon to settle the accounts.

In 1677 Mansart informed Colbert of a labor strike at the Clagny: "You should know, My Lord, that all the stone cutters have left the building and not one has worked since Monday noon; they say their revolt is due to the fact that they are owed four weeks' wages, and that they will do absolutely no work until they are paid, which is a cause of great disorder in the building, of which I felt it my duty to appraise you." Ten years later the château would be abandoned, albeit used on occasion by the Duc du Maine. By the time of the Revolution it had been demolished.

The château de Marly

In 1693 Louis XIV acquired the manor of Marly, in exchange for that of Neauphle-le-Château. This completed an ensemble the monarch had decided upon in 1679 and immediately put into construction, with Mansart in charge. First, ditches had to be dug and the marshes drained, because the land was blessed with several springs. Next, the terrain was leveled so as to produce the unobstructed view required by the King. In front of the central pavilion, completed in 1683, Mansart erected ten smaller pavilions in two parallel rows, to which two more pavilions would be added in 1703 to house the Coronelli globes presented to the sovereign by Cardinal d'Estrées. Marly witnessed its first festivities on 10 September 1684, when the King himself sang, a ballet was performed, and four suppers served, with Louis, the Dauphin, the Dauphine, and Madame each presiding over a table. Promenades, music, collation, dinner, and supper, ballet, lotteries, and theatre—these would make up the menus of what were known as "Marlys," events so prized that people would do anything to get invited, as Abbé de Polignac averred in a 1705 riposte to the King when a sudden downpour spoiled the party: "'Tis nothing, Sire, the rain at Marly does not wet."

For the interior Mansart appears to have found his inspiration in Palladio's Villa Rotonda near Vicenza. The main building was to be square and open on all four sides, where four vestibules—one, on the chapel side, serving as a dining or games room—led into a monumental, octagonal hall at the center, rising the full height of the structure. On the ground floor the cross formed by the vestibules established the placement of four corner apartments. To the right of the main entrance was the King's apartment, composed of antechamber, council chamber, and bedroom, all with a view over the great horse pond. Farther along was the Queen's apartment (occupied by Madame de Maintenon), consisting of the usual three main rooms: antechamber, bedchamber, and *cabinet,* the last an oratory. To the left, near the chapel, Madame, the Duchesse d'Orléans, had her apartment, which would subsequently be occupied by Madame de Maintenon. Finally, there was the apartment of the Dauphin, diagonally across

Louis XIV "promenading" towards the Château's forecourts away from the little Château de Clagny, seen in background.
The King had built Clagny for Madame de Montespan, the most dazzling of his several mistresses, and her ever-increasing brood of royal bastards.
The Clagny residence stood at the head of a reservoir/lake immediately to the northeast of the Château de Versailles.
Anonymous painting (c. 1680).

Overview of the Château de Marly under Louis XV. Designed by Haroudin-Mansart and built between 1679 and 1683,
Marly appears to have been Louis XIV's favorite residence, a place well away from the court and its countless intrigues.
Here the King could live intimately with his family and the privileged few he chose to invite.
The main pavilion at the top of the site may have been based upon Palladio's Villa Rotonda,
but the parallel series of subsidiary pavilions, six on either side of the central perspective, constituted a genuine novelty.
They replaced the wings, courtyards, setbacks, and enfilades found at Versailles, as well as the rigorous etiquette such a system demanded.
And in lieu of the Royal Allée, the Tapis Vert, and the Grand Canal, the main axis is traced out by a stair-step sequence of water terraces,
descending all the way to the Horse Pond at the bottom, where a pair of monumental sculptural groups once proclaimed
the royal glory "on land and on sea." Both the groups by Coysevox placed there in 1702 and the substitute pair by Coustou (1745)
now bring glory to the Cour Marly at the Louvre. Painting by Pierre-Denis Martin.

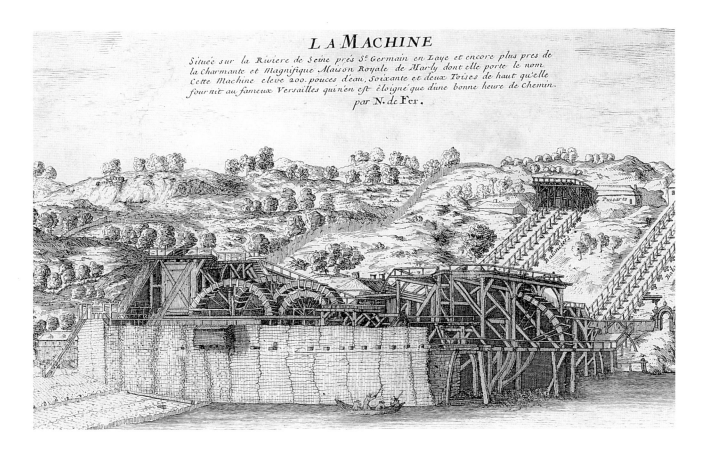

LA MACHINE

Située sur la Riviere de Seine prés St Germain en Laye et encore plus prés de
la charmante et Magnifique Maison Royale de Marly dont elle porte le nom.
Cette Machine eleve 200. pouces d'eau, Soixante et deux Toises de haut qu'elle
fournit au fameux Versailles qui n'en est éloigné que d'une bonne heure de Chemin.
par N. de Fer.

The Marly machine, built by Deville to pump water from the Seine to feed
the Marly fountains, beginning some 100 metres above the source.
Engraving by Nicolas de Fer.

from the King's apartment. Following his untimely death in 1711, this suite would be taken by the Duc de Chartres, son of Louis XIV's brother, Philippe, Duc d'Orléans, and the future Regent of France during the minority of Louis XV. It was carved from the grand staircase giving access to a small suite comprising a tiny antechamber, a bedchamber, and a companion room.

All these rooms faced outwards, while wardrobes and numerous stairways were tucked into the sides of the octagon left free by the vestibules. Upstairs, the layout of rooms was somewhat different, owing to the presence of a hallway circled about the central salon. On this level were housed the Duc and Duchesse d'Orléans, the Duchesse de Lude, the ladies of the court, and the captains of the guard. The list of occupants and the intimacy of everything recall the early years at Versailles. Numerous stairways contributed to the livability of this building, where the King, the Duchesse d'Orléans, and Madame de Maintenon each had an apartment of their own.

The true architectural novelty at Marly lay to the north of the royal pavilion, in that double phalanx of smaller pavilions, all decorated on the interior with trompe-l'œil scenes from mythology. Here, an orderly dispersion of housing replaced the wings, courtyards, setbacks, and enfilades found at Versailles, along with the rigorous etiquette such a system demanded. Everyone sensed the difference, however nuanced, for at Versailles, a place to live had to be obtained, no matter the cost, whereas at Marly only the invited were present. As Louis XIV said to the Bishop of Metz in 1687, "others beg me to take them to Marly, but I beg you to come." Here the idea was to get as close to the King as possible, something unthinkable at Versailles. In 1695 Monsieur de Noyon, François de Clermont-Tonnerre, found himself lodged in one of the more distant pavilions. When asked by the King about his situation, the guest replied: "Marly, Sire? I hope Your Majesty will invite me there some other time, because on this occasion I'm only in the suburbs." Imagine such freedom of expression! Far more than at Versailles, diarists could measure the mood of the royal family, whose members were not all of the same spirit. In 1709, for example, the fairly liberal Madame Palatine waxed indignant over the carefree atmosphere: "You lose track of who you are: when the King goes by, no one takes his hat off. Here, in the salon and in the gallery at Trianon, all the men remain seated in the presence of the Dauphin and the Duchesse de Bourgogne; some are even stretched out on the settees... It no longer resembles court at all."

Apart from the salon's overall décor of pilasters, trophies, and terms, the furnishings within the royal pavilion—all known from the drawings of Robert de Cotte and Le Pautre—were abundant and of the highest quality, just as the paintings were the fruit of carefully placed commissions. On the walls hung scenes of the King's conquests, floral still lifes, portraits, copies of the finest Dutch or Flemish originals in the royal collections, and historic tapestries. This superb decorative tradition would be continued right up to the Revolution.

On the exterior the château appeared to have its back virtually against the forest, with only the Great Cascade, the Horseshoe, and the Crescent of the Winds above it. On the front, the royal pavilion overlooked the sequence of stair-step water terraces extended down the long perspective running between the parallel ranks of secondary pavilions to the Horse Pond at the bottom. Here, Coysevox's equestrian groups entitled *Mercury* and *Fame* would be installed in 1702, far from the gods located high up near the Cascade, and quite alien to the spirit of the Adonis shepherds, the Hamadryade, and the Flora placed near the royal pavilion. At the very gate to semi-private Marly, Coysevox's two monumental groups proclaimed the royal glory "on land and on sea," while also symbolizing the benefits of peace that came with victory. And this near the end of the century. The sculptures—masterpieces both—remained in place only until 1719, four years after Louis XIV's death. Why? In 1745 Guillaume Coustou, Coysevox's nephew and pupil, would replace them with more vigorous-seeming works. Today the two sets can be readily compared at the Place de la Concorde, where casts made from the originals stand (Louvre) near one another, the first two groups at the entrance to the Tuileries and the second pair at the entrance to the Champs-Élysées.

Le Nôtre's Marly gardens also appeared to breathe a new spirit, especially in their diversity. The upper precinct, cut out of the forest, had a vehicle on wooden rails and, as at Versailles, a mall or promenade. Around the château were four "green rooms" with basin fountains much frequented by the King. According to his sister-in-law, it was here, in 1702, that Louis discovered "thirty lovely fat carp. Some are like gold, others like silver, others of a fine rosy blue, others speckled with yellow, white and black, blue and white, golden yellow and white, white and golden yellow with red or black spots; in short, there are so many sorts that it's quite wonderful." Marvels of nature like these were usually gifts sent to the King. In the ever changing groves the court sometimes came upon such playground equipment as a swing or a turning ring similar to the one at Trianon. Most of all, however, the Marly gardens abounded in flowers, thousands of them in such luxuriance that Madame de Maintenon exclaimed in 1698: "Marly will soon be a second Versailles!"

THE KING'S DAY

"The King ordered that no changes, embellishments, or additions be made to the dwellings in the château or any of the other buildings, except at His Majesty's express command, and that those who requested such alterations should make them at their own expense, after approval from Monsieur Mansart." This order came in 1699, and after two decades of interrupted construction, it marked a pause, if only a temporary one. The establishment of the court at Versailles had obliged Louis XIV to set up in his "small apartment." Even so, everyone knew the sequence of rooms—vestibule, guardroom, antechamber, bedroom, *cabinet*—as well as where to slip a message to the King, in the event it had not been possible to leave a petition at the Guardroom on Monday. Meanwhile, Louis still had major projects under way, beginning with the Guardroom and the King's first antechamber, which entailed the removal of the original Queen's Staircase. In addition, a second antechamber, leading to the Hall of Mirrors, had to be installed, after which came the fitting out of the "chair" and wardrobe *cabinets,* the Council Chamber, and the Wig Cabinet, the latter two immediately behind the east wall of the Hall of Mirrors. A billiard room and a picture cabinet were inserted in the north wing facing the Marble Courtyard. Changes in these core parts of the Château would go on continuously until the Revolution, for it was here that the sovereign actually lived, making the sector one in which he enjoyed relative freedom to rearrange things at will.

In the First Antechamber, overlooking the Marble Courtyard and the Queen's Courtyard, Louis XIV took his public meal, an evening supper, often served following any promenade he may have taken, a work session, and time spent across the landing, away from *le gros* (the public), in the

apartment of Madame de Maintenon. The King dined with his back to the fireplace, and if members of the royal family were invited, they sat alternately to the left or right of His Majesty, according to rank. Each monarch found at his place not a glass (drink was served only when requested) but a cadenza laden with spices, a spoon, a fork, and a knife. According to the Duchesse d'Orléans, writing in 1713: "The Duc de Bourgogne [Louis XIV's grandson] and his two brothers were taught to eat with a fork for the sake of good manners, but when they were admitted to the King's table, the King would have none of it and forbade them to do so; I was never forbidden to do so, as I always, when eating, used just my knife and fingers." After the First Antechamber came the Second Antechamber, then known as the Bassano Room. In 1684 Louis XIV moved his bedchamber to the bottom of the Marble Courtyard, and had it decorated with Corinthian pilasters, carved paneling, a handsome fireplace in Languedoc marble, and a silver balustrade modeled by Caffiéri (then melted down in 1689). For furniture, the King kept the gold-fringed, red-velvet pieces used in his previous bedchamber. In 1701 the Second Antechamber and the Bassano Room were combined into a single, large antechamber, known as the Salon de l'Œil de Bœuf, the scene of such important events as the Duc de Bourgogne's wedding ball. This "Bull's-Eye Salon" came into being after Louis XIV decided to transform the King's Salon, in the middle of the central wing overlooking the Marble Courtyard, into his state bedroom, facing east so that the Sun King could rise along with the sun itself. Here the doors to the Hall of Mirrors were blocked and the thickness of the west wall reduced. The lunette above the bed would be filled with Coustou's *France Triumphant* and the walls as well as the shutters decorated with sumptuous white and gold patterns on a lozenged ground. On the walls hung a self-portrait by van Dyck and Valentin de Boulogne's *Evangelists,* pictures retained from the former King's Salon. In addition to the gilt-wood balustrade and the bed fitted out, during the winter, in brocaded velvet and gold-embroidered crimson *gros de Tours* (replaced during the summer by a floral pattern in silver and green), the furniture included three armchairs, twelve folding stools, two floor cushions, and a screen.

The authority of the King over the court found its most symbolic expression in two ceremonies that remained constant until the Revolution, even though Louis XV and Louis XVI slept in a more comfortable bedchamber nearby. Rising and retiring—*le coucher* and *le lever*—provided occasions at which the King could distinguish an officer or a courtier by according him the honor of bearing the candlestick into the royal bedchamber, purely a ceremonial function given the amount of illumination already available in the room. For some, just being there was enough, as Saint-Simon reports: "At eight o'clock, the first valet, who alone had slept in the King's bedchamber, dressed and woke [the King]. The first doctor, first surgeon, and, while she was alive, the nurse, entered at the same time. She went to kiss him, the others rubbed him down and often changed his nightshirt, since he tended to perspire. At a quarter past the hour, the grand chamberlain was summoned or, in his absence, that year's First Gentleman of the Bedchamber, and with them the high nobility. One of these two opened the bed curtains and brought over the holy water from the holy-water basin on the bedside table. These gentlemen were there for a while, and if one of them had something to say or ask the King, the others would move away; when none of them had anything to say, as was usual, they were there just a few moments. The one who had opened the curtain presented the holy water and the prayer book of the Holy Ghost, then everybody repaired to the Council Chamber. Once prayers had been said, the King called for them, and they returned. The same man gave him his dressing gown, while the lower nobility and *brevets d'affaires* entered the bedchamber a few moments later—first the most distinguished, then everyone else—to see the King putting on his shoes; for he did almost everything himself, deftly and gracefully.

The Duc and Duchesse de Bourgogne being served by the Duchesse de Lude. The royal couple became Dauphin and Dauphine of France
after the Grand Dauphin died in 1711, only to survive him by less than a year. Thus, when the long-lived Louis XIV died in 1715,
the crown passed automatically to his great-grandson, five-year-old Louis XV, the Bourgognes' only son.
The Duchesse (Marie-Adélaïde of Savoy) was the most adored member of Louis XIV's court, and her untimely death saddened
the King as few others things in the whole of his existence.
Anonymous engraving.

Chez Trouuain ruë St. Jacques au grand Monarque

M.V

Louis Le Grand Roy de France

On trouue Chez ledit Trouuain tous les Portraits des Dames de la Cour en mode.

se vend Paris chez A. Trouuain ruë St. Jacques au Grand Monarque attenant les Mathurins. aux Pri. du Roy.

Louis XIV, whose daily attire was relatively simple: tight breeches, jerkin, long coat, blue sash, sword, and jeweled shoe buckles, but no rings. The King, in his prime, has been described as a tall, dark, handsome man with a noble look and extraordinary grace in every kind of activity. He appears never to have made an ill-considered or meaningless gesture.

One saw him being shaved every other day; he had a short little wig, and would never at any time, even if he was ill in bed, appear without it in public. "Then came a bedside prayer," with all the clergy kneeling, the cardinals without cushions, "meetings with Mansart or d'Antin in the Council Chamber, and an announcement whether or not the King would attend Mass." One knew to within half a quarter of an hour all that the King was to do. "Louis took lunch in his bedchamber, always in private and often alone, but sometimes with his brother, the Duc d'Orléans, who came from Saint-Cloud and who, again according to Saint-Simon, "much enlivened the conversation."

The Council Chamber was lined with mirrors, and would remain so after the alterations of 1701, the reflecting glass hung between doors and windows and supported by consoles laden with agate vases, beautiful objets d'art, and gems. It was here that Louis XIV spent most of his working hours, engaged with the Council of State on Sunday, Wednesday, and often Monday, and with the Council of Finance on Tuesday and Saturday. After Mass on Friday the King met with his confessor until lunchtime. It was also in the Council Chamber that Louis would spend an hour after dinner with his brother and children before retiring. Moreover, he let it be known that, after supper, the room should be kept for family purposes, as Dangeau remarked in his *Memoirs* (1704): "Monsieur de Torcy led the Elector [of Cologne] by the small staircase to the King's *cabinet,* where all the royal family were gathered, an honor that greatly touched him, and which the King had never accorded to anyone before. The King told him: 'I want you to see me in private, with my family, where you are no stranger, and we are all very pleased to see you.'" The Council Room was, in addition, a place for leisure, which explains the appearance of a couch in 1684, and then, in 1690, a harpsichord painted by the miniaturist Joubert. Here, too, the monarch gave less official audiences, as Saint-Simon reports, writing in 1710: "I found the King alone, sitting on the end of the council table, as was his wont when he wished to talk to someone at his ease and leisure." Next door was the Wig Cabinet, situated like a pendant to the Bassano Cabinet on the south side of the King's suite. Its décor consisted of Classical terms, mirrors, and Charmeton's carved consoles along the walls. Next came the Billiard Cabinet, which, in turn, gave access to the rooms around the interior courtyards. Louis XIV being an avid billiard player, one can imagine the strategic importance accorded this chamber, for a skilled performance here could do a courtier a world of good. Chamillard, an excellent player, obtained a lodging in the North Wing in 1686, an appointment as Intendant of Finance in 1689, and as Controller of Finance in 1699.

On the other side of the wall or the courtyard was the enfilade of State Apartments, where the life of the court went on. In these "planetary rooms" the King entertained lavishly three times a week during the winter on Monday, Wednesday, and Thursday, always in the evening—whenever it was announced that "an apartment" would be held. Reports in *Mercure Galant* or stories told by dazzled courtiers, such as Mademoiselle de Scudéry in 1683, suggest what the events were like: "You have never seen anything to match what is understood by this new word 'apartment'..." Guests were welcome from six o'clock until ten, always free to come and go, linger, play, watch, or even dance with the Dauphine, albeit a privilege available to ladies only. The Throne Room was reserved for music, the Salon of Mercury for the King's game, and the Salon of Mars for all sorts of games, countless according to the Duchesse d'Orléans, including lansquenet, backgammon, piquet, and reversi, as well as some banned by the King. On "apartment" evenings, the billiard table was installed in the Salon of Diana, a brilliant setting, what with its solid-silver furnishings, not only chandeliers, girandoles, and candlesticks but also orange-tree boxes, incense burners, vases, and andirons. The King tallied one success after another against such top players as Vendôme, Villeroy, and Gramont, remorselessly forcing them into mistakes or lining up

OPPOSITE: The Bull's-Eye Salon with Houdon's marble bust of Louis XVI (c. 1780). This superb white and gold room served as an antechamber on the south side of the King's State Bedchamber.

RIGHT: On the north side of the King's State Bedchamber lies the Council Chamber. Among its furnishings is the porphyry *Alexander,* an antique bust mounted in marble and gilt-bronze by Girardon. The décor dates in part to the reign of Louis XIV and in part to that of Louis XV, for whom Gabriel created the large white and gold boiseries.

Louis XIV, the Duc d'Orléans, the Comte de Toulouse, the Duc de Chartres, and the Duc de Vendôme,
Messieurs de Chamillart and d'Armagnac playing billiards in the Salon of Diana.
Engraving by Trouvain.

shots everyone else found incredible. In the Salon of Venus stood tables covered with filigree baskets filled with seasonal fruit, lemons, oranges, or jellies, and everyone could partake at will. Hot coffee or chocolate, liqueurs, sorbets, fruit juices, and wine were served in the Salon of Abundance. Equally splendid was the freedom of speech and movement enjoyed by the select company, to whom the King was delighted to show his collections, thereby indulging the pleasure he always took in artistic matters. The good Abbé Bourdelot found himself led by the Duc d'Orléans into the Cabinet of Rarities, where he encountered the royal family. Struck by how relaxed Louis was, the Abbé wrote: "The main attraction was the King. He was not on his throne; there were three cushions on the edge of the platform, and I was astonished that he should be sitting there so informally."

Once the giddy era of Madame de Montespan had passed, the monarch kept more and more to these interior rooms, or "back *cabinets*" as Saint-Simon called them. Well before Louis XV, Louis XIV constructed, rearranged, and enlarged everything on the north side of the Royal Courtyard, encroaching on the inner courtyards or anything else he could. Along the way, he created a second suite, this one east of the Billiard Cabinet beginning with the so-called "room with the King's dogs," which contained two niches made of "bleached and gilded oak with two dogs and lined inside with red velvet." Next in sequence was the grandiose King's Staircase, behind the north façade of the Marble Courtyard,

The Grand Dauphin, the dowager Duchesse de Conti, the Duc and
Duchesse de Bourbon, and the Duc de Vendôme gathered for one of
the royal soirées know as "apartments". Engraving by Trouvain

until it was destroyed in 1692 and then replaced, farther north on the Bath Courtyard, by a small staircase,
which the King used whenever he left the Château. Also on the Royal Courtyard, but farther east at the
far end of the old Louis XIII wing, Louis created two galleries with walls covered in red velvet and hung
at regular intervals with long gold passementerie strips treated like "flying pilasters." Here the King displayed a superb series of paintings by Nicolas Poussin. His taste for fine objets d'art no doubt reflected
influence from Cardinal Mazarin, part of whose vast collections had been left to the crown. A desire to
exhibit these *gemmes* partially explains the campaign of refection in this part of the Château, which
went on throughout 1692 and 1693. Two *cabinets* were refurbished and two salons, with boiseries by
Noël Jouvenet, fitted out behind them on the Bath Courtyard side. One salon was oval and the other
invested with a splendid cornice of flowers and shells. The first served as a painting gallery, but in 1708
it also boasted two Boulle bookcases embellished with "copper marquetry on a tortoiseshell ground"
and used for storing manuscripts. The second was reserved for sculpture, including scaled-down ver-
sions of the monumental equestrian portrait of the King in the Place Vendôme and four Abductions made
by François Girardon and delivered to Versailles in 1693. For the work done here, the royal building
accounts show payments made not only to sculptors working both outside (Dufour among them) and
inside (Charmeton, Le Goupil, Taupin) but also to the gilder Désauziers. The last received important

sums for his work as well as for the gold supplied to him by the building service and deducted from his invoice. The top-quality gold came to 53 *livres* per thousand and the lesser quality to 30 *livres*.

In the autumn of 1684 Louis XIV took over Madame de Montespan's apartment in the south wing and had the gallery and the salons at either end completely redecorated by the cabinet-maker Gilles-Marie Oppenordt. The project continued for eight years without ever being finished. Did the richness of the scheme finally bore the King or perhaps threaten to ruin him? Certainly, the costs ran into the thousands of *livres*—indeed into the tens of thousands—yet, in the aftermath of the Hall of Mirrors, just finished, nothing appeared to be too good for Louis when it came to hanging his most cherished pictures. Cucci received 18,000 *livres* in 1685 and 10,500 *livres* in 1687, after which his total earnings came to 56,500 *livres* "for work of gilded tortoiseshell, lapis-lazuli, carpentry, bronze ornaments, models and other things done for the gallery of the small apartment." Oppenordt supplied "linen-grey wood from the Indies" and some "red sandalwood" for which he was paid twelve *sous* per pound. Guignard found what must have been a rare treasure, given the sum paid him for two large planks and a log of redwood from the Indies. All this was used to create a true marquetry showcase, with floors and walls recalling the flamboyance of the early Versailles. A combination of mirrors and blue, or red, damask covered the walls, which were finally hung with consoles. In 1692, however, the entire lot was dispatched to the Tuileries and replaced by fine carved paneling finished in white and gold. This new décor became the setting for masterpieces of Italian painting by Raphael, Titian, Albani, the Carracci, and, possibly, "the portrait of Lisa, wife of a Florentine named Giocondo, by Leonardo da Vinci, who took four months to complete it."

To complement this splendor, the Marquis de Louvois, Colbert's successor, recommended Pierre Mignard, who then received the commission to paint the overhead vaults. At the center of the gallery he featured Minerva (in the image of the Princesse de Conti) and Apollo, the latter in the act of distributing gifts to personifications of the Arts and Sciences. All about them the artist painted flowers and allegories of Peace and History. At one end of the composition appeared Mercury, Pegasus, and Vigilance and at the other Prudence and Discretion. Over one salon reigned Apollo driving his chariot and over the other Jupiter enthroned among the gods. Hardly had the ceilings been finished when Audran, in 1686, made engravings of them. These, along with a few ornamental drawings, are all that remain of this suite, which Louis XIV made much less accessible than the State Apartment, admitting only intimates, connoisseurs, and collectors.

The Cabinet of Curiosities, still referred to as the Cabinet of Medals, Jewels, or Rarities, received as much attention as the King devoted to his collections. Louis XIV had learned to appreciate artists, as well as to be demanding of them, but, with equal enthusiasm, he also studied history and science. Having once mastered these subjects, he eagerly celebrated them in specially struck series of medals. At the same time, the sovereign bought medals and engraved stones, three hundred drawers full! The Abbé de Choisy, commenting on the King's passion for medals, wrote: "The King liked to examine his medals after lunch, which greatly increased the standing of Father La Chaise." It matched that of his sister-in-law, Madame, the Duchesse d'Orléans, who, in 1709, admitted: "I can spend days on end admiring them, as with my own antique medals; last Monday, I bought another hundred and fifty with the money the King gave me. I now have a cabinet of gold medals with a full set of all the emperors from Julius Caesar to Heraclius. None are missing, and there are some very rare medals among them which the King hasn't got. I acquired them all for a very good price: I paid for 260 by weight. I have 410 gold medals in all, and I enjoy listening to the arguments of the curious and knowledgeable, and have people tell me the stories written on the back; that interests me greatly."

Buffet laden with vases and magnificent silver plate,
an arrangement suggestive of the sumptuousness of the royal environment at Versailles.
Painting by François Desportes.

Clearly, such a hoard of medals deserved to be kept in a proper place. This was the King's Cabinet, situated on the Royal Courtyard immediately behind the Salon of Abundance. Work, which continued in the room throughout 1681 and 1683, included breaking into the corners so that drawers could be installed. To protect the valuable contents, Dezeustre made a thistle-decorated grille to keep intruders from entering by way of the balcony over the courtyard. The doors were also reinforced by the locksmiths Hasté, Devers, and Roger. Among the furnishings were stuccoed panels, twelve medal cabinets made by Oppenordt, tweezers for handling the treasures, and magnifying glasses for examining them. Bérain designed the desk at the center, while Oppenordt made additional furniture. On top of all this, Houasse and Boulogne decorated the ceiling, while Le Hongre, Mazeline, and Jouvenet provided the cornice. According to Félibien, the walls were hung with paintings by Leonardo, Raphael, the Carracci, and Veronese. Antique vases and silver figurines stood on top of cupboards placed along the lower walls. The corners of the room held semi-octagonal niches for the display of "jade, agate, jasper, cornelian, onyx, and prime emeralds." On the mantelpiece rested the King's *nef,* or "ship," weighing 150 marcs and encrusted, like all the vases, "with pearls, diamonds, rubies, emeralds, sapphires, turquoises, jacinths, garnets, opals, and topazes"—all the perfect complement to a collection of coins dating back to Childeric. Richness, quality, and authenticity characterized a room in which the King's inspiration appears to have matched that already seen in the nearby State Apartment. How could such a collector not be admired?

Louis XIV had to be concerned not only with his own apartments and those of the Queen, but also with transformations elsewhere demanded by everyone resident in the Château. The Princesse de Conti, the King's much-loved daughter by Mademoiselle de La Vallière, obtained permission to have her excellent, ground-floor lodgings in the South Wing expensively updated with boiseries carved by Lassurance and a fresh décor painted by Audran, a project completed in 1699-1700. In 1697-1698 the Comte de Toulouse, the youngest of the sons born to Louis XIV and Madame de Montespan, had minor carpentry done in the Bath Suite, after he moved there with his tutor, the Marquis d'O. For Madame de Maintenon—and for her alone—storm windows were installed and gilded for the winter of 1696. In 1714 she was given a chapel and all the necessary ornaments so that Mass could be said in her own apartment, which consisted of two small antechambers, a bedchamber, and a large cabinet. It was here, in the south wing overlooking the Royal Courtyard, that, for thirty years, the monarch came every day from his own nearby apartment. Here as well he summoned his ministers and attended performances (usually the works of Duché and Molière) arranged by his granddaughter-in-law, the Duchesse de Bourgogne.

The lodgings of the Duc and Duchesse de Bourgogne suggest the complexity of the domestic arrangements at Versailles. At first, the Duke (1682-1712), who would briefly be heir to the throne after his father, the Grand Dauphin, died prematurely in 1711, lived near Madame de Maintenon, Louis XIV's morganatic wife, while his bride, Marie-Adélaïde of Savoy (1685-1712), occupied the Queen's Apartment (whose original occupant, Louis XIV's first wife, Marie-Thérèse of Austria, had died in 1683), which remained unaltered even though the Princess was only twelve at the time of her marriage. In 1699, when the eighteen-year-old Prince was allowed to bed his wife, a "sleeping apartment" was fitted out for him behind the Queen's Apartment. The suite overlooked the Monseigneur Courtyard and comprised a bedroom, a cabinet, and a wardrobe. Meanwhile, in 1701, his wife would have an oratory installed in her interior apartment.

The Dauphin, or Grand Dauphin, Louis XIV's only legitimate son, enjoyed an apartment admired by all, even though it took a while before the heir to the throne found his place. After living on the ground floor below the Queen's Apartment facing the Cupid Parterre, he migrated upstairs

RIGHT: A Copernican sphere designed by Pigeon. Engraving by Picart and Scottin.

BELOW: A table in Louis XIV's Cabinet of Medals, Jewels, and Rarities. The King had a great part of his collections engraved. The sheets are now of immense value, for while works of art—paintings and sculptures—survive, many decorative objects have disappeared.

A screen decorated
with animal motifs by
Blin de Fontenay.
Tapestry woven at
The Manufacture
de la Savonnerie.

in 1680, taking rooms in the South Wing. When the Queen died in 1683, the Dauphine took her apartment, and the Dauphin returned to the main part of the Château, where he lived on the south side directly under his wife, who would die 1690. There he succeeded his uncle and aunt, Monsieur and Madame, who took possession of a beautiful enfilade on the first floor in the South Wing overlooking the Orangery and the Lake of the Swiss Guard. At last, the Dauphin occupied the most agreeable suite in the Château, situated on the ground floor and facing both south and west. It appears that initially the décor was to have been comparable to the marble ensemble devised for the Bath Suite in the northwest corner of the Château. Finally, however, the Dauphin would lead his life—largely independent of the royal entourage—in rooms whose beauty came closer to that of the Small Gallery. The royal buildings accounts suggest the he opted for a degree of luxury already abandoned by the King himself. In 1685 André-Charles Boulle received a partial payment of 10,000 *livres* for parquet and several pieces of cabinetwork. The accounts for 1692 cite some 95,000 *livres* spent on all "these works in the Jewel Cabinet—parquet, marquetry and copper-inlaid chairs, *scabellons,* gilt-copper wall brackets." But *luxe* alone did not suffice; the Dauphin wanted comfort as well, always struggling against the cold and asking Masselin, the boiler man, for "copper machines" to warm the atmosphere. He also struggled against the public, withdrawing behind wrought-iron grillework. Like everyone else at Versailles, the Grand Dauphin never ceased to enlarge his living quarters. After occupying Monsieur's apartment, he added Madame's before annexing the suite of Madame de Thiange to the east. Finally, he laid claim to two rooms from Mademoiselle's suite, which entailed demolition of walls and nonstop work by the decorators of the Small Gallery: Cucci, Le Moyne, and Le Troyen for the walls and Désauziers for the gilding. Mignard, too, got involved, portraying the Dauphin on the ceiling of his large *cabinet,* a room that delighted connoisseurs. Among these were King James II and, probably, Madame de Montespan, who gave the Dauphin a piece of summer furniture and never hesitated to visit his "cave "on the ground floor well away from the State Apartments.

LOUIS XV: TRIUMPH OF THE DECORATIVE ARTS

Louis XV's office (*Cabinet Intérieur*) with the famous Rococo desk begun in 1760 by Oeben and finished by Riesener.

By the time Louis XIV died in 1715, he had outlived both his son, the Grand Dauphin, and his grandson, the Duc de Bourgogne. And so the crown passed to the latter's only son, a five-year-old boy who would eventually reign as Louis XV. Meanwhile, France was governed by the Regency of Philippe II, Duc d'Orléans, Louis XIV's nephew, who preferred to live in Paris, where he installed his royal charge in the Tuileries Palace. Not until 1722 did the court return to Versailles, which had been generally neglected for the past seven years. Young Louis XV discovered the Château complex with awe and dedication, eager to learn all there was to know, beginning with his first visit, which included the Chapel and the gardens. Next he plunged into the history of his great-grandfather, whose image he could observe, while lying flat on his back, on the barrel vault over the Hall of Mirrors. Throughout his reign, everything Louis XV did at Versailles reflected an almost paradoxical desire to preserve or even continue the work of Louis XIV, while also satisfying his own family's demand for comfort. Under Louis XV the decorative arts at Versailles attained perfection, albeit not without the loss of several splendid ensembles. Already in 1685 the Bath Suite had been redone for Madame de Montespan, then again for her daughter-in-law, the Comtesse de Toulouse, and finally for Madame Adélaïde and Madame Victoire, two of Louis XV's unwed daughters. Once Madame de Pompadour's theatre had been closed in 1750, Louis XV allowed the Ambassadors' Staircase to be dismantled for the benefit of his own expanded suite. Mignard's Small Gallery was gradually swallowed up by Madame Adélaïde, then by her father, and finally by Louis XVI. Also sacrificed was Louis XIV's Medal Cabinet. The Regent himself remodeled the Grand Dauphin's ground-floor apartment facing the Cupid Parterre, as would the new Dauphin, resulting in the sale of the Boulle marquetries.

In his official life, Louis XV honored the tradition established by his predecessor. *Levée,* council meeting, Mass, hunting, benediction, supper, and "apartment"—the daily sequence continuing as if by some immutable law. The Hall of Mirrors and the King's State Apartment remained the settings for new acquisitions—a tapestry or a painting—or high diplomatic ceremonies. In 1735 the blue and gold brocade in the Mars Salon was restored, and in 1743 the Slodtz brothers supplied the court with a set of those three-legged tables known as *guéridons.* Commissioned by the Duc d'Antin to finish the Hercules Salon, Robert de Cotte and Ange-Jacques Gabriel introduced colored marbles and a monumental fireplace with gilt-bronze fittings by Vassé, thereby adding fresh lustre to the State Apartment. Their initial project for the ceiling had as its theme "France triumphant from Charlemagne to Louis XV," which would finally be rejected in favor of Lemoyne's enormous *Apotheosis of Hercules,* a perfect companion for the two paintings by Veronese. The full-dress ball held here in 1739 attracted such a throng that the King himself had to restore order and place the guests.

The campaign to decorate the Chapel continued. In 1765 the unstable lantern was taken down from the roof, after which the organ was repaired and the side altars gradually invested with their reliefs carved by Bouchardon, Adam, and Verberckt. The Queen, Maria Leszczynska, the royal Princesses (Mesdames), and Madame de Pompadour had special alcoves made to protect themselves from the winter cold. In 1766 the King gave permission for the Sacred Heart Chapel to be erected behind the main altar, in keeping with the wishes of the Dauphin, who died prematurely in 1765. As all this would suggest, the court still regarded the Chapel as a place of great prestige, the site not only for family ceremonies, daily Mass, and benediction but also for such special events as the presentation of the Papal Golden Rose to the Queen in 1736. Something of the same conservative spirit prompted the decision to have Gabriel redo the Council Chamber in 1755, at the same time that the Wig Cabinet, on the Stag Courtyard (*Cour des Cerfs*), was dismantled. Altogether in keeping with the dignity of the place were Rousseau's splendid boiseries featuring royal insignia and symbols of government. As if these were not sumptuous enough, the room would also be endowed with the great porphyry *Alexander,* a fabulous antique from the Richelieu collection mounted in marble and bronze by Girardon.

The third big project was the Neptune Basin or Fountain at the end of the North Parterre perspective, left unfinished at the death of Louis XIV. Here work went on for several years, while L.S. Adam produced the *Triumph of Neptune,* Jean-Baptiste Lemoyne the *Ocean,* and E. Bouchardon the *Proteus and the Cupids.* There was even a foundry on the site. When completed in 1741, the Neptune Basin was so magnificent that on days when its fountains were played full throttle La Martinière feared this ensemble alone would drain a powerful river. Elsewhere in the gardens Louis XV oversaw essential maintenance, but did not venture much beyond restoring fountains, replanting trees or flowerbeds, and dismantling the Water Theatre, which he judged too costly to keep. Deep in the forest, the King indulged the hereditary Bourbon love of hunting, for which purpose he had fresh trails cut and new lodges built (Butard and Saint-Hubert); he also insisted upon the finest horses as well as a large pack of fast hounds, whose portraits would be painted by Desportes and Oudry. Louis even had his *cabinets* decorated with stuccos representing the royal forests, where stag and deer were his favorite sport.

"I don't like to undo what my fathers have done." Thus, Louis XV went on providing entertainment at court—balls, sleigh races, and gaming. He also controlled the allocation of lodgings as carefully as had his great-grandfather, once declaring: "That man will never have a place to live here as long as I live." Religious ceremonies, with musical accompaniment, unfolded with metronome regularity, which, however, the King himself was capable of disrupting, as on the occasion when he returned to Versailles at half-past eight in the morning, heard Mass in his bedchamber, and ordered that he be woken

Young Louis XV as a pilgrim. Orphaned at two and King at five, Louis XV grew up under the regency of his uncle, Philippe II, Duc d'Orléans.
Young Louis has been described as a pretty boy, silent, reserved, and secretive, but also devoted to his tutor, Cardinal Fleury.
His aunt, the Duchesse d'Orléans, said he had "eyes as black as jet and what one could call a *beau regard*.
His eyes are a great deal gentler than he is, in fact, for he has a violent temper." Louis XV would also mature into a silent,
reserved, secretive man, with an eye not only for attractive, clever women like Madame de Pompadour,
but also for the most ravishing decorative arts ever devised. Anonymous painting.

Details of the Wardrobe or Dressing
Room that Richard Mique and
the Rousseau brothers decorated for
Louis XVI in 1788, a year before the
storming of the Bastille. It has been
called a masterpiece, mainly for the
white and gold boiseries with one motif
scrolling up from below, a different,
star-burst motif suspended from above,
and a delicate, garland-like border.
In this tasteful, aristocratic room,
the excesses of the Rococo are almost
totally banished. The medallion
hung by a casually bow-tied ribbon
is very typical of the Louis XVI style.

only at five in the afternoon. Clearly, the sovereign could bend the rules, giving way perhaps to courtiers who were ever more greedy, disrespectful, and eager to profit from any dissension within the royal family. Yet Louis XV could also exercise authority, reprimanding displays of rude behavior, like that of the Duc d'Harcourt in chapel: "Remove your cushion!" The King insisted on court etiquette and defended it wherever necessary, always citing how things had been under the Louis XIV. He could also show temperament, an example of which came at the engagement ceremony held for Madame Infante, when he forced the men to back up and make room for the ladies. At supper the next day, furthermore, Louis issued a public reminder of the need for courtesy.

Trianon, Marly, the new hunting lodges, and, further afield, Compiègne and Fontainebleau all served as refuges from Versailles, which Louis XV increasingly found burdensome. When not at these secondary residences, he spent more and more time in the Council Cabinet and other rooms that he had refashioned more to his taste. Here the King favored decorative elegance, the intimacy of smaller spaces, and comfort obtained by an ingenious reordering of older volumes. Less stoic than his great-grandfather, Louis XV set about to combat the cold. Thus, Versailles would witness a proliferation of kitchens, baths, wardrobes (the King's a veritable retreat), and bells for summoning the servants. The "flying chair" (chaise volante, a premodern elevator or lift) made by Arnoult for Madame de Pompadour caused a sensation, even though Louis XIV had already commissioned such a "machine."

Louis XV found himself forever trapped in the contrasts of his life—the relative freedom he enjoyed upstairs and the grandeur he preserved on the étage noble. Here the team directed by Le Goupil, who had worked for Louis XIV, and then those under Verberckt or Rousseau would replace the columns and pilasters of the previous era with white and gold boiseries delicately carved with an infinite range of graceful, witty, and picturesque motifs. So elegantly integrated were variety and symmetry, rhythm and richness that majesty radiated from even the most marginal passage. Contributing to the overall effect was the fact that boiseries and furniture were created by the same designer.

In 1738 the rooms along the north side of the Marble Courtyard, near the interior Stag Courtyard, were completely remodeled. The King had Louis XIV's former Billiard Cabinet transformed into a spacious boudoir, although he always returned to the State Bedchamber for the rising and retiring ceremonies. The new bedroom also served as his work place for the next twenty years. The scrolls and shells of 1739 would be supplemented with Classical motifs and sumptuous furniture. Silver-flowered, daffodil brocade, gold-threaded wall fabric with a pattern of crimson flowers, a commode made by Antoine-Robert Gaudreaux, and gilded girandoles by Thomas Germain continued the great tradition of royal commissions. The Clock Cabinet took over part of the onetime Picture Gallery. Initially the room boasted a décor of tapestries, but in 1754, while awaiting the arrival of Lemaire's barometer, it had the distinction of housing the extraordinary pendulum clock made by Passemant and Dauthiau and mounted in a case by Caffiéri. The sphere mimicking the movement of the planets was composed of interlocking circles. Louis XV never failed to be there on New Year's Eve to witness the revolutions, programmed to repeat for 6,000 years.

The former Picture Gallery immediately to the east appears to have become Louis XV's favorite room, where the main alterations occurred in 1738 and 1755. At first it had partitions and served for the display or storage of paintings, precious stones, and medals, for which Gaudreaux, in 1739, provided a cabinet with bronze fittings designed by the Slodtz family. Subsequently, the partitions were cleared away, the boiseries finished, and furniture added, including corner cabinets by Joubert, a red-lacquer desk, to replace the kingwood desk originally there, and a large roll-top desk (secrétaire à cylindre), which, with its complex mechanism, had been made by Œben and Riesener.

The Council Chamber seen here was created in 1755 when Louis XV had Gabriel and Jules-Antoine Rousseau
combine two adjacent rooms, one of them Louis XIV's old Council Chamber.
The elaborate clockcase on the mantel dates from the reign of Louis XV and the vases from that of Louis XVI.

Rest, baths, games, or amours––all could be pretexts for Louis XV to fit out *cabinets,*
laboratories, or terraces. Just behind the study described above, the monarch installed a back *cabinet*
overlooking a small courtyard, where he would work. Around the Stag Courtyard, with its decorative
heads carved by Hardy, the passage, "chair" room, and the Gold Cabinet, designed by Robert de Cotte and
ornamented with reliefs by Dugoulon, were remodeled. The Gold Cabinet, enlarged in 1755 by
integration with the former Wig Cabinet, became the Lathe Cabinet, which the King would later move
elsewhere. Louis XIV's grandiose Bath Suite on the ground floor was to be replaced by a room with two
bathtubs, a bedroom, and, upstairs, a room equipped with a water tank. At Versailles the baths never
remained anywhere for long. In 1728 they faced east on the first floor overlooking the Stag Courtyard;
in 1738 they were made smaller; in 1750 they migrated upstairs to the southwest corner; in 1755 above
the Council Chamber facing the Marble Courtyard; in 1763 on the east side of the Stag Courtyard, again
on the upper storey; in 1765, after the death of the Dauphin, the west side of the Stag Courtyard, now on
the first floor in the former Lathe Cabinet; and, finally, in 1770, in the former apartment of Madame Adélaïde on the south side of the small courtyard created by the elimination of the Ambassadors' Staircase.
Here, Rousseau's boiseries, with their decorative motifs from nature, hunting, and bathing and their three-
gold gilding by Brancourt, were fine as well as expensive enough to suggest that Louis XV may have
finally hit upon the baths he wanted. The library, hardly less migratory, was in the attic on the north side

LEFT: This magnificent marble fireplace, installed in the Dauphine's apartment, may have once been in the first-floor suite of Marie Leszczynska, Louis XV's Queen.

OPPOSITE: A Rococo *lit à la polonaise* designed by Nicolas Heurtaut.

Details of the Gilded Chamber decorated for Madame Adélaïde, who wanted to live near the suite of her father, Louis XV, on the north side of the Marble Courtyard. It replaced the former Little Cabinet designed by Mignard for Louis XIV. The new décor was created in 1753 by Gabriel and Verberckt, who revived the trophy chutes favored by Hardouin-Mansart but with earth and water themes—fishing tackle, gardening tools, etc.—rather than military ones. The panels added in 1769, when Louis XV reclaimed the room for himself, display musical motifs, recalling that Madame Adélaïde had studied music here under the supervision of Beaumarchais. One afternoon in December 1764 the royal family gathered here for a recital by a child prodigy, Wolfgang Amadeus Mozart.

of the Stag Courtyard. In 1726, it comprised a *cabinet,* a gallery, and a large room, which, in 1732, would be augmented by a new room as well as an annex, the latter crammed with every sort of history book and map. Then, in 1763, the whole of this collection was moved to the bottom of the Marble Courtyard.

The decoration of the Small Gallery on the second floor began in 1735, during the heyday of Madame de Mailly. It included hunting scenes painted by Boucher, Lancret, van Loo, de Troy, and Parrocel, all set in gilded paneling. This was the large salon where King and company assembled after their hunt, for suppers described by the Duc de Croÿ. It would undergo several modifications before finally disappearing in 1767. The organization of the winter dining rooms on the second floor and the summer ones on the third floor, not to mention rooms for buffets, gaming, and wardrobes—all demanded by the King—proved an ongoing headache for the architect, who also had to accommodate the wishes of successive royal mistresses, of a puttering monarch jealous of his laboratories and kitchens, and, finally, of the entire royal family.

THE QUEEN AND THE CHILDREN OF FRANCE

Alongside the luxury arranged by the King for his comfort as well as that of Madame de Pompadour or Madame du Barry, the Queen—Marie Leszczynska—undertook to have her own State Apartment renovated by Robert de Cotte, Gabriel, and Verberckt, changing the furniture to use the new pieces given her by Louis XV in 1743. They featured bouquets of flowers "according to the new taste." After transforming the Salon of Peace into her card room, she set about installing a series of *cabinets* over the Dauphin Courtyard that would be as numerous and complicated as those of the King. Here, amidst a surfeit of pictures, chinoiseries, and decorated ceilings, the Queen led her quiet life. It was not the Queen who tormented Louis XV so much as their numerous children. The Dauphin lived, by turns, in the South Wing during his first marriage, then during his second marriage, to Marie-Josèphe de Saxe, in the main part of the Château on the ground floor, where he had also grown up. Here the apartments of both the Dauphin and the Dauphine, located below the Queen's suite and the Salon of Peace, were decorated with gilded or polychromed boiseries. Among the rooms were a blue and white library and an interior cabinet finished in soft green. The princely couple turned the courtyard into a garden, which could only contribute to the overall sense of joy and spontaneity generated by the marquetry furniture and brightly colored fabrics.

The lodgings of Mesdames, Louis XV's two unwed daughters, yielded complications of another order. The King enjoyed their company and wanted them to be well treated. And so they lived, by turns, in the South Wing, on the ground floor towards the south end, but also towards the north end in the former Bath Suite; then on the first floor in the onetime apartment of Madame de Montespan, where the last vestiges of Mignard's Small Gallery vanished, as would its memory in the wake of the splendid Gold Cabinet overlooking the Royal Courtyard. The Princesses's lodgings would be further augmented by a rear *cabinet,* an oratory, baths, and a library. On the ground floor, west and north, was a warren of small rooms, corridors, servants' quarters, libraries, and mezzanines, to which Mesdames increasingly laid claim. Meanwhile, on the other side of the Marble Courtyard, in the southern sector of the Château, Versailles had a new Dauphin, who, after studying the physical sciences, would shortly marry the last Dauphine of France, Marie-Antoinette of Austria. She, too, would learn to evolve away from the majesty of the State Apartments towards the more intimate suites, bringing her own ideas about how to renovate them.

The former *cabinet*
of Marie Leszczynska.
Marie-Antoinette had it refitted
with naturalistically painted boiseries
taken from the inner *cabinet*
of her husband's late mother,
Marie-Josèphe de Saxe.

LEFT: Jean-Joseph Lemaire's barometer, commissioned by Louis XV in 1772.

OPPOSITE: The bedchamber of the Dauphin, Louis XV's son, decorated with paneling by Verberckt and a fireplace mounted with gilt-bronzes by Caffiéri. This beautifully situated room gives directly onto the Water Parterre on the garden side of the Château.

OPPOSITE: The Dauphin's ground-floor library as decorated in 1755. The boiseries, with their bright, spring-like colors, were finished in *vernis Martin,* which had just been invented by the Martin brothers. The medium was appreciated for its ability to simulate the hard, gleaming effects of Oriental lacquer.

RIGHT: The inner *cabinet* of the Dauphine. The commode, made by Gaudreaux, and the writing desk, signed by B.V.R.B. (Bernard Van Ryssen Burg II), were commissioned for Louis XV's daughter-in-law, the first wife of the Dauphin, the Infanta of Spain, who died in 1746.

LEFT: The Marquise de Pompadour, as portrayed by Carl van Loo. A clever bourgeoise with an appetite for art and letters, Madame de Pompadour (*née* simply Jeanne Poisson) became Louis XV's official mistress in 1745 and retained his regard until her death in 1764. Together with her brother, the Marquis de Marigny, whom the King made superintendent of royal buildings, the Marquise was in large part responsible for redirecting contemporary taste away from Rococo fantasy towards a more refined classicism, as exemplified by the architecture and design of Ange-Jacques Gabriel. It was for her that Gabriel built the Petit Trianon, completing it, unfortunately, the year in which she died. At the Château, Madame de Pompadour enjoyed the royal favor, in part, because of her gift for creating an atmosphere of relaxed intimacy, animated by wit and charm. She also amused the famously bored monarch, especially in her role as theatrical impresaria, staging play after play in the King's *cabinets,* a series so popular that Louis XV decided to have Gabriel build a proper theatre/opera house.

OPPOSITE: The salon of the Comtesse Du Barry (*née* Jeanne Bécu), Louis XV's official mistress after the death of Madame de Pompadour. She too lived in the *petits appartements* on the attic storey above the King's private *cabinets,* albeit surrounded by the white and gold splendor designed by Gabriel in 1772.
It was this kind of low-ceiling, intimate room that Louis XV adored. Madame Du Barry had none of the intellectual interests of her famous predecessor.

Boiseries created in 1770-1774 by Jules-Antoine Rousseau for Louis XV's Bath Suite and the last interior of the reign. The motifs—bats, birds, geese, dolphins—are comparable to those of Rococo design, but the simplicity of their treatment anticipated the more classical Louis XVI style.

Details of Madame Adélaïde's inner *cabinet,* which Louis XV revamped as his Bath Suite. Louis XVI, in turn, transformed the little back room into his Privy Purse Office, well removed from public scrutiny. Like those seen overleaf, the gilded reliefs reproduced here are the work of Jules-Antoine Rousseau, who also had a hand in designing Louis XVI's Wardrobe (page 173). Although made for Louis XV, the panels, with their straight lines and broad expanses of white ground, would have made Louis XVI feel very much at home within his own time.

GABRIEL AT VERSAILLES

The tribune colonnade
inside the Theatre
or Royal Opéra
designed by Gabriel.

In 1759, even before Gabriel had been asked by Louis XV to build him an entire châ-teau, at Compiègne, the royal administration was already talking about the Petit Trianon, a short distance from the Grand Trianon. The King new the area well, having loved it since childhood, and he often went there with Madame de Pompadour to check on the everyday process of maintenance. Moreover, his passion for the gardens equaled that of Louis XIV. In 1749 he authorized the creation of a flower garden and a "menagerie," the latter consisting of a dairy, a farm, a cowshed, and a sheepfold. Close by there would also be a cruciform pavilion—the French Pavilion—with a central hall for games or parties and four rooms: a kitchen, a heated salon, a boudoir, and a wardrobe. The floor paved in marble mosaic reflected the royal taste for opulence, but Verberckt's carved boiseries and cornice, finished in 1750, acknowledged the King's pastoral interests and botanical ambitions. The sovereign had an aviary built, as well as hen runs and a pergola or trellised pavilion. Fascinated by agricultural research and acclima-tization, Louis XV, in 1750, recruited the well-known botanist Claude Richard for the new Trianon kitchen garden, a *potager* designed to complement the one at Versailles, where figs, coffee, and pineapples were already being grown. Greenhouses—some heated, others not—were built, while strawberry-growing was improved and experiments carried out leading to new ways of ploughing and handling wheat grain.

In 1759 Louis XV summoned the botanist Bernard de Jussieu, known throughout Europe for his studies of plant families best suited to botanical gardens. His arrival marked the beginning of a major scientific program, involving expeditions abroad, explorations, and experiments. The mood was such that anything could be tried. The botanist Antoine Richard, having discovered a few tulip-tree seeds imported from Virginia in 1732, managed to plant them and realize a successful outcome. A similar result had already been obtained with the wax tree brought back from Louisiana by La Galissonière. From China, India, and Cayenne came bushes and large, pearly beans, cocoa and vanilla, marine wallflower

and Gilbraltar oak, the last unequal to the deep freezes of 1879. Nearly 4,000 different botanical specimens, ranging from cedars of Lebanon to boxed orange trees, could be found at Trianon, where the King sought to create a *coin vert,* naming it in English: Evergreen. Antoine Richard and his cousin Louis traveled all over Europe and the Americas, finally returning with new varieties of potato, as well as with flowers from the Alps and the Middle East.

Having launched these projects, Louis XV decided to build something larger and more ambitious than his French Pavilion. For this purpose, groves and gardens were laid out, displacing the aviaries and hen runs installed in 1768. For the new château—what would be known as the Petit or Small Trianon—Gabriel retained the elevation then canonic at Versailles: tall basement or ground floor, *étage noble* (first floor), and attic crowned by a balustrade concealing the roof.

For the ground floor the King ordered a billiard room, as well as service quarters. He also took a personal interest in the design of the grand staircase, its wrought-iron railing decorated with the royal cypher, fleurs-de-lis, and trophies. The wall would be swagged with massive oak-leaf garlands carved by Joseph Vernet's brother-in-law, Guibert. The first floor comprised an antechamber, a small dining room as well as a large one, a drawing room, the King's *cabinet,* and a botanical library, all decorated with pastoral motifs, French blossoms, sunflowers, lilies, and fruits, rendered in white on a soft green ground with gold accents. Everything at the Petit Trianon had been done under the careful guidance of Madame de Pompadour, who even contributed two mantelpieces from her Paris residence, the Hôtel d'Évreux (today the Élysée Palace). After the Marquise died in 1764, Louis XV saw to it that the decorative program was completed in a manner consistent with her taste. Thus it would be in the décor commissioned in 1768 for the dining room with its four large scenes of hunting, fishing, harvesting, and grape-picking, executed by Vien, Doyen, Pierre, Lagrenée, and Hallé. The pastoral element seen here had already appeared at the Grand Trianon, where the loves of the gods commissioned by Louis XIV were now supplemented with a profusion of flowers. In addition to the painters cited above, Lépicié and Monnet worked at the new Trianon, where they painted the overdoors, again in light, pastel colors. All these artists represented nature in the fanciful way of Boucher, even while modeling figures rather more firmly, *à l'antique,* with a grace symptomatic of dawning Neoclassicism. For the next few years Madame du Barry enjoyed the Petit Trianon, a dwelling where every last detail denoted a change of fashion in the decorative arts. Still, luxury reigned supreme, as can be seen by the presence of damask, crimson *gros de Tours,* and furniture made by Riesener. The Petit Trianon even provided an occasion for experimenting with new technology, such as the "movable mirrors "(recently restored) and the "flying tables" invented by the academician Lorito, the latter devices planned but not executed. As at Choisy and La Muette, these would have ensured the comfort of intimacy in the dining rooms, where, by a system of counter-weights, tables prepared downstairs could have been lifted into place without the intrusion of domestics. The Petit Trianon had now become a place for leisure. Madame Du Barry had no interest in becoming a patroness of either artists or scientists. No one summoned Jussieu, and while Richard worked at improving the gardens, he had no mandate to do more than reproduce them. Already the taste for variety was giving way to an appreciation of landscape, the first hint of an obsession with the singularities of nature, soon to be reinvented at the Hamlet grotto or at Versailles itself.

The Petit Trianon, built by Gabriel fifteen years after his French Pavilion nearby, shows the evolution of the architect's style towards a purer form of classicism. This small château in the Versailles park is a tribute to the success of Madame de Pompadour in her campaign for greater refinement in the decorative arts. Unfortunately, the Marquise died in 1764, just as Gabriel was completing the Petit Trianon, which would not have an occupant until Marie-Antoinette claimed it following the accession of Louis XVI in 1774. The Queen adored living there as much as she despised the stifling formality of Versailles.

The King's bedchamber at the Petit Trianon, hung with crimson and white lampas woven with a *musique chinoise* theme. The *lit à la polonaise,* with its carved lion heads, replaced the original bed, designed *à la turque* by Foliot.

THE THEATRE

At Versailles, entertainment was paramount. Festivities had been staged in the gardens and in the Marble Courtyard, but now the time had come for a proper theatre. In 1681 a temporary solution had been tried on the ground floor of the small building (only thirteen by eight metres) built as a link between the South Wing and the main part of the Château. Situated between the gardens and a courtyard, it was lighted by six windows and entered by way of the Princes's Staircase. It boasted nine gradated rows of seats ranged about a wide semicircle, a free space for the "*horsqueste*," and a shallow stage with three doors and two loges or boxes for the First Gentlemen of the Chamber. These courtiers played an important role all their own, since it was they who chose both the plays and the actors. A low mezzanine made it possible to install a tribune for the royal box, which the King and his family could reach by a small staircase leading down from the Merchants' Salon. This hall, located over the theatre, was the route by which the inhabitants of the South Wing made their way to the Château. Needless to say, it would soon be thronged with makeshift stalls selling trinkets, embroideries, books, and jewelry, all very useful to those caught unprepared. To modern eyes, they also suggest quaint precursors of the luxury-goods galleries found in today's hotels. For a while, Louis XIV attended performances in a theatre set up in the right wing of Mansart's Trianon. In 1685 the King approved plans for the construction of a large theatre at the far end of the North Wing, only for it to rise no higher than the foundations. In 1745, under Louis XV, the Slodtz brothers and Perrot fitted out the riding school at the Large Stable as a theatre, where Rameau scored a tremendous hit with, first, the *Ballet de la Princesse de Navarre* and then the *Fêtes de l'Hymen,* works performed to celebrate the two marriages of the Dauphin. This *salle* would succumb to fire on 3 September 1751.

As early as 1740 Gabriel had submitted plans for refashioning the "old wing" of the Château (on the southside of the Royal Courtyard) as a theatre. In 1751, after the fire in the Large Stable, thought was given to building something near the Small Stable on the Avenue de Sceaux. In the end, however, the court had to make do with Louis XIV's old theatre. In 1725, 1748, and 1762 a fair amount of construction went on in preparation for the brilliant carnivals, organized, like the one in 1763, by the princes of the blood, offering programs of both old ballets and rustic diversions full of flowers and picturesque details. On 7 February the theatre was packed for a ball. The King, the Queen, their retinues, officers of the Swiss Guard, the princes of the blood, the captain of the guards, and various princesses filled the loges, twelve to the box. In addition, there were Mesdames, the Dauphin, the officers, and the dancers, all of them moving through their steps on both the stage and in the hall. Altogether there must have been some 300 people who, to satisfy their curiosity, risked death by suffocation.

This theatre was so lacking in comfort and style that the whole court had been intent on finding a better solution. Madame de Maintenon allowed the Duchesse de Bourgogne to perform regularly in her apartment. A generation later Madame de Pompadour produced plays in the King's *cabinets,* beginning on 16 January 1747 with Molière's *Tartuffe* in the Small Gallery. The monarch and a privileged few (the Queen, the Dauphin, and Mesdames, all crowded onto chairs and benches) sat near the Oval Salon, while the actors changed costumes in "portable retrenchments with canopies." This scene was repeated every Monday for a year, the events proving so popular that Louis XV resolved to enlarge what was yet another stop-gap arrangement. Thus evolved the tradition of daily entertainment at court, with concerts given on Monday and Saturday, French drama on Tuesday and Thursday, and Italian comedy on Wednesday, Thursday, Friday, and Sunday. In 1748 Madame de Pompadour asked for a stage both

Sketch for a production at the Versailles Opéra (1753).

deeper and equipped with machinery. After delivering the new stage, the engineer Arnoult declared that, in the event of a ceremony, it could be dismantled within fourteen hours and then reassembled within twenty-four. The success of the enterprise was all the more considerable given the great number of performances included in the series. During a two-year period, Rameau, Destouches, and Voltaire all saw their works performed in Madame de Pompadour's theatre.

Meanwhile, Louis XV had become serious about a more ambitious project, nothing less than the revival of Vigarani's project for a theatre at the end of the North Wing. From 1748 to 1763 Gabriel drew up plans, designed and redesigned the elevations as well as the décor. Work began on the basement floor, then continued on the street façade. In 1767, Papillon de La Ferté, the intendant of the Menus-Plaisirs (that department responsible staging ceremonies and entertainments at court), projected "likely expenditures during the next three or four years for the wedding of Monsieur le Dauphin… These will be wasted if it is not decided to complete the great theatre at Versailles." Gabriel reviewed his plans and soon thereafter had the worksite reactivated, a process further stimulated by the fact that Arnoult had just finished the theatre at Fontainebleau.

At the far end of the North Wing the architect composed a monumental façade over-looking the reservoirs, with an avant-corps whose pediment, carved by Pajou, rose into the attic level. Construction, machinery installation, and embellishment moved forward at a breakneck pace, but at such

PAGES 200-201:
The Royal Opéra,
designed by Ange-
Jacques Gabriel and
decorated by the painter
Louis Durameau and
the sculptor Augustin
Pajou. Charles de Wailly
created the magnificent
Royal Tribune.
The stage machinery
developed by Arnault
made the Versailles
Theatre a technological
marvel. Commissioned
by Louis XV, this most
beautiful of court
theatres was
inaugurated in 1770 as
part of the celebrations
marking the marriage of
the Dauphin Louis to
Marie-Antoinette of
Austria.

LEFT: The grillework
gates on this central box
enabled Louis XV to
attend performances
more or less incognito.
The secretive King,
always reluctant to show
himself in public,
preferred sitting here
rather than in the Royal
Tribune directly above.

cost that the balance could be settled only by issuing bonds, on which Louis XVI would continue to pay interest. Gabriel decided not to recruit the mason Thévenin, who was already deep in debt from having worked for thirty years at Versailles without ever being paid. The scale of the project harked back to the euphoric days of Louis XIV's major building campaigns. By the end of the construction phase in 1769, some 250 masons were involved. One innovation, however, saved both time and expense, and this was the use of wood to build the auditorium. The King wanted the theatre to be unique, larger and more beautiful than any court theatre in Europe, every one of which an expert, Chaumont, would examine. On 9 July 1769, following Mass, Louis XV went to the Hôtel des Menus-Plaisirs and reviewed a scale model of Gabriel's theatre, at which time he consented to have the *salle* constructed of wood rather than stone and marble. It would also be inscribed within an oval truncated along the edge of the side boxes and the stage. So that the theatre might be used for balls or banquets, jacks were installed under the floor, thus allowing it to be raised level with the stage and the first ring of boxes. On such occasions, the stage itself could be transformed into a small theatre with boxes. The upper, third-tier gallery hung behind an Ionic colonnade reflected in mirrors set within tall arches. The wooden elements would all be finished in faux-marbre painted by Durameau, who had to "decide on all the tones and mixtures needed to obtain overall harmony and fine execution." For the walls and columns he used blue, rose, and yellow with gold highlights. Augustin Pajou carried out the extensive program of decorative sculpture: Olympian gods, Muses, putti, signs of the Zodiac, sphinxes, swans, trophies, and lapis-lazuli urns. All formed part of a scheme consistent with the composition on the ceiling, where Durameau painted a trompe-l'œil sky filled with *Apollo Making Crowns for Illustrious Figures of the Arts* and *Loves of the Gods*. The delicate palette, the gilding, the excellence of the sculpture (for which Pajou added the cabinetmaker Delanois to his team), the acoustics, the stage machinery, the floor mechanism—all of it the King found most pleasing. On 7 May he indicated how the chandeliers might be used, partly lit so that the auditorium and its ceiling could be admired. The up-to-date technology, the architectural amplitude, recalling that of the State Apartments and the Chapel, and the superb craftsmanship made the new *salle,* in the opinion of everyone, "the finest theatre in Europe," as the Duc de Croÿ put it. Such was the concern for quality that Pajou had found only ten assistants sufficiently qualified to help him, for a project that included the foyer, where the master executed large allegories in painted wood. Alas, the Versailles theatre cost so much to operate that relatively few events were ever held there. Lighting alone required 3,000 candles backed by polished metal, optical lamps with mirrors, and reflectors to increase the overall brightness. The theatre was inaugurated with a performance of Lully's *Persée,* to celebrate the marriage of the Dauphin to Marie-Antoinette of Austria on 17 May 1770.

THE QUEEN
IN HER GARDEN

Respect for tradition, affirmation of the right to privacy, and enthusiasm for new ideas—all these characterized Versailles during the last twenty years of the Ancien Régime.

As for building, Louis XVI very quickly got involved with the so-called "great project," intended to harmonize the Château façades on the urban side, an ambitious idea rejected by Louis XIV almost a century before. Le Vau considered the problem, as did Mansart, whose plans and suggestions called for entrance elevations uniformly composed of a tall, arcaded basement, a single storey with round-headed windows, and a crowning balustrade. Ornamentation amounted to little more than pedimented avant-corps, niches flanked by columns, and military trophies on the balustrade. The overall effect would have been a more compact-looking Château.

For Louis XV, Gabriel had prepared two plans, the first in 1759 and the second in 1771, the latter partially accepted by the monarch. It would have meant rebuilding the Chapel wing. Then came Louis XVI, who, following through on earlier initiatives, announced a competition in 1780. For the next several years, various architects worked on what would have been a complete reconstruction of the entrance courtyards: Mique, Peyre senior (who had just completed the Odéon in Paris), Peyre junior, Boullée, and Pâris, as well as less well-known aspirants: Potain, supervisor of the Fontainebleau worksite, Darnaudin, and Huvé. As their benchmark, all the aspirants adopted Gabriel's 1759 proposal, which entailed a grand, colonnaded façade in the Classical manner, totally concealing the brick, stone, and slate ensemble inherited from Louis XIII. This project had made some headway, but only because a reluctant Louis XV, having determined to shore up the Chapel, accepted the revised proposal of 1771, i.e., "a general plan of decoration [on the urban side] analogous to that on the garden side." Gabriel could not have been more pleased. The competition prize went to Peyre the Younger, whose idea was to redesign the forecourt as a piazza with a pair of embracing, semicircular colonnades similar to those created by

Bernini at the Vatican in Rome. On the south side, the colonnade would have swung all the way to the Grand Commun, with this matched or symmetrically balanced on the north side by a "new building for the ministers." Meanwhile, the two long wings flanking the forecourt would have disappeared. Peyre also wanted to extend the North and South Wings as far as a colonnade separating the Royal Courtyard from the Marble Courtyard. On the garden front, finally, the Château's central block was to have been slightly enlarged, with the State Apartments giving onto an Ambassadors' Courtyard, closed on the North Parterre side, and onto a Princes' Courtyard, closed on the South Parterre side. Boullée would have immersed the Château behind a long series of façades, with avant-corps either domed or pedimented, at the bottom of an immense *place* confined by double rows of columns. Pâris, a less theoretical architect, stuck to a few well-defined objectives: a more majestic entrance, with a pair of enormous buildings designed as concave crescents and, on either side, a wrought-iron gate for access to or from the Place des Armes, its decorative program composed of fountains, obelisks, and colonnades. Pâris proposed leaving the Chapel intact, while redoing everything else (the Old Wing rebuilt like the Gabriel Wing), or perhaps sinking it within a new structure. Further modifications included closing off the Marble Courtyard and dividing it, by means of a monumental stairway, into two courtyards, the King's on the north and the Queen's on the south, as Mansart had suggested in his grandiose plan submitted a century earlier.

Here, as a second objective, the architect hoped to reduce the tiresome inconvenience of the palace complex, which would have required radical transformations of the spaces within. The State Apartments could not be touched, but the small apartments and interior cabinets, all the products of successive additions and remodelings, would have more or less disappeared and been replaced by two symmetrical parade chambers on each of the new courtyards. As a pendant to the Chapel, a theatre would have been erected on the Princes' Courtyard. In 1787, after reviewing the scope and cost of such an enterprise, the court paid the architects and then put their plans aside in the hope of better times.

Louis XVI changed nothing in his State Apartment, although he did commission for the Hall of Mirrors a set of white and gold curtains like those hung by Louis XIV. Marie-Antoinette redecorated her State Apartment but made almost no other alterations. In the bedchamber the Queen merely freshened up the Rococo boiseries, while also ordering new silks: crimson and gold brocade for winter and, for summer, "white-ground *gros de Tours* brocaded with bouquets of flowers, lilacs, roses,

A project drawing
of 1780 for a
reconstruction of the
Château's eastern or
entrance façades.
This was only one of
many proposals for the
harmonization of the
urban face and
forecourts, the series
beginning far back in
the reign of Louis XIV
and continuing right up
to the eve of the
Revolution.

and ribbons interlaced with spreading peacock tails, the whole framed by a superb green border garnished with rich fringes."

In the Nobles' Cabinet, Mique retained only the Corneille ceiling but replaced everything else, albeit inexpensively, with a décor of boiseries, mirrors, and suitable furnishings supplied by the cabinetmaker Riesener and the *bronzier* Gouthière. The Salon of Peace, joined to the Queen's Apartment since the time of Louis XIV, was at much greater risk, since the new Queen preferred clarity and gaiety over grandeur. Thought was even given to replacing the marbles and metal trophies with boiseries and a mirror, as well as to the installation of a false ceiling decorated with a clear, blue sky, in place of Le Brun's dome. The latter had come to resemble "nothing so much as large black stains, especially by daylight," despite numerous attempts to restore the painting. Durameau, when consulted, persuaded the court to maintain the Peace Salon in its original state.

Private cabinets and apartments

In his private suite, Louis XVI made few modifications. In 1774, however, he transformed Louis XV's Games Room into a library, with boiseries by the Rousseau brothers and a fireplace by Boizot and Gouthière, appropriated from Madame Du Barry's old apartment at Fontainebleau. Here, in a room that was not truly private, the King expressed something of his own taste, for reading, reflection, mechanics, geography, and the ideas of the day. On the large table, he even placed an image of Montesquieu, among other biscuit statuettes. In 1774 Louis XVI installed his bathrooms next to the Council Chamber overlooking the Stag Courtyard. As for his inner *cabinet* (his working office), the King changed nothing, apart from hanging van Blarenberghe's gouaches representing Louis XV's military campaigns. Here as well he placed the famous "American Independence "candlestick made of bronze and porcelain. In his grandfather's former bathroom, Louis XVI fitted out a remote *cabinet* known as the Privy Purse Room (*Pièce de la Cassette*), where he kept his private accounts, far from public scrutiny. This retreat lay behind Louis XV's old cabinet, which Louis XVI preserved and had regilded in 1784. The far end of the King's private suite always grew particularly animated in December, when Louis had the dining

OPPOSITE: Louis XVI's Games Cabinet was installed in the space once given over to Louis XIV's Medal Cabinet. The chastely sumptuous room now boasts most of its pre-Revolution furniture, including four superb corner cupboards delivered by Riesener in 1774 and many of the thirty-six silk-covered chairs bought from Boulard in 1785.

RIGHT: Louis XVI's library, the last interior designed by Gabriel for Versailles, with boiseries executed by Jacques-Antoine Rousseau. Realized in 1774, the year of the young King's accession, the library announced the style that would prevail to the end of the *ancien régime.* In the foreground is a collection of small-scale copies in Sèvres biscuit of the Great Men of France series commissioned during the reign of Louis XVI by the Comte d'Angiviller, successor to Marigny in the post of superintendent of the King's buildings. The pieces rest on a table designed by Riesener.

LEFT: Marie-Antoinette's Gilded Cabinet decorated in 1783 with boiseries designed by Mique and executed by the brothers Rousseau. Although very similar in style to the King's Wardrobe, the Gilded Cabinet appears more self-consciously antiquarian, thanks to such delicately rendered motifs as tripods, sphinxes, and palmettes. The Queen often entertained privately here, giving concerts in which she herself both played the harp and sang.

OPPOSITE: The décor of the Queen's State Bedchamber is lavish but far from homogeneous (see also page 225). Overhead, for instance, the compartmented ceiling dates from the time of Marie-Thérèse of Austria, Louis XIV's Queen, the grisaille medallions by Boucher from the early reign of Louis XV, when they were painted for Marie Leszczynska, and the corner reliefs carved with the arms of France and Austria from the era of Marie-Antoinette. As for the boiseries, they were executed for Marie Leszczynska by a team that included Robert de Cotte, Degoulon, Gabriel, and Verberckt. De Troy and Natoire painted the overdoors, installed in 1734. The sumptuous bed and canopy replicate the arrangement in place at the time of Marie-Antoinette's departure in October 1789.

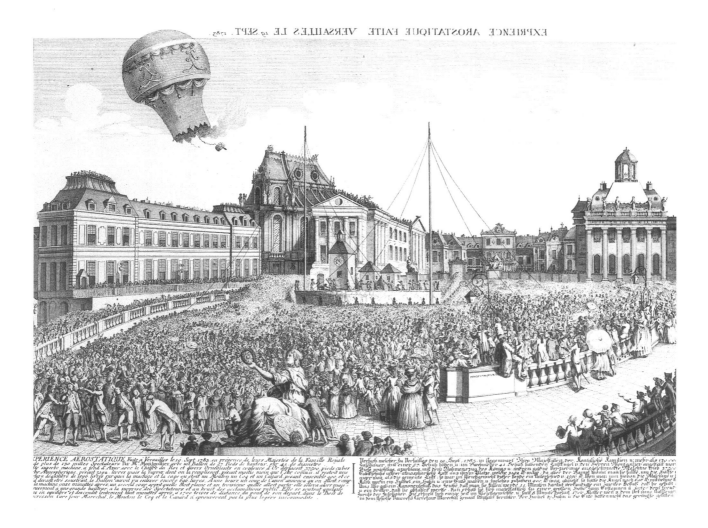

The aerostatic experience at Versailles in 1783.
The entire royal family gathered to watch as Montgolfier's hot-air balloon rose above the Château.
Its passengers—a sheep, a cock, and a fox—were none the worse for their eight-minute flight
after the vehicle landed in the Vaucresson woods.

room turned into a showcase for the latest productions from the Sèvres porcelain manufacture. On either side of the Billiard Cabinet, born of the changes made to the west landing of the former Ambassadors' Staircase, was the Buffet Room, another product of the staircase's demise, where the King and his intimates relaxed, supped in the dining room, or played cards in the salon next to the Salon of Abundance overlooking the Royal Courtyard. In 1775 the Buffet was hung with van Blarenberghe gouaches from the same series found in the sovereign's inner cabinet. Corner cabinets by Riesener and tables for playing backgammon or whist contributed further to a sense of intimacy quite at odds with the other end of the private apartment.

Finally, on the very eve of the Revolution, Louis XVI had his wardrobe redecorated with new boiseries featuring—along with the usual allegories of the Arts, Sciences, War, and Agriculture—such carefully rendered scientific instruments as electric or pneumatic machines, agricultural tools, compass, and goniometers. These reflected an obsession with scientific research on the part of a monarch who was altogether as secret as his predecessors.

Upstairs, Louis XVI kept a series of *cabinets* entirely for his own personal use, all ranged about the Stag Courtyard, on two and even three floors, and all subject to continual revision. On the first floor could be found a library, the Geography Cabinet, the Map Corridor, and the Artillery Cabinet. Above were another *cabinet,* the Geography Gallery, the lathe and carpentry shop (a symptom of the family love of puttering), and, later, the Electricity Gallery. The Attic Library on the third floor, overlooking the Marble Courtyard, had an annex and two neighboring rooms: the Physics Cabinet and the Chemistry Cabinet. Finally, in the attic itself, were the Locksmith Cabinet, the Mechanics Cabinet, and several kitchens. All these little rooms, linked by narrow corridors and brief stairs, were—already under Louis XV—the sole place at Versailles where the King could be his own master. Louis XVI arranged them according to his own taste, which was that of a country-squire King, fascinated by science and the latest discoveries, military and naval innovations, models of which he had made by the score. He also took an interest in research and explanations of the new concepts found in the *Encyclopédie,* a copy of which he had acquired in 1771, paying for it out of his privy purse. Under Louis XVI, the latest discoveries were sometimes put to daily use at Versailles, where frigid air, the common enemy, made it worthwhile to try the Franklin stove, a Swedish solution, or a combustion regulator, to fight the cold or, once this had been conquered, the smoke. In June 1789, a month before the storming of the Bastille, Louis XVI even decided to install two stoves in the royal tribune in the Chapel.

Marie-Antoinette was no less eager to escape the court and its etiquette, "longing to be alone when she wishes, without bothering her servants or being bothered by them." In 1779 she had her private suite redone, those rooms, that is, strung along the back of the Queen's State Apartment. This campaign began in the Large Cabinet, for which Mique supplied furniture with flower-decorated boiseries and silks. Next came the Mediterranean Cabinet, which the Queen insisted be octagonal in plan, with a mirror-faced alcove. To make the room brighter, she also cleared the window of the trellis that had been there since Marie Leszczynska's time. The space could be accessed by two doors, both of them equipped with monogrammed sash bolts, devices indicating a determination to live there in peace and quiet. Around this nucleus, beginning in 1776, Marie-Antoinette annexed a mezzanine room for billiards and a boudoir hung with *toile de Jouy.* Everywhere the décor was both refined and luxurious, including a large gold and silver table service, which the Queen would have the Royal Mint melt down on 20 September 1789. By this time much good food had been consumed, judging by the outlays for provisions and table candles.

In 1782, after the death of Madame Sophie, Louis XV's youngest daughter, Marie-Antoinette took over her ground-floor apartment on the Marble Courtyard, which she could reach directly by way of stairs leading down from her own floor. Here she made a self-contained, comfortable apartment comprising both a bedroom and a library, decorated with green wall fabric and mahogany furniture by Jacob and Riesener.

Thus, Versailles in the 1780s saw little construction but considerable refitting and refurnishing, with much evidence of silks and passementeries, hardstone objets d'art mounted in gilt-bronze, and floral motifs on everything from bronzes to capitals. Also characteristic was a taste for mechanical furniture, convertible tables, and adjustable lamps. Riesener, Georges Jacob, Daguerre, and Robin worked wonders to satisfy the Queen's fantasy. Simultaneously, they also cultivated both exquisite craftsmanship and classical restraint, in the face of a royal weakness for Austrian Rococo, not to mention the German variety put forward daily by the artisan Mercklein.

THE GARDENS

Despite their plea for privacy, neither Louis XVI nor Marie-Antoinette led a solitary existence. The King hunted with a mad passion, on a domain he extended on every side, beyond Trianon, Saint-Cyr, Satory, and Clagny. He rode together with his brothers, who were equally committed to

For Marie-Antoinette, Richard Mique designed the boiseries in the octagonal Mediterranean Cabinet, which were then executed by the Rousseau brothers. The *guéridon*, made of petrified wood embellished with gilt-bronze and steel, was a gift to the Queen from her mother, the Empress Maria-Theresa of Austria. The room could be accessed by two doors, both of them equipped with monogrammed sash bolts, devices indicating the Queen's determination to retire there in peace and quiet.

The Queen's State Bedchamber, now
restored as it was when the Marie-
Antoinette left it in October 1789, is
remarkably luxurious, especially the
1787 *gros de Tours* brocaded and
embroidered with bouquets. For her
interior *cabinets,* Marie-Antoinette
preferred an elegant but less opulent
décor, like that of the inner *cabinet*
designed by Richard Mique. See also
pages 204 and 211.

the sport of Kings, as witnessed by the sovereign's diary for 1787 concerning Trianon: "Thursday 16th: stag hunt at Pont de la Ville-Dieu, took one, missed the other... Saturday 18th: deer hunt at the Costeaux-de-Jouy, missed several and killed 15... Monday 20th: stag hunt at Pont de la Ville-Dieu, took 2... Wednesday 22nd: shooting at le Fours-à-Chaux, killed 79... Friday 24th: stag hunt at Dampierre, took 2..." Usually Louis XVI returned to Trianon for dinner and to Versailles for the night. One day in the Bull's-Eye Salon, the Duc de Croÿ may have mistaken Louis XVI for a "kind of priest," but there was nothing lymphatic about this King. Early in his reign, he took on the colossal task of replanting the park. A poster dated 20 November 1774 announced "the sale and auction of the wood from full-grown timber trees, the trees along the allées or those used for decoration, with both brushwood and thickets, planted in the gardens of Versailles and Trianon."

So momentous was the event that the court asked Hubert Robert to record it in two paintings, both exhibited at the Salon of 1777, offering to the world a glimpse of the perspective along the Royal Avenue to the Grand Canal and the installation of the Baths of Apollo, under way at the time. In 1782 Delille mourned those "masterpieces of a great King, of Le Nôtre, and the passage of time," while the Duc de Croÿ pointed out the garden sculpture, then more visible thanks to the disappearance of all the splendid trees. The great project had been carefully studied, as a result of which it was understood by all that Le Nôtre's work would not be destroyed. Morel, the French authority on English gardens, insisted that the replanting take place "on the old lines." Still, the Dauphin and Girandole groves would be redesigned as quincunxes, the Labyrinth replaced by the Queen's Grove, and the hedges by rows of trees. An effort was made to analyze the soil for the purpose of determining the most suitable species: plenty of oak but also beech, ash, and elm to form an enclosure around the park. Yet, Le Roy, Lieutenant of the King's Hunt, had advised that "the best tree to use, and that which will produce the most even effect throughout the gardens, is the oak alone." Meanwhile, several gardeners, far from Trianon, proposed setting out a few exotic specimens, among them tulip, cedar, maple, and pine, all of which would find a home in the Queen's Grove.

The new Baths of Apollo were another matter altogether. They involved the marbles originally made for the Grotto of Thetis, which Louis XVI decided to reinstall north of the Latona Fountain on the site of the former Marsh Grove so beloved by Madame de Montespan. After first consulting Mique, the King approached Hubert Robert on 1 June 1777 and requested an economical solution, nothing more perhaps than a leafy background for the white sculptures, set off by "pedestals, bowls, shells or rosettes, given that the forms are good and the materials precious." The artist must have seen the figures placed there under canopies designed by Carlier in 1705, for very quickly he suggested a setting composed of "a rock adorned with waterfalls and arranged so as to allow the placement of the three groups." This required much reterracing and then construction of a quasi-Classical, semi-ruined grotto reflecting the period taste for nostalgic reflections on Time, the master of Nature.

For the new grotto, Hubert Robert built a pool to collect water from a cascade, assisted in the project by Yves-Éloi Boucher, nephew of Louis XV's official court painter, to whom Robert remained loyal. When completed in 1780, Robert found himself rewarded not only with a fee of 6,000 *livres* but also with a court title: Designer of the King's Gardens. Already in 1778, he had been granted a much-coveted lodging in the Louvre, no doubt an enabling measure given that he had been placed in charge of both the King's pictures and the vast work of remodeling the Louvre's Grand Gallery.

Elsewhere, Louis XVI busied himself with such important projects as the restoration of the reservoirs and the pursuit a new waterproof cement for the Orangery, whose vaults still tended to

OPPOSITE: Marie-Antoinette's Billiard Room, on the second floor, has been reconstructed from evidence found in old documents.

219

The Versailles park during the replanting of the trees ordered by Louis XVI in 1774.
To record the event the King commissioned Hubert Robert to paint this landscape and the one opposite.
Note the Grand Canal in the distance, Mansart's Colonnade in the left mid-distance,
Coysevox's *Castor and Pollox* on the near left, and Puget's *Milo of Cortona* on the near right.

In the right foreground are the sculptures for the Baths of Apollo, then under construction as the replanting of the Versailles park was under way.
Standing tall in the mid-ground are marble figures from the Great Commission of 1674, ordered for the Water Parterre but transferred to the North Parterre, seen here.
The painting, a pendant to the one opposite, is by Hubert Robert (1775).

The Baths of Apollo,
installed in 1774
by Hubert Robert,
using sculptures
salvaged from
the Grotto of Thetis:
Apollo and Nymphs
by Girardon and
Regnaudin; and
Horses of the Sun
by Guérin and Marsy.

leak. Meanwhile, the King worried about the effect of such expenses and such splendor on the French people. Thus, on 14 August 1789, one month after the assault on the Bastille, Louis had the fountains turned off at Versailles, in response to complaints from millers in the nearby Bièvre and Yvette Valleys about the current drought, which made it difficult for them to produce enough flour. The sovereign decreed that the fountains should remain dry "until the town of Versailles and the environs are suitably provided with flour." As this suggests, Louis XVI was a far more serious man than the mere locksmith the caricaturists have wanted the world to believe. Indeed, it was thanks to him that the Versailles gardens came through the Revolution relatively unscathed.

In 1774 Louis XVI gave Trianon to his wife, Marie-Antoinette, who proceeded to make it very much her own private domain. The Queen took particular interest in the gardens, which, almost immediately, she redesigned, at such length, moreover, that a special budget had to be set up "for the works of the Queen's Garden." In 1775, near the Petit Trianon, she had Mique create a Chinese-style ring game with dragons and peacocks. In 1777-1779 came the construction of a "rock," a lake, and a river, all artificial and on the site of Louis XV's large hothouse. So important was this enterprise that the Duc de Croÿ, an amateur botanist, could but regret all the modifications: "Never can two acres of land have been so transformed or cost so much money"—except perhaps the Baths of Apollo! At the same time, Mique was constructing a whole series of buildings for the Trianon complex, among them the Temple of Love, built low on an island. Within its Corinthian colonnade would stand Bouchardon's *Cupid Carving a Bow from the Club of Hercules.* And then a theatre, for which Mique received approval in 1775, with the recommendation from the Queen that he model it after the *salle* at Choisy. In 1779, following a year of construction, the ceiling was ready for Lagrenée to mount his painting entitled *Apollo Surrounded by Muses and Graces.* On its exterior, the theatre, built in the *communs* flanking the Petit Trianon forecourt, boasted only an entrance pediment carved by Deschamps. Inside, Marie-Antoinette's private theatre was, and remains, an enchanting jewelbox, its foyer adorned with bas-reliefs and its auditorium an ensemble of gilt and blue watered silk. On either side of the stage stand torchères held aloft by carved female figures, while lion-head consoles support the balcony, cherubs part the draperies hung from the flat proscenium, and fairy-like figures gather up the garlands draped below the circle of twelve bull's-eye windows punched through the coving.

On 1 June 1780 the Queen inaugurated her theatre, the evening launched with garden illuminations and a supper. In the *salle* the program consisted of a "prologue" by Despréaux, who took as his subject the competition among the various dramatic arts. In a scene of utter chaos, stage hands went about their business while Opera and Tragedy quarreled over who should first test the acoustics, the one singing ever louder and the other declaiming at the top of his voice. At the same time, their son, Opéra Comique (opera with both sung music and spoken dialogue), struggled to reconcile them by warbling dainty airs. Finally, Monsieur Machine *(deus ex machina)* descended from the flies and urged them all to make up. Despréaux's prologue was the first of many productions and performances staged in the Queen's Theatre right up to the Revolution. Typically, Rousseau's *Pygmalion,* a parody of Gluck's *Iphigénie en Tauride,* Marmontel and Piccini's *Dormeur éveillé* derived from *A Thousand and One Nights,* and Sacchini's *Dardanus* alternated with plays by Sedaine.

Under the direction of Vaudreuil, Marie-Antoinette organized a company that, on the advice of Campan, included the Comtesse de Châlons, the Polignacs, the Comte d'Artois (the younger of the King's two brothers), Count Esterhazy, and the Comte d'Adhémar, the French Minister in Brussels. The audience usually consisted of the King, several princesses, and Mercy, a spy for the Queen's mother,

OPPOSITE: Marie-Antoinette entertaining in the Queen's State Bedchamber. Gouache by Gautier-Dagoty.

225

Marie-Antoinette's private theatre at the Petit Trianon, where the original eighteenth-century stage machinery is still almost intact. And so is most of the exquisite interior, with its gilded décor fashioned mainly of papier-mâché. This jewelbox setting was designed by Richard Mique, the Queen's favorite architect, who received the commission in 1775. By 1779 Lagrenée could mount his ceiling painting entitled *Apollo Surrounded by Muses and Graces.* On either side of the stage stand torchères held aloft by carved female figures, while lion-head consoles support the balcony, cherubs part the draperies hung from the flat proscenium, and fairy-like figures gather up the garlands draped below the circle of twelve bull's-eye windows punched through the coving.

Empress Maria-Theresa of Austria, but not the Princesse de Lamballe, so notoriously implicated with Marie-Antoinette in the coming Terror, or yet many others, to whom Her Majesty said: "I have already advised you of my wishes for Trianon. I do not hold court there. I live privately." The Queen wished to be with people she could trust.

THE HAMLET AT TRIANON

The whole of the eighteenth century sang pastoral or exotic hymns of praise to the beauties of nature. Urged on by Jean-Jacques Rousseau, the time had arrived for a new, "English" style of garden—"natural" or "picturesque" gardens studded with "follies," those fanciful constructions simulating Gothic or Classical ruins, Chinese pagodas, Dutch windmills, etc. The most ambitious of the follies—in which rusticity always seemed combined with luxury—were *hameaux* or "hamlets," and these were all the rage. The Prince de Condé built one at Chantilly; the Comtesse de Provence (the King's sister-in-law) had hers at Montreuil; and the Duc d'Orléans at Le Raincy. And so why not the Queen of France, who would indeed have the biggest and most complete of all, created at Trianon by three artists collaborating at the top of their form: the painter Hubert Robert, the architect Richard Mique, and the gardener Claude Richard. What they created was a Normandy-like ensemble of thatched roofs, rough-cast or half-timbered walls, small leaded windows, and everywhere white faïence jars emblazoned with the Queen's blue cypher. The "farm" consisted of *potager* enclosures reserved for fruit trees, raspberry bushes, beans, and cauliflower. Love of the exotic coincided with the period's Anglomania, and so the Hamlet would have its Marlborough Tower, constructed on the edge of the lake in tribute to Beaumarchais, who had introduced the popular ballad *Marlborough s'en va-t-en guerre* into *Le Mariage de Figaro,* which, ironically, had been banned. This, of course, obliged the entire court to go about humming the tune. The tower was crowned with crenellations as well as an arcaded loggia, approached by way of a wrap-around, counter-curving stairway. At the dairy next door the Queen and her ladies-in-waiting churned butter, not far from the farm and its cowshed, chicken run, aviary, dovecote, and separate sheds for the Swiss herd (cows, bull, and calves), the nanny goats, and the sheep. There was a roof for the pigsty, as well as a hutch for rabbits, a curing hut for cheeses, and a cottage for the cowherd. Also present nearby were a cottage for the guardian or gatekeeper and a large dairy, both of which have vanished.

On the other side of the lake stood a cluster of separate dwellings: a boudoir, a mill with a wheel that turned in the stream, and a service building *(réchauffoir)* with kitchen, office, laundry, linen closet, and larder. Finally, the largest of the structures—the Billiard Hall and the Queen's House—overlooked the lake, where they were linked by a first-floor balcony made of wood. The former contained an upstairs apartment with a library, which Mique himself appears to have fitted out. The ground floor of the second comprised a dining room and a backgammon room, while the upper floor was given over to a Chinese *cabinet* and two salons.

The Queen's Hamlet was no doubt a stage-set affair, an imaginative pastiche worthy of operetta; yet, beginning on 1 July 1785, it was also a place where families lived and worked, growing fruits and vegetables. The furniture Jacob made for the Queen was very simply decorated, with such motifs as flowers, ribbons, and trellises. It was all rather artificial, and certain, moreover, to disorient the rare visitor. The Queen, in fact, planned to entertain no one here but her family. After performing in Beaumarchais's *Le Barbier de Séville* (in which she took the leading role: Rosine), Marie-Antoinette never

Marie-Antoinette's Hamlet near the Petit Trianon. In 1783-1785 Richard Mique, in collaboration with Hubert Robert and the gardener
Claude Richard, built for the Queen a complete Normandy-style *hameau*—a tiny, half-timbered, thatch-roofed farming village.
This exercise in make-believe rusticity included a dovecote, a gardener's cottage, a mill with a turning wheel, a barn,
a dairy, a working farm, a house for Her Majesty, a reception cottage, and a billiard cottage.
There was even a place for the local *seigneur,* at least in the symbolic or ceremonial form of the Marlborough Tower,
so-called for the popular song *Marlborough s'en va-t-en guerre.* Nothing could be more symptomatic of the eighteenth century's
Rousseau-inspired taste for picturesque nature and pastoral simplicity. Painting by Wallaert (1803).

LEFT: The farm at Marie-Antoinette's Hamlet near the Petit Trianon.

OPPOSITE: The Queen's house in the Hamlet near the Petit Trianon.

The Marlborough Tower in Marie-Antoinette's Hamlet.
Engraving by Nattes and Hill (1809).

again appeared on the Trianon stage, but she did continue giving her regular Sunday ball at the Hamlet, as the Comte de Vaublanc tells us: "All persons properly dressed were received, and above all the maids with the children. The Queen would dance a quadrille to show that she shared the pleasure to which she invited the others. She would call for the maids and meet the children, speaking to them of their parents and showering them with presents. Usually almost all the royal family were with her… I observed, with one of my friends, that a few persons of high society took part in these bucolic gatherings; a greater mix would have produced a better effect." The balls were so popular that Marie-Antoinette decided to erect a large marquee, supported by twenty-four columns, with galleries for circulating and gradated stands for spectators. A covered passage linked the tent to the Petit Trianon and one of the houses used for service.

What Marie-Antoinette invented at Trianon was nothing less than a new life-style, a new *art de vivre*. And no one appreciated the peace and quiet the Queen insisted upon than Louis XVI: "The King would come every morning, alone and without the Captain of the Guards, to have breakfast with the Queen, returning to Versailles for his *levée,* and come back again at two o'clock for lunch before repairing to the garden to read in a grove, sometimes spending the whole day like this, only returning to Versailles for his affairs or council meetings, then coming back for dinner at nine. Afterwards he would play a game and leave at midnight to go to bed. As there were scarcely any dwellings at Trianon, all the guests would go and sleep at Versailles." A cozy, comfortable life. Here, Louis XVI and Marie-Antoinette managed to create for themselves what Louis XIV and Louis XV could only fantasize. Dismissing protocol, the Queen imposed her own, less burdensome etiquette, as described by Madame Campan: "She entered her salon without the ladies having to abandon the pianoforte or their tapestry looms, and without the men having to interrupt their game of billiards or backgammon."

At Versailles itself, the tone was very different. Here the King worked or withdrew to his laboratories, while the Queen found herself at odds with a court incapable of simplicity. Monsieur, the Comte de Provence (and future Louis XVIII), lived in grand style, whether at Versailles, Brunoy, or near the Pool of the Swiss Guards. His architect, Chalgrin, built the Château de Montreuil and laid out the domain for Madame. Everywhere on the estate, theatre, music room, bath suite, games rooms, and gardens with grottoes rivaled in splendor what the Queen had achieved at Trianon. Equally imaginative were the projects undertaken by the Comte d'Artois (future Charles X), Marie-Antoinette's favorite brother-in-law, not only in his South Wing apartment, renovated in 1781, but also at the Temple in Paris and then at Bagatelle, today one of the gems of Paris's Bois de Boulogne.

This was a young court. When Louis XV died in 1774, the three brothers who were the old King's immediate heirs were between twenty and seventeen years old, and Mesdames, their aunts, still under forty. The young Queen and her brothers-in-law frequently ran off to Paris in search of amusement. Marie-Antoinette even had an apartment done up for herself at the long-neglected Tuileries, seeing it as an opportunity to escape the rigor of Versailles. And she did indeed kick over the traces by organizing such unbridled games that they shocked her brother, Emperor Joseph II, one day at the Comtesse de Guéménée's. The sober Joseph scolded the Queen for what he saw as a gambling den full of license and indecency, and she took the lesson to heart, according to Mercy. By the beginning of 1777, Marie-Antoinette's debts had mounted to 487,000 *livres,* which Louis XVI paid from his privy purse.

The Queen recruited Campan to take charge of her library, which had overflowed on several fronts and was still growing. The catalogue, published in 1779, abounds in poetry and fiction, but it also records such sumptuous works as the Abbé de Saint-Non's *Voyage pittoresque… de Naples et de Sicile,* illustrated by Fragonard. For intimacy the Queen retired into the heart of her private *cabinets.* Here, surrounded by harp, harpsichord, music scores, and chinoiserie objects, Marie-Antoinette received privately, not only ladies but, even more, musicians. Gluck, Grétry, Mozart, and Salieri could all be heard in the private suite, where the German harpist Hinner played regularly, and also gave lessons to the Queen. Another frequent performer was the singer Steibelt. It was also in these little back rooms that the sovereign sat for her favorite painter, Madame Vigée-Lebrun, who recalled the royal patron's kindness: "One day, I failed to come to a session she had arranged because, being at the time far advanced in my second pregnancy, I suddenly felt most unwell. Next day I rushed to Versailles to apologize. Her Majesty was finishing her toilette and was holding a book in her hand to go over a lesson with her daughter, young Madame… 'Don't leave,' said the Queen, 'I don't want your journey to have been in vain'." With this the Queen picked up the palette and brushes the nervous painter had let drop. Sessions with an artist or a musician, Mass, coping with everyday etiquette or unexpected events—these made up what were, on the whole, quite full days.

LEFT: The Belvedere, built in 1778-1779 by Richard Mique near the Petit Trianon for Marie-Antoinette. The little garden "folly" boasts four pairs of guardian sphinxes, triangular pediments, and garlands. The interior is lavishly decorated with painted stuccos by Leriche and a flower- and putti-embellished ceiling painted by Lagrenée.

OPPOSITE: The period taste for domesticated nature manifests itself in the mill at Marie-Antoinette's Hamlet, constructed after 1783.

FROM ONE REVOLUTION TO ANOTHER

The Hall of Battles
in the South Wing.

Even before the fateful month of October, 1789 had been an eventful year at Versailles. Here the Estates-General convened for the first time since 1614, after which came the Tennis Court Oath, presaging a showdown between the King and the Assembly, the abolition of privilege, and finally the Declaration of the Rights of Man. The Convention had good reason to assert, on 7 Brumaire II (28 October 1790), that "Versailles deserves well of the nation." A year earlier, France had lived through a tense summer, made worse by a poor harvest, creating an atmosphere in which the least breach of tact could very well spark public demonstrations. The trigger came on 1 October when the Bodyguard, in the presence of Louis XVI and his family, welcomed the Flanders Regiment. According to Gorsas's *Courrier de Versailles,* the Flemings drank to "the health of our King, our master, and may no one recognize another!" Next, they saluted the Queen's cockade rather than the tricolore rosette. The Parisian mob soon heard about it and began marching towards Versailles, as did the Marquis de Lafayette and the National Guard, albeit too late to restore calm. On 6 October the great Château would see its last royal day. At six in the morning an enraged throng entered the park through the Princes' Passage, swarmed across the Royal Courtyard, and mounted the Queen's Staircase, only to find the antechamber door locked on the inside and defended by the Bodyguard. In the hope of mollifying the crowd, Lafayette persuaded the King and Queen to appear on the balcony at the center of Marble Courtyard, outside the King's State Bedchamber. In the afternoon, however, Louis XVI and Marie-Antoinette found themselves in a carriage rumbling towards the Tuileries, escorted by Lafayette, the Comte d'Estaing, and the noisy rabble. Along with "the baker, the baker's wife, and the little apprentice [the Dauphin]," the insurgents had also seized cartloads

of wheat and flour. As he was leaving the Château, the King said to his Minister, Comte de La Tour du Pin: "You remain the master here; try to save my poor Versailles." Initially, life went on at the Château, albeit without the court. The renovation of the Queen's new apartment on the ground floor continued, as did the preparation of a suite for Madame Royale, the monarchs' only daughter, then eleven years old. The Tuileries, a Renaissance palace at the western end of the Louvre complex, had long been uninhabited and needed to be refurnished, once it became clear that the royal family had come to stay for some time. When they did quit Paris, their destination would be Saint-Cloud. Some furniture and objets d'art were moved from Versailles to the Tuileries, leaving the most valuable pieces to be stored in the furniture ware-house on the Rue des Réservoirs. Meanwhile, certain paintings were removed to the Hôtel de la Surin-tendance, where visitors departing the Château could view them. After 10 August, however, it became so common to shift art works to the Louvre—only later the Central Museum of the Arts—that the people of Versailles, backed by Madame Roland, persuaded the Convention to stop the consignments, beginning in September 1792. Then, on 22 October, came the order from the Committee of Alienation authorizing the sale of all furnishings found in the royal residences, as well as those belonging to émigrés and religious orders. Only scientific instruments and art works were to be kept. From 25 August 1793 to the spring of 1796, a great wealth of craftsmanship was dispersed in 17,182 lots. Lists, inventories, and catalogues were drawn up, and a number of objects given as payment to state suppliers, among them Lanchère, who had the responsibility for military convoys, and Alcan, provisioner to the Rhine-Moselle Army. Many things were bought back by their makers. Riesener, for instance, acquired part of his own production and then resold it from his workshop at the Arsenal in Paris.

The concerned citizens of Versailles began to mobilize. Aware of the grave disad-vantage their town would suffer were the Château to be left empty, they secured an agreement, dated 8 July 1793, whereby the royal residence could be used as a depository for works listed by the Arts Com-mission. Thanks to this arrangement, the buildings were not sold off, as urged several months earlier by Manuel, the receiver for the Paris commune, or yet demolished as demanded in certain quarters. Charles Delacroix, father of the great Romantic painter, had even argued for ploughing the royal domain under. Also not among the Château's most ardent defenders was the father of the poet Alfred de Musset. Life, however, did not entirely vanish from Versailles following the King's departure. As early as 6 October 1789, Lafayette ordered the Lieutenant-Colonel of the Versailles National Guard to look after the Château and the surrounding estate. Outside, at the gates, war veterans stood guard, as did the Swiss until they were imprisoned on 10 August 1792. Inspector Le Roy, onetime architect for the Superintendence sug-gested that identifying arm bands or badges be worn by the eight grove-keepers authorized to show people around the sealed-off areas of the park. Finally, however, the prospect of earning money from curious visitors led to the formation of a network of park guides.

As all this suggests, Versailles appeared to be well managed, but life at the Château could not entirely escape the turmoil of what was a critical time in France. In 1792, nearly seventy occu-pants—former courtiers, chambermaids, and guards—found themselves expelled, even though the admi-nistrative personnel remained, some of them even holding onto their rooms and apartments. Couturier was put in charge of Versailles and Marly, assisted by three inspectors: Le Roy, who oversaw the Château and "national garden"; Loiseleur, who took care of the national buildings and the small park in town; and Devienne, whose mandate extended to the fountains and the great park. Boucheman, the porter under Louis XVI, remained at his post until 1793, when he, too, went to prison, making way for the musician Giroust, who, in 1799, would also be replaced. Richard, the gardener long responsible for the hothouses

A caricature of the royal family's journey from Versailles to the Tuileries in October 1789.

and botanical gardens at the Petit Trianon, was reassigned to the garden at the Grand Trianon and made responsible as well for planting fruit trees in the Château gardens. The gondoliers and sailors, under the captaincy of Gosse, continued to maintain and protect the boats, while also seeing to the fountains, which made it possible for the *grandes eaux* to be played regularly. Who today could recall that in 1797 the Versailles park was host to a festival lasting several days, staged in honor of the Ottoman Ambassador? For this occasion an entire orchestra played atop the rock over the Baths of Apollo. Finally, a team of thirty-two sweepers and thirty-two polishers kept an eye on things, insofar as they could given that, by 1793, their number had dwindled to a dozen and then only six. On 19 October 1794 Le Roy informed members for the district of pillage and vandalism, resulting in the loss of windows, locks, and even doors. Most of all, there was "no end of filth."

Outside the Château, the statues remained in place, but all about them things began to fall apart. In January 1790 Louis XVI, from his exile at the Tuileries, agreed to hire 800 unemployed workers to clean the Grand Canal, but soon ran out of money to pay them. In 1792 thought was given to the possibility of transforming the Canal into a swimming school or into farmland, an option agreed upon in February 1795. The paved banks were demolished, the channels drained, and the whole divided into three fields for pasture and cultivation. Large numbers of trees were cut down for firewood as well as for use by wheelwrights and the military. Richard transformed the parterres into vegetable gardens and the areas around both the Canal and the fountains into orchards. At Trianon the gardens gradually disintegrated, despite the efforts of Richard.

On 26 April 1794 the Menagerie lost its animal population to the National History Museum in Paris, after which its buildings would be auctioned off in 1801. Only the farm remained, although given in lieu of cash payment to Sieyès. At the Orangery a collection of trees continued to be maintained, and even augmented by species appropriated from princely houses near Versailles. By 1796 the Orangery produced so many herbs that it took 291 days to complete the harvest and supply the Central Pharmacy on the Champ-de-Mars in Paris.

Not even the Château entrance was spared. On 1 August 1794 Le Roy received orders requiring him to remove the wrought-iron fence around the courtyards. Next, the cobblestones would be taken up and replaced with "four squares of greenery," their grass thick enough in 1797 to tempt an opportunistic Versaillais in search of pasture for his flock of twenty-eight sheep. The municipality reacted by informing him that "it would be indecent for beasts to graze in the courtyard of a national palace," in front of which a Liberty Tree would be planted in 1798. It appears that each person adopted his own make-shift arrangements, among them the billeted soldiers, who, according to a 1796 report from Le Roy, set a bad example "by washing their clothes in the fountains, known as buffets, at each end of the terrace, beating them on the marble tablets, then hanging them to dry on the hedges."

The Château, so abruptly emptied of its inhabitants, nonetheless escaped destruction, remaining more or less imperturbable. Although some officials would have loved to see it razed, others made sure that the royal residence would be maintained. In 1791 scaffolding went up in the Hall of Mirrors so that the ceiling could be restored. At the same time, heaters were installed and the Queen's Apartment painted and regilded. On 5 May 1794 the Convention designated the Château "a national house preserved and maintained at the cost of the Republic as a place for popular festivities and establishments useful to agriculture and the arts." Everyone cast about for causes the Château could be made to serve. The sheer size of the premises made it possible to establish several different institutions there. One project or program succeeded another, none of them lasting long enough to become a solution to the Château problem. Early on, it was decided to eradicate the fleur-de-lis from both the Château and the town, despite some hesitation and the objections of Rubeis, Louis XVI's curator of paintings, who tried to prove that those "feudal signs" were in fact the arms of France, not merely the emblems of French royalty. One of the Rousseau brothers, who had decorated Marie-Antoinette's *cabinets,* Dejoux, an assistant to Pajou at the Versailles Theatre, and the painter/gilder Dutemps set about obliterating fleurs-de-lis, crowns, and inscriptions related to the royal past. Meanwhile, Charles Delacroix could hardly wait to replace the Louis XIV medallion on Guidi's *Fame* with Republican fasces. Roland dismissed the idea of a museum of masterpieces, which would be reserved for Paris.

One of the first projects undertaken was a library on the ground floor of the South Wing, its collection of 28,000 volumes begun with books once owned by Mesdames, Louis XV's three daughters. A second project was a museum, intended for the North Wing and composed primarily of curiosities collected by Fayolle, former Naval Commissioner, and purchased by the Comte d'Artois, one of Louis XVI's younger brothers, to form a natural history *cabinet* for his children.

In 1793 the Committee of Public Safety considered a proposal from Barère that the Château be transformed into a school. "It would be splendid to see citizens taught to hate tyranny in the tyrants' palace. Lebrun's salons would become a drawing school, the Menagerie a riding school, the Canal a swimming school." Thirteen arts commissioners busied themselves classifying the palace collections. As Durameau prepared to hang the pictures, he had to fend off Alexandre Lenoir's endless demands for yet more transfers to his Museum of French Monuments in Paris. Duplessis and Durameau, both court painters under the *ancien régime,* and Dardel, a Pajou pupil, found themselves frequently accused of being lax in their conservation of art works in the park, seen to be "damaged by the humid atmosphere." The Arts Commission wanted these replaced by less valuable pieces.

This was a time for confusion as well as for projects. On 27 October 1793 the Versailles municipality, keen on the idea of establishing a regional grammar school, called for the demolition of the Old Wing, the Gabriel Wing, and virtually all of the Marble Courtyard. The following year, on 3 August, the district of Versailles decided to open, for two days every ten days during the summer, the depository of "precious effects from the national furniture collections in the county." The Chapel became a music school, while the North Wing housed a "school of living models." Finally, on 16 March 1797, Bénézech, Minister of the Interior, decided, after much hesitation, to create a "Special Museum of French Painting" as a complement to the Central Museum of Arts and the Republic at the Louvre. Once more pictures had to be moved, with only those by David, Girodet, and Gérard left in Paris. The new museum would not be opened to the public until the fall of 1801, and not actually completed until 1803, the year in which the process of returning works to churches, to Paris, or to the provinces began. Later Napoleon, alerted to the danger arising from the uncertain status of the Château's contents, recommended a policy that all subsequent Versailles curators would adopt: "Hold firm against appeals from other departments which, as is their wont, will make every effort not to return anything."

In 1798 the Directory government took up the problem of Versailles, asking the Council of Five Hundred to decide finally what should be done with the palace, now that it had lost its royal emblems and assumed a character more worthy of the French people. Once again, no final solution could be found. The First Consul, Napoleon, proposed that wounded soldiers be housed in the Château and the Ministers' Wings, once precautions had been taken to ensure the "conservation of the monuments and the art contained in the Château, and the upkeep of the French Museum." Artists from the National Institute opposed the idea, fearing the consequence of wear and tear on the buildings.

Yet, after the wounded soldiers departed in 1802, it was clear that they had done no damage whatever to aging Versailles. The time had now come for rehabilitation. After 1800, the Comédie Française gave regular performances in Hubert Robert's theatre (today destroyed), staging such plays as Voltaire's *Zaïre.* Moreover, the great waterworks began to draw crowds just as they do today, with 1,300 arriving on a single day in 1801, followed by 20,000 visitors the next year. Attitudes appear to have relaxed after the Peace of Amiens (1802), with numerous foreigners making a pilgrimage to see what remained of the *ancien régime*'s most dazzling site. All were struck by the empty frames, the obliterated royal emblems, the unhinged doors and windows, and, of course, the famous portraits.

In her *Mémoires,* Madame Vigée-Lebrun recalls the fate of one of her own pictures, then among the most famous in the world: "Under Bonaparte, the large portrait I had made of the Queen with her children was relegated to a corner of the Château at Versailles. One day I left Paris to go and see it. I arrived at the Princes' Gate, where a guard led me to the room where it was kept, which was closed to the public. The keeper who opened the door recognized me, as we had met in Rome, and exclaimed: 'Ah! I'm so happy to welcome Madame Lebrun!' He quickly turned my picture around, as the figures had been placed against the wall after Bonaparte had ordered its removal when he learned that so many people wanted to look at it. As you can see, this order was not exactly carried out, and the work continued to be shown, to such an extent that when I offered to give the guard a tip, he stubbornly refused, saying I helped him earn enough as it is."

A view of the Royal Courtyard in 1814 during the refurbishment of the Old Wing, so called because of its status as the sole complete structure facing the entry courtyards to have been erected under Louis XIV. Indeed, it dates from 1661, when the architect Louis Le Vau took charge of the young King's first building campaign at Versailles. On the opposite or north side of the Royal Courtyard stands the Gabriel Wing (1771), the only realized part of the Grand Design proposed by Ange-Jacques Gabriel for harmonizing the various eastern façades. The plan was to rebuild them in stone, thus eliminating the "archaic" Louis XIII combination of brick, stone, and tall slate-covered roofs. At the request of Louis XVIII, the architect Pierre Fontaine demolished Le Vau's end pavilion, after which Alexandre Dufour transformed the Old Wing into a mirror image of the Gabriel Wing, by restyling or "classicizing" it in the elegant Gabriel manner, complete with a new end pavilion, flat roofs, pediments, and tall colonnades rising from a high basement.

Thus ended all practical attempts to carry out a Grand Design on this side of the Château de Versailles.

Watercolor by Drahonnet.

It was around this time that Madame Lebrun sent her *Apotheosis of the Queen* to the Vicomtesse de Chateaubriand, whose husband, the great Romantic writer, described a visit to Versailles in his characteristically visionary manner: "The palace by itself is like a large town, with marble staircases that seem to rise to the clouds, and the statues, fountains, and trees are falling apart, covered with moss, rotted, or chopped down. The warrior's noble misery has succeeded courtly splendor; pictures of miracles have replaced profane paintings... It is fitting that the ruins of Louis XIV's palace should house the ruins of the army, the arts, and religion."

Napoleon and Louis XVIII

Napoleon, in his *Mémorial,* admitted to ambiguous feelings about Versailles: "I condemned the creation of Versailles, but I dreamt of using it and, in time, turning it into a sort of suburb... a sight of the great capital... I would have driven all those tasteless nymphs and fancy ornaments from the noble groves, and replaced them with stone panoramas of all the capitals we had entered in triumph, and of all the famous battles won by our armies, eternal monuments to our triumph and glory." Hardly had he crowned himself Emperor when Napoleon ordered the restoration of Versailles, beginning with the expulsion of the institutions set up there. Only in April 1811, however, did Denon finish stacking all the works from the Special Museum of French Painting in the foyer of the Opéra. With Versailles now added to the civil list, the Emperor launched several major projects, despite his horror at how much restoration and improvement were required. From the Buildings Department, he wrested the Hôtel des Réservoirs, the stables, which would be used as a riding school for grooms, and the Grand Commun, long given over to the manufacture of arms. As for the domain, it had to be reconstituted, which meant buying back the farms at the Menagerie and the Faisanderie, both given to Sieyès, as well as those at Satory, Chèvreloup, Le Désert, and Galie, stretching all the way to the Hell Hole (*Trou d'Enfer*) and the Butard Lodge. Finally, the Emperor had an estate of over 2,300 acres.

In the gardens, Napoleon ordered the statues and their ornaments repaired, also the fountains and their pipes. The banks around the Grand Canal were rebuilt and the poplars surrounding the site replanted. On 7 April 1801 water once again flowed into the Grand Canal, which meant that Little Venice could also be revived. The flotilla set sail for the first time in years, joined by the *Marie-Louise,* a galley named for the new Empress. There were plans to rehabilitate the principal groves (Colonnade, Ballroom, Dome, and Water Allée) and to eliminate others (Three Fountains, Triumphal Arch, and Royal Island), but the cost (26 million) proved too much even for an Emperor. Trepsat may have been the architect in charge of Versailles, but it was Gondoin who appears to have enjoyed the Imperial favor. Together with Alexandre Dufour, Gondoin oversaw the repairs made to the roofs and the park façades (columns on avant-corps and statues) and the removal of trophies, with the explanation that "even under the *ancien régime,* there had been orders to examine them frequently and destroy those which threatened public safety." The balustrade was shored up and whitewashed "with milk, oil, and quicklime." By December 1810 the ruined south wall of the Guardroom and its sculptural decoration had been fully repaired.

After his divorce from Joséphine and his marriage to Marie-Louise, like Marie-Antoinette an Archduchess of Austria, Napoleon toyed with the idea of making Versailles an Imperial residence, and indeed he did review several proposals for enlarging the palace. In the course of discussing the merits of the Gabriel Wing, Napoleon deemed it to be "in bad taste and feeble in effect," but he also felt that erecting a pendant would be too expensive. Dufour, who took charge of the great project, even suggested razing the Gabriel Wing and building an east façade centered upon a large pavilion housing a throne room, with a colonnaded pavilion at either end and a theatre sited like a pendant to the Chapel. Finally, however, the Emperor abandoned all idea of major changes to the Château, primarily for fiscal reasons. "Better not to do anything if one cannot do something that rivals the part built by Louis XIV," he noted in 1811.

A totally different situation prevailed on the interior, where the Emperor took account of the grandeur and asked that antique statuary taken to the Louvre during the Revolution be restored to the Hall of Mirrors, because "we would miss them if we installed anything modern." By 1811 nothing had come of the various proposals made earlier by Peyre, Potain, Gondouin, Pâris, and Dufour, all of whom at least agreed that the apartments overlooking the Marble Courtyard should be eliminated. As for Percier and Fontaine, the pre-eminent French architects under the Empire, they would have retained only part of the decorative program in the State Apartments. The Salon of Hercules would have become a sort of guardroom embellished with wall hangings and military reliefs, leaving the Salon of Abundance ceiling to be endowed with a scene dedicated to Victory—the successes of the Italian and Egyptian campaigns. The "planetary salons" were to retain their décor (but hung with new portraits), and the Salon of Apollo was to remain the throne room. In the Hall of Mirrors, Percier and Fontaine wanted to replace a lunette representing the 1672 alliance between Germany, Spain, and Holland with a scene from Classical antiquity. For the Empress, they proposed redecorating and refurnishing the Queen's State Apartment, supplemented with a two-storey banqueting hall at the far end, where a balcony would have been supported by caryatids. The architects called for even greater modifications to the former apartments of the Dauphin and Dauphine, located on the ground floor below the Empress's Apartment. Under the Banqueting Hall, the Emperor's Guardroom would have led through a bronze door to the vestibule of the Queen's Staircase, and thence to a suite of rooms with coffered ceilings and pictures representing *Caesar, Zenobia, Dido,* or yet cavalry charges in the manner of Van der Meulen. For the Emperor's study there were to have been sumptuous boiseries and a Neoclassical décor composed of pilasters, atlases, and torchères. For the King of Rome, the lone child born to Napoleon and Marie-Louise, and his cousins, there were to have been thirteen princely apartments strung along the ground floor of the South Wing.

These ambitious plans all remained on the drawing board. Even so, 85,000 yards of silk had been shipped from the weavers of Lyons, some 10,000 yards of which would be used at the Élysée Palace in Paris and the Monte Cavallo in Rome. The rest survived intact for the benefit of the Bourbon Restoration, beginning in 1815. Recent exhibitions organized by France's Mobilier National, marking the publication of an inventory of its collections, have revealed the utter splendor of the Napoleonic commissions, the peerless craftsmanship they summoned, and a host of other elements recalling the wealth of invention seen earlier in the furnishings produced under the *ancien régime.* The Throne Room boasted heavy gold and crimson brocade with a laurel-leaf motif, and the Empress's Grand Salon a blue and gold ensemble featuring crowns and other ornaments. The Emperor's *Cabinet de Repos* was done up in gold-brocaded *gros de Tours* and matching silk woven with a pattern of rosettes, bluebells, cameos, and swans. For her Small Apartment, the Empress had white satin embroidered with flowers and birds. Clearly, the sense of quality and harmonious color remained constant, albeit placed in the service of Neoclassicism's love of Greco/Roman antiquity. At the Petit Trianon, Napoleon commis-

OPPOSITE: The "King's Garden" was installed under Louis XVIII after 1815 on the site of the former Royal Island.

sioned Trepsat to reconstruct the Chinese ring game and restore the Queen's house, where the decorative painting would be executed by Dubois-Drahonet. Gabriel's masterpiece would then be occupied by Pauline Borghese, Napoleon's sister, while the Emperor made frequent sojourns at the Grand Trianon with Joséphine. Queen Hortense (of Holland), Joséphine's daughter by her first husband, Alexandre de Beauharnais, describes a dinner given there on 25 December 1809, following the annulment of the Imperial couple's childless marriage: "The Emperor wished to keep her [Joséphine]. As usual, he sat opposite her. Nothing seemed to have changed. The Queen of Naples and I were the only guests. The pages and the Prefect of the Palace attended as usual. A profound silence reigned. My mother could eat nothing, and I saw her on the point of fainting. The Emperor dried his eyes two or three times without saying anything, and we left straight afterwards." In 1810 Marie-Louise moved into the Dauphin's former apartment, and Napoleon into Madame de Maintenon's. Most of the furniture commissioned at the time has been preserved.

"When they are up on the scaffolding, if they happen to sneeze, blow their noses, or cough heavily, they find themselves showered with Venuses, Marses, and Fames with their trumpets and all the glory of Louis XIV's *Grand Siècle,* now blackened with dust and draped in cobwebs." Thus wrote Fontaine, reminding us that the Restoration (1814-1830) was indeed an age of restoration, beginning with Louis XVIII, Louis XVI's younger brother, who launched a major campaign. By October 1814 some 900 workers were busy re-endowing Versailles with its royal emblems and wrought-iron gates, working on the pediment atop the Gabriel Wing, under the direction of Lange, the Louvre conservator responsible for antiquities, and finishing the Dufour Pavilion. Inside, the State Apartments were freshened up with new painted décors, but the main objective was to restore the ceilings, which Durameau, as early as 1788, had already found to be in poor condition. Now, despite his efforts to retouch *The Capture of Ghent* above the Hall of Mirrors, the scene had to be entirely repainted. The artists involved were Ducis, Heim, Vafflaard, and Paulin-Guérin, assisted by less able practitioners, such as Boisfremont and Vaysse de Villiers, whose work came in for some criticism. Vaysse de Villiers, for example, was asked to explain what "Venus's flowing blond tresses had in common with the tumbling yellow corkscrew curls he had given [the goddess]."

LOUIS-PHILIPPE: MUSEUM FOUNDER

In 1833 the German poet Heinrich Heine wrote: "Apart from the King of Bavaria, Louis-Philippe is, among all princes, the one who most appreciates the fine arts." Following the overthrow of Charles X (1830), the last of Louis XIV's direct heirs to wear the French crown, Louis-Philippe came to the throne, by reason of his descent from Philippe I, Duc d'Orléans, Louis XIV's younger brother. The accession of the Orléanist monarch rekindled hope among the Versaillais for an economic revival. Already in 1831, the Chamber of Deputies began expressing a desire to transform Versailles into a museum. This brought out a number of old projects, among them a proposal from the Prefect of the Seine and Oise, who assumed that the "Citizen King" would live in the State Apartments. Elsewhere in the Château, however, there could have been a "chronological and historical collection of the best painters of the French School," for the purpose of "bringing this vast palace back to life and turning Versailles into a city of the arts and sciences, and attracting more and more students and foreigners."

When Louis-Philippe visited Versailles on 26 July 1833, he told those accompanying him of his plans for the former royal residence, which had become part of his personal estate as of 2 March 1832. Meanwhile, Montalivet, Intendant-General of the Civil List, could scarcely have been more wrong when he noted how lucky it was that Versailles "had not suffered overmuch from being left abandoned for so long." After all, both the Empire and the Restoration had done their best to keep the great pile dry and in good repair. Nor would the "King of the French" escape criticism, articulated by sophisticates unduly concerned about good taste, but whatever its errors, the July Monarchy need not apologize for work undertaken to save an old but still magnificent building.

On 1 September 1833 Louis-Philippe signed a report submitted to him by Montalivet in Cherbourg, four days before it would be published in *Le Moniteur*. In this way he dramatized his solemn decision to give to the nation the Château de Versailles, that arch-symbol of the *ancien régime* which had also become the cradle of the Revolution. Now a museum, Versailles would reflect both a new artistic sensibility and a moment of national reconciliation.

Louis-Philippe made almost 400 visits to the Versailles worksite, each of them recorded by the architect Frédéric Nepveu, whose surviving reports tell much about the genesis of this museum, "dedicated to all the glories of France." They also reveal the King's hesitations, the disagreements among his associates, and the scope of a project that would continue for fifteen years.

Before final plans could be drawn up, the King had reviewed a variety of proposals submitted by Nepveu, a pupil of Peyre and Percier. Thus, with the aid of Dubuc, his Director of Buildings, and with Fontaine, onetime architect to the Emperor and now the King's advisor, Louis-Philippe had the means to consider how the work should proceed. By July 1833 there were vague ideas about a library in the North Wing, adjacent to a "collection of rare and curious objects that might provide a worthy conclusion to the foreigner's visit." Also envisioned were the apartments hung with "a logical succession of pictures, statues, books, and models, to make up a museum of art." In August, finally, it was settled that Versailles should assume a new national and historical purpose; simultaneously, the idea of transforming it into a residence was abandoned. The galleries dedicated to French history would make the nation take account of itself, its history, and, by none too subtle implication, the legitimacy of a monarch whose father had voted for the execution of Louis XVI, his near cousin.

A gallery of battle pictures would be installed in the South Wing, which had to be fitted out with halls large enough to display vast canvases. Another high priority was the creation of a circuit making it easier to control the flow of visitors. This concern made it seem wise to lower the level of the Marble Courtyard and to rationalize the basic plan of the châteaux of Louis XIII and Louis XIV. The two museographical necessities led to a complete redesign of both the ground floor of the central building and its two wings. Only the State Apartments and, to a lesser extent, the sovereigns' private apartments and inner *cabinets* escaped this radical process, which otherwise eliminated the princes' apartments and the mezzanine in the South Wing, formerly allotted to the Children of France and the King's brother. On the ground floor, the apartment of Marie-Antoinette facing the Marble Courtyard vanished, as did those of Mesdames on the site of Louis XIV's Bath Suite.

Unlike his predecessors, Louis-Philippe did not recoil before the prospect of colossal expense, nor did he flag, over a period of nearly fifteen years, in his programmed effort to open new rooms, beginning with the South Wing. Already in 1833, a space was created on the first floor for the Hall of Battles. The iconographic scheme would be completed in an adjacent gallery, built of stone along the east side and invested with a series of busts and statues. Meanwhile, on the ground floor, thirteen rooms were organized for the display of an impressive collection of 528 portraits—full-length images, busts, and heads—of the constables, marshals, and admirals of France. On 29 June 1834, however, these works would be superseded, "provisionally" at first but then "definitively," by such major depictions of the Napoleonic experience as Girodet's *Revolt at Cairo,* Gros's *Battle of the Pyramids,* Carle Vernet's *Austerlitz,* Regnault's *Portrait of Jérôme,* and Benvenuti's *Court of Élisa Bacchiocci.* Today, all these galleries remain virtually as they were established under Louis-Philippe, their walls entirely covered with pictures. Reinforcing the continuity of the enfilade along the South Parterre is the ubiquitous presence on the windowed side of a decorative repertoire inspired by Le Brun. This shows that, from the outset, Louis-Philippe was determined to present French historical painting within a suitably monumental setting.

Here Louis-Philippe brought together two Versailles specialities: the traditional one of framing art works in some dramatic manner, such as the gilt-bronze garlands in the Salon of Diana, or the rich, sculptural borders carved by Verberckt, like those surrounding the Veroneses in the Salon of Hercules; and the new, museographical tradition, whose launch was assigned to Jean Alaux. The setting he formulated comprised a decorative repertoire of arabesques, acanthus leaves, trophies, volutes, chimeras, and putti, all gilded, set forth upon a ground of bronze or ox-blood red, and spread the full length of the walls. The vigorous design and strong colors tend to upstage the smaller pictures, such as those by Guyon, Gué, and Adam, who copied works by David and Gros. Yet, the setting proved less overwhelming than the Mannerist *grotteschi* painted by Stürmer and Mucke at Heltorf Castle. Throughout these galleries, especially those preserved today, or perhaps because of them, what impresses most is the originality of the décor, which prompted one of the more generous critics to compare the museum to a bazaar where decoration is all: "On every side, paste jewels set in real gold."

Above these rooms ran a very long gallery. Numerous plans and drawings prepared by Nepveu and his team, all preserved at the National Archives in Paris and the Office of the Château Architect at Versailles, attest to the various solutions taken under consideration. Walls and vaults were to have been entirely covered with immense pictures, except on the window side, where portraits were thought preferable to a monotonous repetition of trophies. Early on in the planning there arose a concern for effect, which yielded the idea of replacing the barrel vault with a coffered ceiling, of using dormer windows to light the space, etc. Finally, in 1835, a decision was made to fill in the wall windows and to light the gallery, throughout its great length, "by means of a skylight cut into the barrel vault and made entirely of iron." At the Pont des Arts in Paris, the aesthetic potential of metal architecture had already been demonstrated, but at Versailles the metal structure would be concealed, relegated to a purely technical role.

Work on the long gallery proceeded at a good pace, so that by the end of 1836 thought could be given to the task of hanging the collection. The pictures would be placed flat against the wall, not exactly set within panels but, rather, framed in carton pierre and separated by tall, reed-thin columns. Beginning at the north and continuing clockwise, they formed a sequence of thirty-three episodes retracing French history from Tolbiac to Wagram. The program was not so much premeditated or artistically determined as an eclectic narrative desired by a King who, in matters of painting, preferred verisimilitude over exceptional quality. Below Abel de Pujol's grisaille friezes and coving, the full-color pictures by Delacroix, Vernet, the Scheffer brothers, and Heim exhibit remarkable restraint, without flights into Romantic or picturesque extravagance, the better to narrate a history peppered with anecdotes taken from Thierry, Michelet, Thiers, and Guizot.

What remains of the most grandiose project undertaken at Versailles by the July Monarchy reveals virtually nothing about the King's own taste. What was in fashion at the time can be glimpsed from certain kinds of documentation, such as orders for alterations issued by the royal counselors in the aftermath of a Salon exhibition (Évariste Fragonard) or an honorarium paid to an artist for checking some topographical detail (Bouchot in Zurich). Everywhere in Europe, people were rediscovering their national history, a trend set in motion by American independence, glorified in the paintings of John Trumbull, as well as by the French Revolution. During the Restoration, such Napoleonic artists as Girodet, Gros, and Regnault had joined together in a didactic history program developed by the Comte de Pradel, Director of the King's Household. Once completed, the "lessons" would have been given to 200 people at a time, all "comfortably seated." Although the scheme came to nothing, it found a logical successor in the Hall of Battles, the notices published about the pictures, and Gavard's long series of engraved views of Versailles's historical galleries.

A sense of history is rarely without political motive. For proof one has only to consider the incredible array of portraits, battles, and other scenes hung throughout the three storeys of the Château. Given this, it is just as well to recall the political situation of Louis-Philippe. An Orléanist destined to promote the home of the Bourbons, the King had to rally about himself a number of differing factions. During the "July Days" or "Three Glorious Days" that brought him to the throne, beleaguered Parisians witnessed barricades and street fighting, the pillage of the episcopal palace, and a general descent into anarchy, symbolized by the black flag briefly flown from the Hôtel de Ville. Such were the confused excesses that kept the republicans from seizing power, in 1830. The son of Philippe-Égalité and thus heir to a liberal tradition, Louis-Philippe had only to pick up the scattered reins of government, following a moment of hesitation characteristic of an age given to Romantic posturing. After he swore to maintain the Charter, Viennet exclaimed: "The extreme right was joyless, the extreme left was hardly gay, but powerful voices from the center have now silenced the extremists... We could not do better."

Versailles became an occasion for combining art and history. The King, as a moderate and a Man of the Enlightenment, understood the need to surround himself with brilliant personalities. Soon, this lover of grand building schemes would be recruiting architects (Fontaine and Nepveu), historians (Vatout, Trognon), and artists (Granet), all competent talents eager to work with utter dedication, though occasionally disconcerted by shifting instructions. The account books as well as the diaries of Fontaine and Nepveu reveal the many rivalries at play, not to mention a driven, authoritarian King forever faced with mounting costs but always pushing the whole enterprise, as stubbornly as Louis XIV "forcing nature" or assigning regiments to dig the Lake of the Swiss Guard. And who could forget that "father of artists," Baron Taylor, mobilizing Delacroix, Ingres, Géricault, and Vernet to take part in his monumental *Picturesque and Romantic Journeys through Old France*? The man who outdid himself to create the Louis-Philippe gallery at the Louvre, with its 450 paintings, which might very well have perished during the Iberian troubles of 1835-1837, would certainly have been prepared to advise the creator of the Versailles museum. Too, the man who first imagined the Luxor obelisk at the center of Paris, and then discussed its acquisition with Mohammed Ali, could be counted on for ideas about how to arrange a gallery about the door brought from Rhodes. National unity was also to be affirmed at Versailles, as declared in the highly official *Journal des Débats*: "Here are all the great families of France: those dating gloriously from our revolution of 1789, those whose origins are lost in the mists of time, those grouped around the throne of the July Monarchy, and those which honorable regrets or unabated passions have condemned to retirement. All are represented with their arms, titles, trophies, and history in this vast Pantheon to all

The Royal Opéra in 1855 during a supper given by Napoleon III in honor of Queen Victoria and Prince Albert, then on a state visit to France.
Painting by Eugène Lami.

the exploits and heroes of France. The King has forgotten no one! He has brought together the great French Family, uniting all periods and reconciling all origins."

The opposition press did not hesitate to cite the overall artistic mediocrity, noting as well that military leaders were more in evidence than intellectuals. Critics thought the project a historical hodgepodge; moreover, they asserted that the call for national reconciliation was nothing more than an artful, ostentatious way of papering over difficult social problems. The galleries devoted to the July Monarchy, for example, concentrated more on military glory than on the daily lives of Lyons's silk weavers. But whether deemed propaganda or popular instruction, Louis-Philippe's great enterprise took its first spectacular step with the celebratory inauguration of the Hall of Battles in 1837.

Thereafter the royal undertaking continued apace. In addition to the large galleries of famous men, generals, constables, admirals, kings, and queens, where full-length or bust portraits hung side by side or in tiers, the King planned several ensembles entirely as coherent as that in the Hall of Battles because history is politics, or propaganda. Thus, in 1834 work began on the rooms commemorating those revolutionary years 1792 and 1830, as well as on the Coronation Room. In 1837 planning got under way for the Crusades Room, a project that would take a decade to complete. Two years later came the series on the Estates-General, and, finally, the big African halls, launched in 1842.

The former Swiss Guards' Room was reserved for the Volunteers of 1792. This gallery alone could be seen as a summary of the King's program, for here, rubbing shoulders along the paneling, were Lafayette, Dumouriez, and most of the future marshals of the Empire, along with the Duc de Chartres (future Louis-Philippe) and Bonaparte, their reigns depicted as if they were the glorious outcome of hard-won battles. The hall was devoted neither to the Revolution (curiously absent are the Tennis Court Oath, the Storming of the Bastille, and the Night of 4 August) nor to the only campaign of 1792. Moreover, the pictures representing Valmy and Jemmapes, both copies of Vernet paintings commissioned by Louis-Philippe for the Palais-Royal during the Restoration, evoke the King's role as military commander during the last days of the old monarchy. Primarily, however, it was the virtues of an army loyal to the nation which this hall celebrated. Louis-Philippe himself gave Cogniet the subject of his painting entitled *The National Guard of Paris Leaving for the Army in September 1792,* its subject an event that took place at the height of the Terror. For Louis-Philippe, the picture constituted an occasion for proclaiming the merits of *juste-milieu,* or centrist, patriotism, given that the volunteers were neither extremists nor allies of the enemy, towards whom the King, in his *Mémoires,* accused Louis XVI of having been somewhat sympathetic: "The King's duty, as well as his true interest, was to carry out frankly and effectively what he announced in his speeches. As Head of State, whatever his actual title, his duty was to defend the State and oppose foreign invasion; he ought therefore to have put himself at the head of the national movement, and postponed the miserable question of whether he would exercise a greater or lesser part of his authority, and reign as 'King of the French by the Grace of God and the constitutional law of the State,' or as 'King of France and Navarre' purely and simply by the 'Grace of God,' without the State having any 'constitutional law,' which was the 'utopian' view held by émigrés and many foreign courts." It could not be more clearly stated. Louis-Philippe, who took part in the battles of this campaign, declared himself to be the Citizen King, a patriot more concerned with his country's security than with political disputes. Once again, he had asserted his willingness to perform his national duty. To the official press, this gallery was, in some measure, the "Golden Book of France."

At the southern end of the Hall of Battles would be the Hall of 1830, its dimensions fixed on 18 January 1834. Here, more than elsewhere in the museum, it took a while before the iconographical program could be sorted out. After Louis-Philippe made his nineteenth visit to Versailles, on 18 October 1834, Nepveu reported as follows: "I explained to the King that, after all the work and sacrifices made by His Majesty for the restoration and new role of the palace of Versailles, I thought that one could, without excessive pride, set aside this final room to receive, at its most apparent point, the marble equestrian statue of the King and, all around on the first floor, hang paintings retracing the major aspects of His Majesty's life, representing the army's various weapons between the attic pilasters. This program did not displease the King. I had studied it with all the interest it deserved: I would have loved to carry it out, but the King gave me orders not only for another manner to crown the room, but also for a different decorative scheme, as he wanted it to be used for pictures of the main events of the July Revolution."

The coving, suspended from an iron framework, would be decorated from drawings prepared by Fontaine. All about were red walls embellished in an eclectic style featuring emblems of industry and the fine arts reminiscent of the style developed for the table service used by the French Philhellenic Committee and executed at the Montereau pottery in 1830. Larivière, in his picture entitled *The Arrival of the Duc d'Orléans at City Hall,* attempted to convey a popular enthusiasm that, in fact, everyone knew was lacking. Alongside it hung *The Deputies' Declaration* and *Louis-Philippe Sworn in at the Chamber,* in which the eponymous scenes come across as galleries of stilted portraits. Such topical paintings were no doubt aimed primarily at impressing visitors, especially since the gallery lay not far from the large Guardroom, glorified by two David masterpieces: *The Coronation* and *The Army's Oath of Allegiance.* Overhead the ceiling offered *The Nation* and *The Fundamental Virtues of Truth, Justice, and Wisdom Defending the Charter,* the latter scene restating a solemn pact between the King and the people, and, finally, *Order and Liberty.* On the walls, the importance of the city and people of Paris was signaled, also, once again, the loyalty of the army, in this instance symbolized by a meeting between the King and his son, the Duc de Chartres, at the toll barrier on the Place du Trône, where the Duke, at the head of his hussars, is said to have declared: "I would have had too many regrets if any other regiment but mine had arrived in Paris ahead of me bearing the national cockade."

Also in process at the same time as the Hall of 1830 were the transformations effected in the Great Guardroom. In 1834-1835 these provided consolation for Nepveu, who had not been able to express loyalty to the King after his panegyric scheme had been turned into a "simple" reminder of those July days in 1830. Today the Guardroom looks peaceful enough, but at the time it was the cause of a sordid struggle between Nepveu, always on assignment at Versailles, and Fontaine, who was based in Paris, where he had more opportunities to press his case before the King. As the hub of the circulation route within the museum, the Guardroom was hung with a select group of spectacular pictures sure to move anyone nostalgic for the Empire: *The Coronation* and *The Army's Oath of Allegiance,* both painted by David for the Tuileries Palace, where the Emperor had made his Paris residence, and Gros's *Battle of Aboukir,* which Murat had installed in the royal palace at Naples. It was in Naples that Stendhal saw the heroic canvas "spread out on the floor of a vast room, with people walking across it in order to see the principal figure." The decoration of this superb room had come to Nepveu as a kind of obligatory gift, a consolation prize. Right away, he persuaded the King that the ceiling should be a work of architecture and therefore subject to his control. Plantar designed the trophies executed in carton pierre around *The Battle of Aboukir,* but was not allowed to produce a frieze of shields. To Alaux, Nepveu assigned a floriligium of personifications (Industry, Navigation, War, Peace, Law, and Abundance) to complete a series of medallions retracing the career of Napoleon Bonaparte: *Castiglione, The Concordat, Rivoli, The French*

Standards on the Banks of the Nile, Alexandria, Marengo, The Army's Oath of Allegiance, Austerlitz, The Treaty of Leoben and *The Monuments of Assembled Art.* At the museum's inauguration on 10 June 1837, the King's guests all stopped in this room to pay homage to "one of those immortal geniuses who are always the men right for their time."

In addition to the ensembles still in place today, there were also portrait galleries throughout the attics and much of the ground floor. In them hung reassembled collections—from the Sorbonne, the French Academy, the Royal Academy, the Hôtel de Toulouse (admirals), etc.—all arranged without much concern for décor. As for the State Apartments, some of which had suffered (as in 1834, when the fireplaces were removed from the Queen's Bedchamber and the Queen's Salon of Nobles), they were hung with paintings from the former royal collections. To perfect this ensemble and "fill in the gaps," Louis-Philippe had casts made (at Brou or Fontevrault) and paintings copied, but he also bought works. Today no one can study Le Brun, Rigaud, Nattier, Vigée-Lebrun, Gros, or Vernet without going to Versailles.

The paintings in the Africa Rooms, located in the middle of the first floor of the North Wing, were mainly the work of Horace Vernet, assisted by Féron and Victor Adam. The series, however, would never be finished. *The Assault of Constantine* attracted considerable attention at the Salon of 1839, and the public could hardly have been more enthusiastic about *The Capture of the Smala of Abd el-Kader,* where the Duc d'Aumale distinguished himself. After completing 14 pictures covering over 300 square metres, Vernet received the cross of Commander of the Legion of Honor from the hands of Louis-Philippe himself. He also heard his work praised for its "extraordinary tenacity and facility; he has drawn all the figures in his immense composition of 66 feet by 15." Inaugurated in 1842, the African Rooms display almost nothing of an Orientalist character, and this at a time when Delacroix was painting his *Jewish Wedding* and *Sultan of Morocco.* The coving over the Constantine Room is decorated merely with mounted cannon and monochrome flags. Only in the overdoors of this gallery and on the coving over the neighboring Morocco Room did Vernet and his team achieve a colorful, picturesque style prefiguring that of Gérôme or Regnault.

The Crusades Galleries are another matter altogether. Until this time, the subject had rarely been adopted for major pictorial cycles, except when touched upon in certain episodes from the lives of Saint Louis or Saint Francis. Nevertheless, the period still had wide popular appeal, which explains the King's commission for 150 paintings. Every French person longs to have an ancestor who had taken part in the Crusades, a dream very likely shared, most of all, by members of the Legitimist family, with whom the Orléanist King had found it so difficult to achieve conciliation. A second reason was, again, the general revival of interest in history. The writers of the seventeenth and eighteenth centuries, for all their devotion to literature, had disdained neither ideas nor history. During the Revolutionary period, however, both the latter came very much to the fore, thanks to enthusiasm for the Revolution and an eagerness to export its concepts throughout Europe, or even overseas. Also relevant were the Egpytian expedition, with its great scientific import, and Bonaparte's Australian dream, both pre-Romantic manifestations that found their literary equivalent in Chateaubriand's *Journey from Paris to Jerusalem,* while also stimulating a thirst for knowledge. The prestigious School of Chartres turned out historians who busied themselves classifying, studying, and publishing old documents. Mérimée and Viollet-le-Duc sought to repair and maintain the nation's architectural heritage, in the wake of so much revolutionary vandalism and neglect. Most of all, there was a resurgent passion for national history, a feeling that gripped the whole of Europe, where every society appeared intent upon reinforcing its identity by exploring its roots. Doors therefore stood wide open to Romanticism and reverie. In 1822 came the publication of Michaud's *History of the Crusades,* a narrative that fired the popular imagination. Although sometimes steeped in tradition more than in verified facts, the Michaud book constituted an ongoing source for the galleries at Versailles.

The first installation was modest, carried out on the first floor of the Gabriel Wing near the Hall of the Estates-General. Still, work went on for three years, without ever being finished; moreover, the pictures fell short of a homogenous ensemble. Was this merely an experiment? In 1837, Louis-Philippe shifted his attention to the North Wing, where he decided to fit out a large, monumental hall on the ground floor. Now the decorative element proved so important that it would not be completed until 1843, while Nepveu was still very much involved with the four adjacent rooms. For once, the archives are fairly explicit about the royal desire for a décor in keeping with the subject. The task became easier after Sultan Mahmoud II presented the King with one of the doors from the hospital of the Order of Saint John of Jerusalem on the island of Rhodes. Louis-Philippe advised Nepveu "to start work on the design only after the doors have arrived from Rhodes, since their dimensions and ornament should serve as a point of departure." During 1838 Morel and Plantar spent 267 days restoring, or even reconstituting, the lower part of the door.

Meanwhile, various decorative schemes were under way, involving pilasters, cornices, window casings, ceilings, palm-leaf capitals, bronze portraits of twenty-nine French kings, and armorial escutcheons, whose placement still engaged the King as late as 1842: "To reserve a margin of error and satisfy the demands of families who might later appeal against involuntary omission, His Majesty has decided to replace simple crosses with escutcheons on most of the panels of the four new ceilings." Poor families! They were duped by a clever businessman named Courtois, out to make his fortune at the expense of more than one nobleman's vanity. In 1842 Courtois flooded the Paris market with hundreds of acts, each duly sealed and certifying numerous participants in the Crusades. The operation unfolded in several phases, one of which included types of documents that historians realized had never existed. With this came rumors of fraud. Nevertheless, the painter Jorand, after designing a series of 176 shields, painted them in natural colors with gold accents on a wood support.

The royal taste for the Middle Ages proved ostentatious enough to attract even the hold-out Legitimists to the Orléanist monarchy. However, the truth that Louis-Philippe valued in painting could not be so easily satisfied. Was Jerusalem really captured by Jacques de Molay in 1299? Jean Richard, historian of the Crusades, is not convinced. Yet, the décor commands interest because, in the whole of this museum, it remains the only one that, again in the name of a certain kind of truth, is neither eclectic nor purely academic. Rather, the décor is entirely, and quite properly, at one with the period it evokes. The homogeneous neo-Gothicism even embraces the furniture. In 1840 the upholsterer Charles Munier delivered eighteen benches with neo-Gothic ornament. In 1841 Chaumont installed two giant chandeliers with Gothic figures, both of which, in 1846, would be transferred to the castle at Pau, a Bourbon stronghold, and then replaced by Gothic-style arms, again made by Chaumont, this time in association with Marquis. As for the huge painting commission, which would not be fully executed by the time the July Monarchy collapsed during the 1848 Revolution, Louis-Philippe planned to augment it in a new gallery extended northward towards Gabriel's theatre, a gallery "containing new escutcheons, new pictures, and above all funerary monuments dedicated to the Crusaders." Although sometimes a bit picturesque, the Crusader works constitute an original ensemble.

The Crusader paintings illustrate nothing to be discovered in the works of either Walter Scott or Dante, nor do they betray any trace of Italian emotion, or the grandiloquence of the

The Château de Versailles and the Water Parterre
under Louis-Philippe. Painting by Ricois.

Niebelungen in Munich, or yet the colorful Orientalism of David Roberts's travelogues painted in the Holy Land. Rather, they are the products of conscientious craftsmen, who put into their pictures events then believed to be true, capturing in more than a few details their contemporary love of archaeological reconstruction. This can be seen in Granet's Temple or the rendering of the Madeleine Church in Vézelay before its restoration by Viollet-le-Duc. The Crusader artists kept their personalities in check, whatever the generation of each. Thus, we find Papety, Signol, and Blondel muting their taste for luminism. Gallait, in his *Coronation of Baldwin,* embraced the high ambition of history painting, doing so on a grand scale and proving himself worthy of his role as head of the Belgian School. Only Delacroix, in *Crusaders Entering Constantinople,* captured the pain of the vanquished and the grandeur of the victors, thanks to his mastery of chiaroscuro effects and the lyricism these bring to a subtle, iridescent, richly chromatic palette. During the fortunate period when it hung here, this work must have been a glowing presence at the end of the great hall.

At Versailles, Louis-Philippe and his team left not one room untouched. When Gabriel's theatre reopened in 1837, the original blue and gold décor had been redone, by Cicéri, in red and gold, providing ample evidence of the King's self-confidence. In 1845, however, some hesitation arose when it came to Nepveu and Vernet's plans for the Morocco Room. Vernet proposed "a single composition divided into three parts by two half-columns set against an openwork balustrade, through which one can glimpse the near ground." In 1846 the concept still remained under discussion, and even in 1848 Louis-Philippe seemed more interested in detail, forever resisting anything theatrical, which might have lent the museography of Versailles a touch of the avant-garde. In his approach to the Morocco Room, the conventional Vernet, who always placed every element of his painting in the foreground, as would Manet later, proved himself to be a true Versailles master, always concerned for the overall décor. For a precedent, one has only to recall the transformations made on the ceiling of the Queen's Bedchamber in the eighteenth century. Should Vernet be included in that long line of master decorators who, at Maser or Blenheim, insisted upon interweaving art and ornament? Did he see himself as a forerunner of those mural artists at the end of the century, among them Max Klinger who, in 1885, made his *Last Judgment* as decorative as it was lyrical?

Louis-Philippe's Versailles was therefore little more than a Château rescued, an album of images. It was an ambitious enterprise whose weaknesses the King himself acknowledged. "My successors," Louis-Philippe admitted, "will change the paintings, but first I wanted to put something in the frames." With this, he pre-empted the criticisms of Balzac and Baudelaire, as well as Victor Hugo, who wrote that "the Bourgeois King's grey hat and umbrella cost more than the crown of Charlemagne." For the "Bourgeois King," however, restraint always went hand in glove with ambition. At Versailles the frames were never anything other than purely ornamental, whereas fifty years later, at Goslar Castle, Wislicenus framed his historical series devoted to the German emperors with veritable scenes, or compartments featuring three-dimensional elements reminiscent of the base of the Virgin tympanum at Longpont as much as the eclecticism of H. Lebas's design for the altar in the Holy Sacrament Chapel at Notre-Dame-de-Lorette, completed in 1823. Such is the context in which Louis-Philippe's museum, with all its complexity, becomes significant, a place where, on every side, originals cohabit with copies. But such a program was not new, having already been realized in the seventeenth century by Gaignières and in the eighteenth by Horace Walpole at Strawberry Hill.

Décor, like painting, reflected the same urge towards historicism. Fortoul, while admiring King Ludwig I's reconstructions in Munich, advocated a French vocabulary for expressing

French ideas, rather than the scrupulous erudition shown by German architects. Yet, he also reproached his fellow citizens for the narrowness of their artistic views, as did Alfred de Musset, who had no patience with the lack of invention in eclecticism. Was Fortoul aware that, about this time, the Germans had discovered, to their great consternation, that Gothic had not originated in Germany, that Amiens had been a model for the Cologne cathedral, and that neo-Gothic could scarcely exist without reference to medieval France and thus to Catholicism? Gothic was therefore to be viewed as a French and Catholic art form. Fonthill Abbey in England, the writings of Chateaubriand in France, the Catholic conversion of Pugin in 1834 and Newman in 1845, and the construction of numerous Gothic-style buildings finally led to a triumphant form of medieval academicism that would last until the dawn of the twentieth century.

"If genius is rare, talent is common." Thus did Théophile Gautier summarize the general attitude towards Louis-Philippe's Versailles—academic, Orientalist, military, political, national historical, didactic, glorious, and all of it without excess. At this Versailles one would seek enthusiasm or fantasy only in vain. And Louis-Philippe made sure of it, ordering Évariste Fragonard, for example, to modify the color harmony in his *Marignan,* at the time of its exhibition at the Salon. In 1840 Granet moaned that "Franque is working for the King at the Louvre, enlarging old pictures and touching up new ones that lack the required qualities; in short, earning more than for doing Greeks or Romans."

Skepticism, disappointment? Not on the part of Nepveu, who, in 1847, returned from Italy still under the charm. "Books and pictures float in space, with each statue in its niche, its chosen place, I could even say its temple, as the galleries of Rome and the halls of the Vatican immortalize everything they contain." At Versailles the public may have found what it wanted, but what about the artist or poet? While Ruskin was writing about the organic forms of architecture in *The Poetry of Architecture* (1837), and later in *The Seven Lamps of Architecture* and *The Stones of Venice,* while the feverishly erudite literature of the 1840s was making a vigorous argument for the prestige of Greece, and while the Classical example of Mansart and Gabriel lay all about, Louis-Philippe found no occasion at Versailles to heed the monumental lesson of Greece. Just as in Munich or at the Houses of Parliament in London, we find—on the very eve of the Parnassians' celebration of *le beau idéal*—government bureaucrats making decisions about the suitability of forms and decoration, leaving visitors to long for the enlightened artistic patronage of the Popes, the Medici, or Louis XIV. Nevertheless, Louis-Philippe's history taught by image is not without charm or things to appreciate. And the overall ensemble has ceased to be despised. Having decided to create a whole, Louis-Philippe never faltered in his resolve, relying over and over on subject matter, historical continuity, and various sequences. Language for characterizing the results arrives unbidden: talented, solid, illustrative rather than pretty, intellectual rather than sensitive, punctuated here and there with brilliant works. This leads to paradox, and rightly so, since the very idea of national continuity finds its plastic equivalent along the walls of the Hall of Battles, where the only bright spot is Delacroix's *Battle of Taillebourg.* And, despite the title of Museum, the monumental concept at work here involves far more than a mere assembly of magnificent collections.

The museum was not the whole story of Versailles under the July Monarchy. Louis-Philippe also had Nepveu restore and refurnish the Grand Trianon, where the King regularly stayed with his family. For this kind of bourgeois use, the château had to be provided with service corridors and cellars. Further manifestations of the new life-style are Alphonse Jacob's family tables, with their drawers numbered for each member of the royal family. Louis-Philippe had a chapel built in Louis XIV's former billiard room at Trianon-sous-Bois, where the wedding of Princess Marie d'Orléans, a Catholic, with the Duke of Würtemberg, a Lutheran, would take place at nine in the evening on 18 October 1837.

From the Second Empire to Today

Beginning with the Second Empire (1852-1870), curators strove to maintain the ensemble, be they painters like Granet and Gosselin, or scholars like E. Soulié and Clément de Ris. During the Franco-Prussian War (1870), the Château served as a military hospital, before witnessing the proclamation of the German Empire, staged in the Hall of Mirrors on 18 January 1871. Two months later, during the Paris Commune, the National Assembly and various ministries took up residence in the Château. The deputies met in Gabriel's theatre, while their staff slept, dormitory style, in the Hall of Mirrors. Communard insurgents found themselves imprisoned in the Orangery. In the Fall of 1873, Marshal Bazaine was tried for treason at the Grand Trianon, whose peristyle was hung with green repp and heated with stoves to create a hall for spectators. The vote ushering in the Third Republic was taken in Gabriel's theatre on 30 January 1875. The *salle* became home to the Senate, leaving Joly to construct an assembly hall for the deputies in the South Wing. The two representative bodies would return to Paris on 2 August 1879.

Since then Versailles has never again been the seat of government. The Château, however, would see many events planned there for the prestige it could bestow. Among these was the signing of the Treaty of Versailles at the end of World War I, receptions for visiting heads of state, and the elections of French Presidents. The time had come for conservation, for organizing an increasingly popular museum, and presenting special exhibitions such as the splendid ones devoted to Le Brun, French diplomacy, and Marie-Antoinette. The new era has also meant appealing to the generosity of donors who appreciate the beauty of the Château and everything it stands for. The large-scale restorations undertaken since the turn of the century have been made possible by support from Percy Singer, Gordon Bennett, and others with near-mythic names like Rockefeller, Schlumbeger, and Mellon, as well as many benefactors who remain anonymous. Thanks to their generosity, the roofs are waterproof and the Royal Bedchambers or the Hall of Mirrors can still help visitors imagine etiquette under the *ancien régime*. Even now every effort is exerted to track down the original furniture, canvassing dealers or private collectors—or just searching through the archives! Protecting sculpture, opening rooms, or renewing attempts to persuade government ministers and officials to relinquish a major piece—Versailles's civil servants share a passionate commitment to their task. A bond of love exists between Versailles and all the very diverse personalities who have labored for it. Some of them, such as Pierre de Nolhac and Gérald van der Kemp, devoted most of their lives to Versailles. The groves have now been replenished, and music is performed more and more often, thanks to the determination of Philippe Beaussant. Some researchers even feel themselves unfaithful whenever another subject catches their interest. Such is the hold Versailles has on those devoted to it. When they return, it is to measure the power of the Château's appeal.

GROUND FLOOR

DAUPHINE'S APARTMENT
1. First Antechamber
2. Second Antechamber
3. Great Cabinet
4. Bedroom
5. Inner Cabinet
6. Duchesse d'Angoulême's Back Cabinets

DAUPHIN'S APARTMENT
7. Library
8. Great Cabinet
9. Bedroom
10. Back Cabinet
11. Second Antechamber

12. LOWER GALLERY

MADAME VICTOIRE'S APARTMENT
13. First Antechamber
14. Nobles' Room
15. Great Cabinet
16. Bedroom
17. Inner Cabinet
18. Library

MADAME ADÉLAÏDE'S APARTMENT
19. Inner Cabinet
20. Bedroom
21. Great Cabinet
22. Hoquetons' Room
23. Vestibule of Ambassadors' Staircase
24. Réchauffoir
25. King's Guardroom
26. King's Stairs

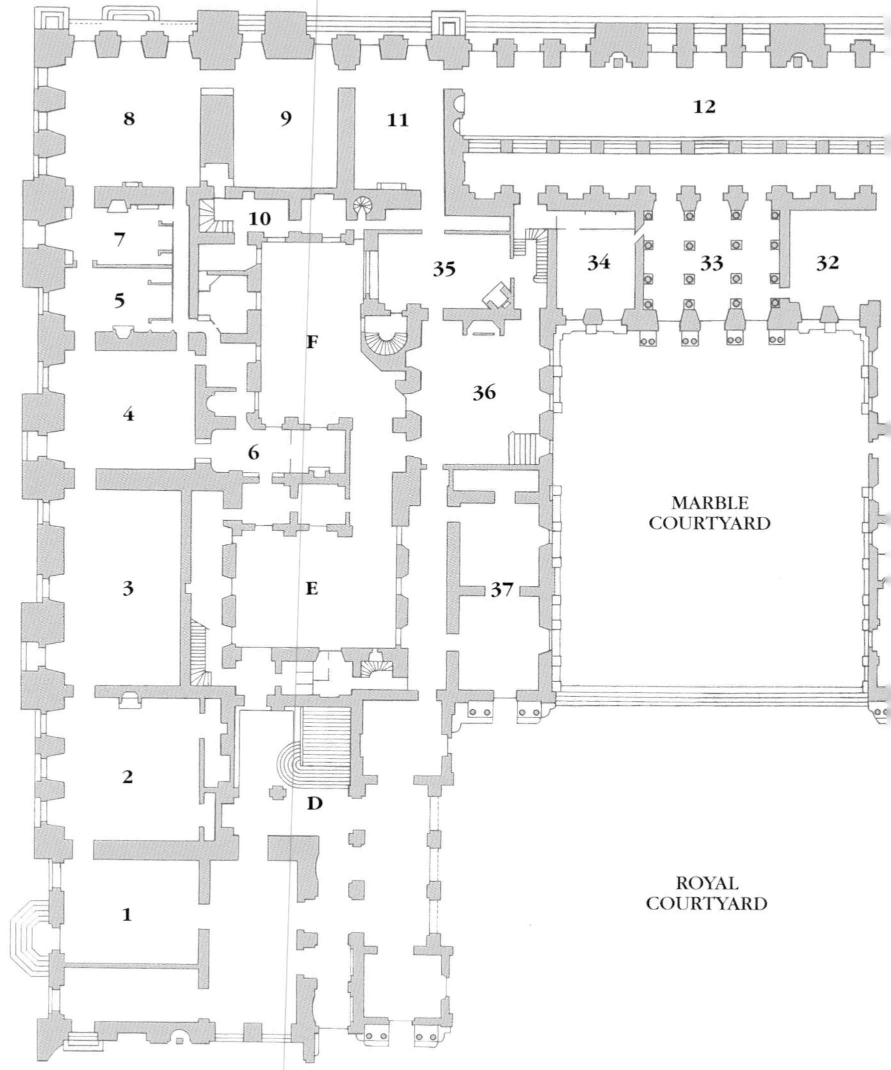

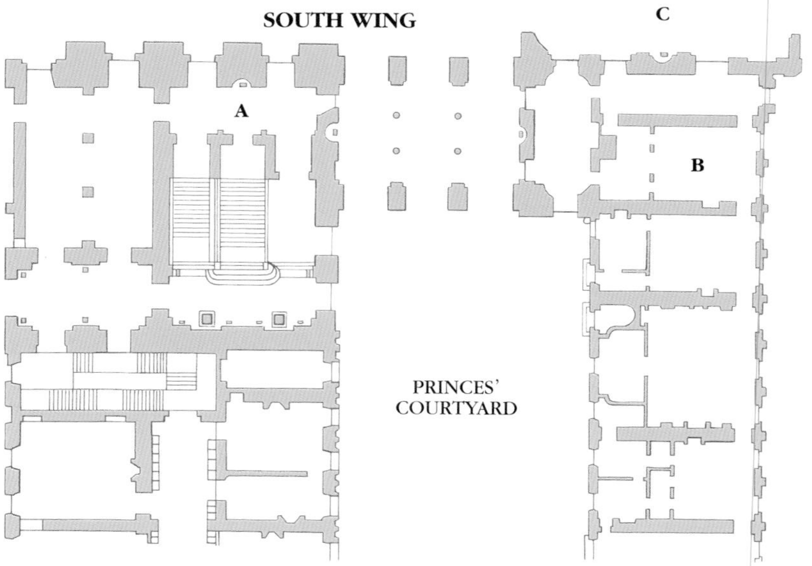

8
9
11
12
10
7
35
34
33
32
5
F
36
4
6
MARBLE
COURTYARD
3
E
37
2
D
ROYAL
COURTYARD
1

SOUTH WING
C
A
B
PRINCES'
COURTYARD

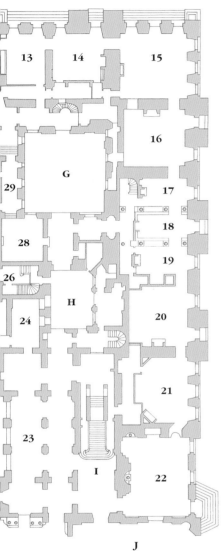

13 14 15

29 G 16

17

18

28 19

26 20

H 24

21

23

I 22

J

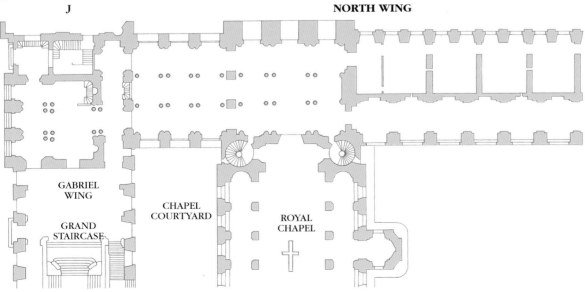

**CAPTAIN OF THE
GUARDS'
APARTMENT**
27. Great Cabinet
28. Antechamber
29. Inner Cabinet
30. Bedroom

**MARIE-ANTOINETTE'S
APARTMENT**
31. Chambermaids'
     Room
32. Queen's Bedroom
33. Marble Vestibule
34. Bath Suite

**ANTEROOMS TO THE
DAUPHIN'S
APARTMENT**
35. First Antechamber
36. Guardroom
37. KING'S
     DRESSING ROOM

A. Princes' Staircase
B. Old Wing
C. South Passage
   to Gardens
D. Queen's Staircase
E. Monseigneur Court
   or Queen's Court
F. Dauphin Court
   or Queen's Court
G. Stag Court
   or Mesdames' Court
H. Small King's Court
I. Louis-Philippe Staircase
J. North passage
   to Gardens

NORTH WING

GABRIEL
WING

GRAND
STAIRCASE

CHAPEL
COURTYARD

ROYAL
CHAPEL

FIRST FLOOR

STATE APARTMENT (PLANETARY SUITE)
1. Salon of Abundance
2. Salon of Vénus
3. Salon of Diana
4. Salon of Mars
5. Salon of Mercury
6. Salon of Apollo
7. Salon of War

QUEEN'S APARTMENT
8. Salon of Peace
9. Queen's bedchamber
10. Great Cabinet or Nobles' Salon
11. Antechamber or Public Dining Room
12. Guardroom
13. Quen's Staircase or Marble Staircase
14. Loggia leading also to the King's Apartment

KING'S APARTMENT
15. Guardroom
16. First Antechamber or Public Dining Room (Grand Couvert)
17. Second Antechamber or Bull's-Eye Salon
18. King's State Bedchamber
19. Council Chamber

SOUTH WING

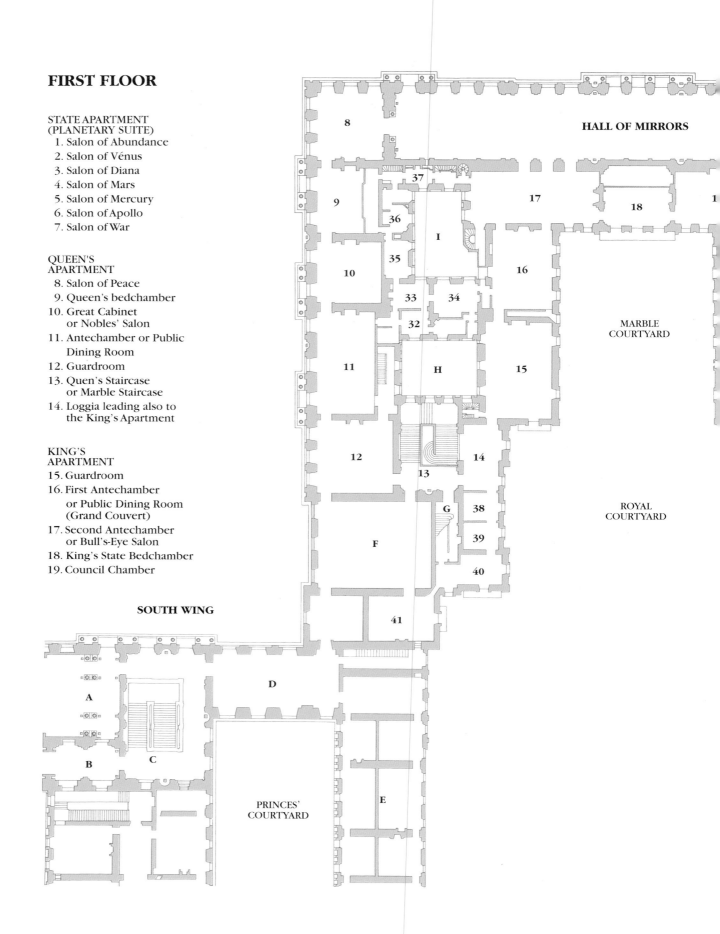

HALL OF MIRRORS

MARBLE COURTYARD

ROYAL COURTYARD

PRINCES' COURTYARD

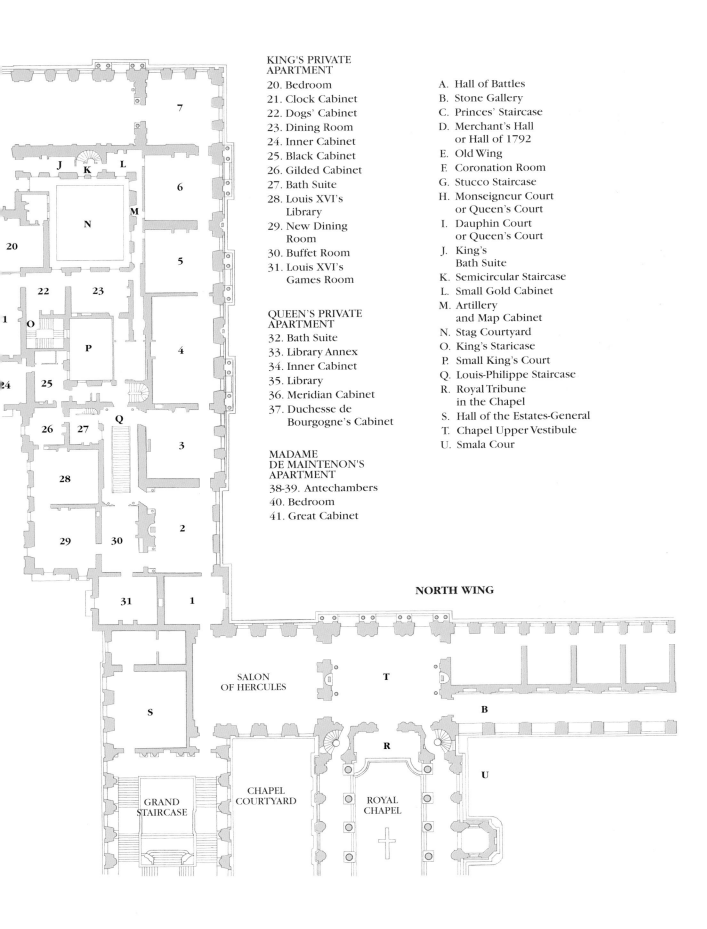

KING'S PRIVATE
APARTMENT
20. Bedroom
21. Clock Cabinet
22. Dogs' Cabinet
23. Dining Room
24. Inner Cabinet
25. Black Cabinet
26. Gilded Cabinet
27. Bath Suite
28. Louis XVI's
    Library
29. New Dining
    Room
30. Buffet Room
31. Louis XVI's
    Games Room

QUEEN'S PRIVATE
APARTMENT
32. Bath Suite
33. Library Annex
34. Inner Cabinet
35. Library
36. Meridian Cabinet
37. Duchesse de
    Bourgogne's Cabinet

MADAME
DE MAINTENON'S
APARTMENT
38-39. Antechambers
40. Bedroom
41. Great Cabinet

A. Hall of Battles
B. Stone Gallery
C. Princes' Staircase
D. Merchant's Hall
   or Hall of 1792
E. Old Wing
F. Coronation Room
G. Stucco Staircase
H. Monseigneur Court
   or Queen's Court
I. Dauphin Court
   or Queen's Court
J. King's
   Bath Suite
K. Semicircular Staircase
L. Small Gold Cabinet
M. Artillery
   and Map Cabinet
N. Stag Courtyard
O. King's Staircase
P. Small King's Court
Q. Louis-Philippe Staircase
R. Royal Tribune
   in the Chapel
S. Hall of the Estates-General
T. Chapel Upper Vestibule
U. Smala Cour

NORTH WING

SALON
OF HERCULES

GRAND
STAIRCASE

CHAPEL
COURTYARD

ROYAL
CHAPEL

THE GARDENS

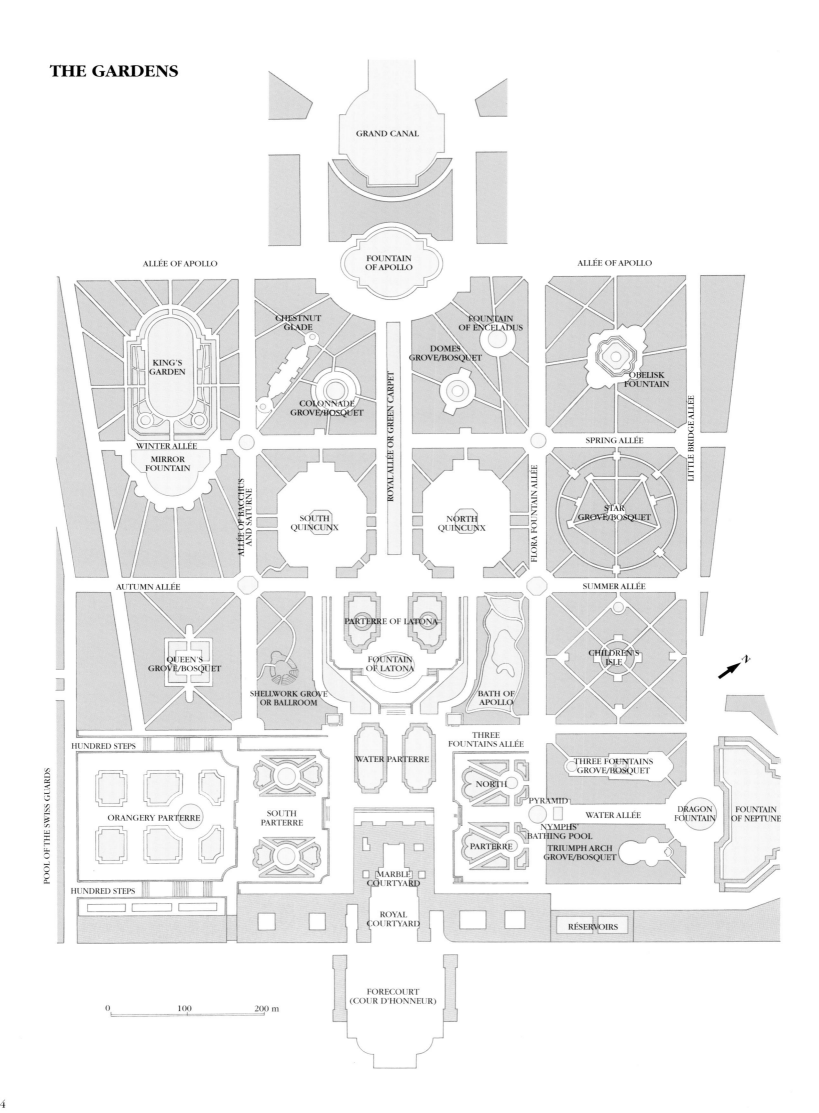

GRAND CANAL

FOUNTAIN
OF APOLLO

ALLÉE OF APOLLO

ALLÉE OF APOLLO

CHESTNUT
GLADE

FOUNTAIN
OF ENCELADUS

DOMES
GROVE/BOSQUET

OBELISK
FOUNTAIN

KING'S
GARDEN

COLONNADE
GROVE/BOSQUET

WINTER ALLÉE

MIRROR
FOUNTAIN

SPRING ALLÉE

LITTLE BRIDGE ALLÉE

ROYAL ALLÉE OR GREEN CARPET

ALLÉE OF BACCHUS AND SATURNE

FLORA FOUNTAIN ALLÉE

SOUTH
QUINCUNX

NORTH
QUINCUNX

STAR
GROVE/BOSQUET

AUTUMN ALLÉE

SUMMER ALLÉE

PARTERRE OF LATONA

QUEEN'S
GROVE/BOSQUET

CHILDREN'S
ISLE

FOUNTAIN
OF LATONA

SHELLWORK GROVE
OR BALLROOM

BATH OF
APOLLO

HUNDRED STEPS

THREE
FOUNTAINS ALLÉE

WATER PARTERRE

THREE FOUNTAINS
GROVE/BOSQUET

POOL OF THE SWISS GUARDS

NORTH

PYRAMID

DRAGON
FOUNTAIN

WATER ALLÉE

FOUNTAIN
OF NEPTUNE

ORANGERY PARTERRE

SOUTH
PARTERRE

NYMPHS'
BATHING POOL

PARTERRE

TRIUMPH ARCH
GROVE/BOSQUET

HUNDRED STEPS

MARBLE
COURTYARD

ROYAL
COURTYARD

RÉSERVOIRS

FORECOURT
(COUR D'HONNEUR)

0   100   200 m

1 Plan of the château and gardens in 1663. Drawing. The small Louis XIII château is ringed about by a moat, with two servants' wings by the entrance. Note the three vistas "cut" through the sloping woods.

2-3-4 Three projects for altering the Marble Court. 17th century drawings. High roofs with tall chimneys; Italianate balustrade; attic or proper second storey; huge central dome… Only a few of the many solutions designed to enlarge the Château de Versailles.

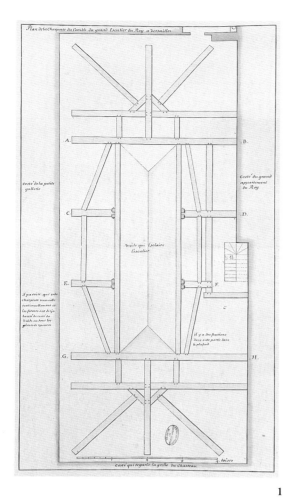

1 Glass roof of the Ambassadors' Staircase. 18th century drawing. One of the first major examples of overhead lighting.

2 Floor design for the Bath Cabinet.

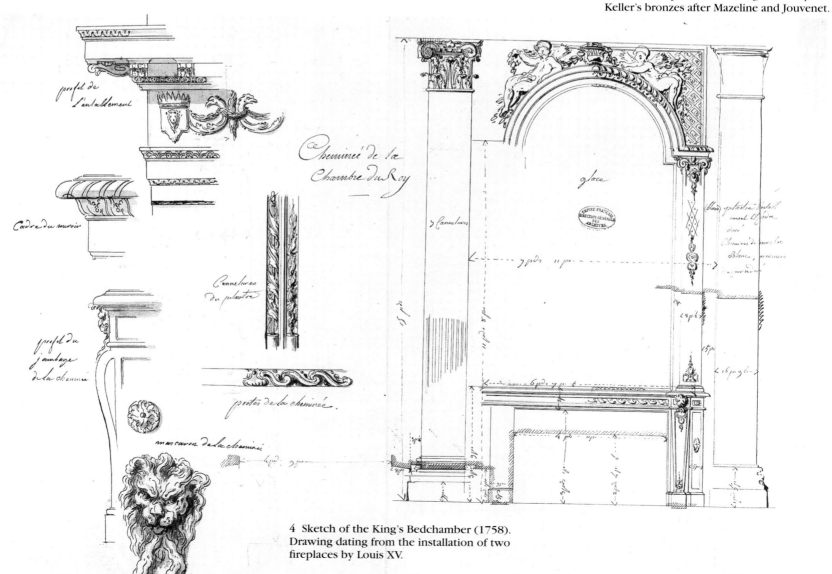

3 Niche design for the Salon of Diana. Drawing (1685). Bernini visited Versailles in 1665, at which time he made the bust of Louis XIV, its presentation heightened by Keller's bronzes after Mazeline and Jouvenet.

4 Sketch of the King's Bedchamber (1758). Drawing dating from the installation of two fireplaces by Louis XV.

4

1

2

1 Project for the throne in the Salon of Apollo. Drawing by the Slodtz brothers. This model was proposed to Louis XV. The carved and gilded woodwork was upholstered in crimson brocade. The canopy was crimson in Winter, and gold, silver and blue in Summer.

2 Elevation of the Jupiter Throne in the Hall of Mirrors (1715). Drawing for the audience of the Persian Ambassador.

3 New arrangement of the Hall of Mirrors for the audience of the Turkish Ambassador in 1742. Drawing. Protocol changed little from one ceremony to the next, as such drawings show: witness the form of the stairs and the size of the boxes for the royal family.

3

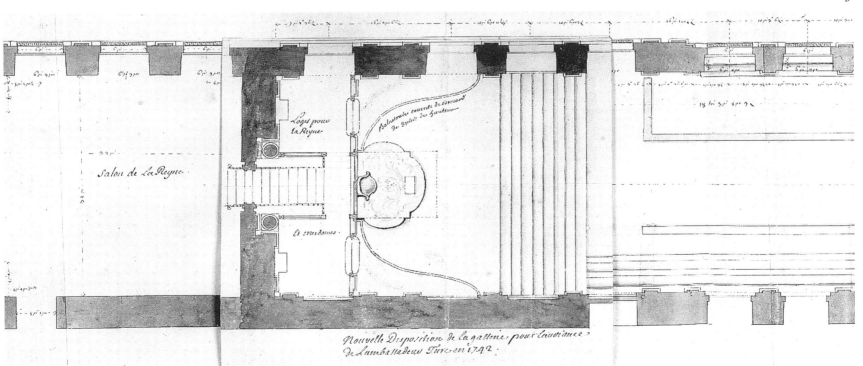

1 Bed for the Cupid Bedchamber in the Porcelain Trianon (1672). Drawing by N. Tessin the Younger. The Swedish architect visited Versailles in 1687, at which time he was shown around by Le Nôtre, Girardon and Bérain. He even witnessed the demolition of the Porcelain Trianon. This "extraordinary" bed with all its curtains, ribbons, and cardboard cherubs is one of the few items of the interior décor known to us.

2 Chapel elevation (c. 1700). Drawing.

3 Cross-section of the Chapel (c. 1700). Drawing.

3

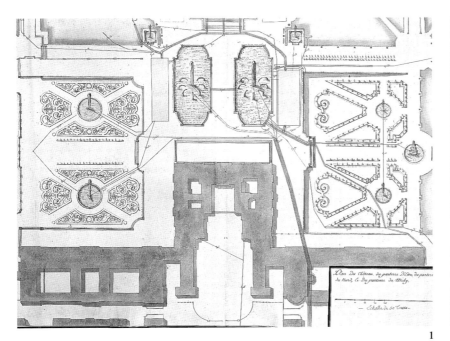

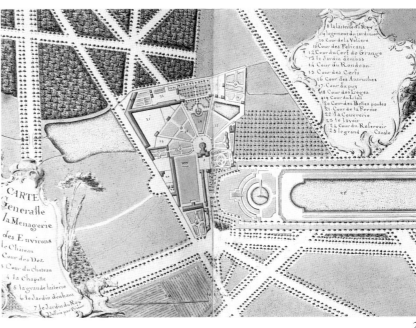

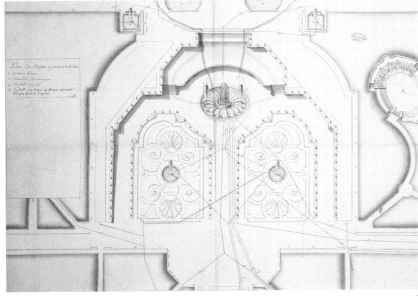

1 Map of the Château and gardens. The unevenness of the terrain obliged the planners to resort to an artificial symmetry both in their general plan and the decorative details.

1

2 Plan of the Menagerie. Until the end of the *ancien régime*, Versailles remained a country residence with a number of farms.

2

3

4

3 and 4 These drawings of the Parterre of Latona suggest the complexity of the water system installed for the most sophisticated fountain in the Versailles gardens.

5

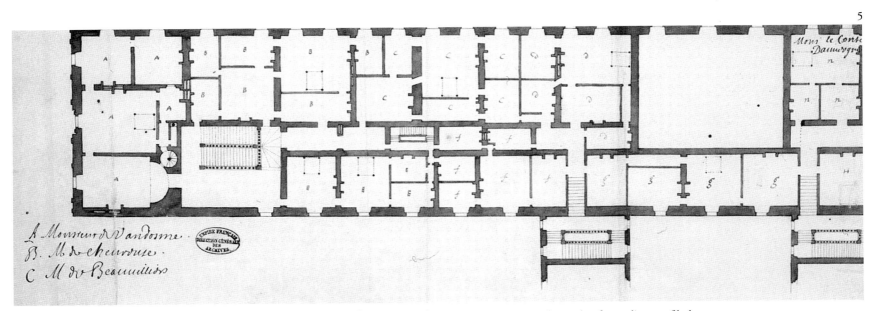

5 Plan of part of the South Wing (1680). The Château was not composed merely of grandiose enfilades. In the South Wing, the Ducs de Vendôme, Chevreuse, and Beauvilliers, as well as the Comte d'Auvergne, had the run of apartments that would be continually refitted and subdivided until the Revolution.

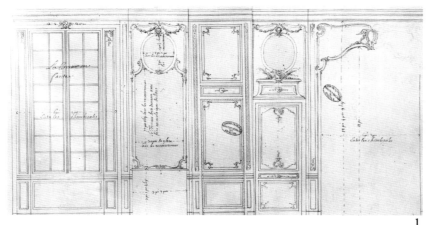

1

1 The Queen's small *cabinet* (1747). Behind the Bedchamber and Nobles' Rooms, a warren of more modest rooms was being reconfigured and refurbished for such sequential occupants as the Duchesse de Bourgogne, Marie Leszczynska, and finally Marie-Antoinette. In these intimate, private quarters, the Queens and Dauphines established their baths, poets' rooms, oratories, and libraries, using them as retreats in which to withdraw momentarily from public life.

2 Elevation of the Clock Cabinet (1738). The wall of the circular section boasted dials by the Prior of Saint-Cyr that showed the rising and setting of the sun and moon.

3 The Door to the Dauphin's Apartment in the South Wing (1671-88). The decoration of the two doors, bearing the arms of each of the occupants, is a reminder that Monseigneur left this apartment to his uncle, Monsieur (Philippe II, Duc d'Orléans) around 1685.

4 Project for the ceiling of the King's Corner Cabinet (1738).

5 Project for the Bull's-Eye Salon (1758). During alterations to the King's Bedchamber, Gabriel proposed installing a stove.

2

3

4

5

1

2

3

4

5

1 Cross-section of the King's private apartments giving onto the Stag Courtyard (1732). Above a bathroom revetted in Dutch tiles was a library with paneling carved by Le Goupil's team and a complementary suite of furniture made by the *ébéniste* Lalliée. The terrace wall at the top was painted with an illusionistic perspective.

2 Elevation of the Queen's Bedchamber. Drawing by Robert de Cotte. In 1725 the room was considerably altered for Marie Leszczynska, the daughter of King Stanislas of Poland and the bride of Louis XV. It was here that the Queen dined in private (sometimes with the King), dressed in public, died, and was laid out for burial.

3 Elevation of the Queen's Bedchamber. Drawing by Robert de Cotte (1725-35).

4 Design for the ceiling of the Queen's Bedchamber. To François Boucher would go the commission to paint the Virtues for the grisaille medallions.

5 Trellis (c. 1725). The balcony around the Queen's Courtyard was adorned with trelliswork, planters, and shrubs, as well as tiny gardens full of sweet-smelling flowers.

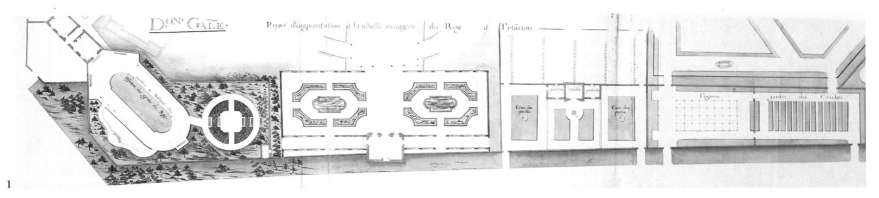

1

OPPOSITE:

5 Boxes in the former theatre (c.1748). The modest hall in the Princes' Courtyard was still in use when the Cabinet Theatre was installed on the Ambassadors' Staircase.

6 Design for the royal box at the Royal Opéra (1750-1753).

7 *Apollo in His Chariot,* a preparatory study for the ceiling of the Dauphine's Bedchamber (1770). The idea may have been to echo the treatment of the same subject in the Salon of Apollo in the King's State Apartment.

8 Elevation of the new wing pavilion (1759).
Drawing for the "Grand Project."

9 Façade of the new wing pavilion (1772).
Drawing for the "Grand Project."

2

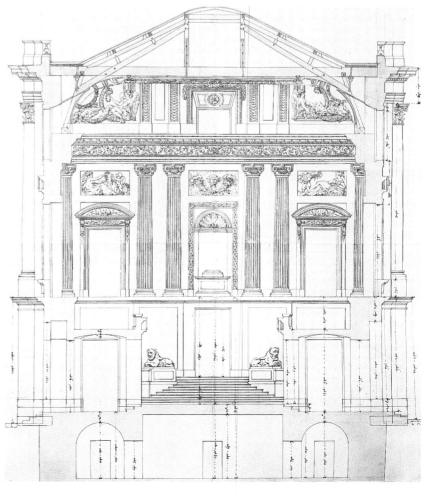

3

1 Plan for an extension to the new Trianon Menagerie (1751).
The aviary, fig orchard, and nursery garden testify to the agricultural aspect of the Trianon ensemble.

2 Map of the picturesque garden at Trianon (c. 1785). A Rousseau-like ruin and folly were planned but never built.

3 The private garden at Trianon (c. 1771-73). Gabriel altered the paths and created groves.

4 Cross-section of the Grand Staircase (1772).
Design for the "Grand Project."

4

5

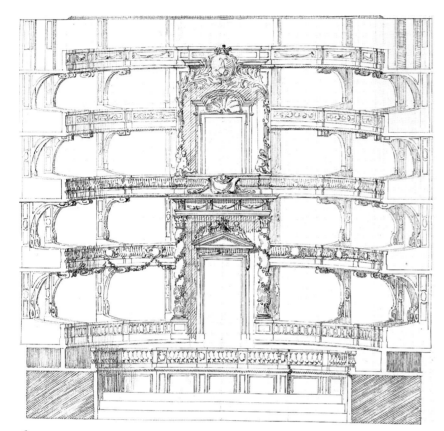

6

7

8

9

AD MAJORA VERSALIA

Although the French Revolution deprived Versailles of its political importance, Louis-Philippe gave the Château a new lease on life by turning it into a great museum. Today, tourists have replaced the old courtiers as the principal inhabitants of the greatest royal residence in Europe.

The Revolution also broke up the royal domain, so that now only the Château, the gardens or park, and Trianon claim the interest of historians, for their beauty, the quality of craftsmanship found there, or the fairy-tale life of the court itself.

A recent administrative reform (1995-1997) has redefined the limits of the Versailles domain, which now approaches the form it possessed under the *ancien régime*. Various buildings scattered throughout the town of Versailles, such as the Grand Commun, the Large and Small Stables, the Jeu de Paume, the Hôtel des Menus-Plaisirs, and the Hôtel de Madame de Pompadour, have already been reunited with the Château. They have also been liberated from some of the administrative services they once housed. The Hôtel des Menus-Plaisirs is presently home to the Music Department, whose ambitious program includes performances of ballet, opera, and tragedies from France's Classical era, all staged at the Château. One particularly memorable event was the "Lully Day" in 1988.

Similarly, the buildings and all the facilities of the Fountain Department, the water tower, the Fountain Staff House, the Filter and Spring Pavilions, and the Montbauron Reservoirs are being returned to the Domain, little by little. Moreover, the roles of the Royal Kitchen Garden and the Chèvreloup Arboretum have long been established. Facing them, near the Pool of the Swiss Guards along the Saint-Cyr Road, are stretches of land known as the Camp des Matelots and the Camp des Mortemets, both of which appear safe from building speculation, now that they have been returned to what official documents refer to as the "Versailles Public Authority."

As all this would suggest, there are good reasons for optimism. The reorganization of this vast yet fragile complex of nearly 2,500 acres will go on for about twenty years. The plans have aroused widespread interest and fired the enthusiasm of the huge, 500-member team who work under the direction of the Domain's President, Hubert Astier, and its Director-General, Pierre Arizzoli-Clementel. Various major projects lie ahead of them:

Preparing to accommodate greater numbers of visitors, which will require rearranging the collections and, if possible, organizing more itineraries to relieve the congestion in those parts of the Château most frequently visited. Not that it will ever be easy to persuade visitors to forego the splendor of the Hall of Mirrors in favor of an educational tour of Louis-Philippe's historical galleries!

Protecting and restoring the buildings, maintaining over 25 acres of roofing, replanting 250,000 trees (a task begun after the terrible storm of 1991), and modernizing the electrical heating, and water systems. Although less than glamorous, such housekeeping is essential for reasons of safety and comfort.

Utilizing refurbished structures for exhibitions and scientific gatherings related to life at court and the Château's collections. The Chapel, for instance, will be host to events involving the collection of musical instruments, and discussions are under way concerning an Equestrian Academy to be located in the Stables. The Royal Kitchen Garden (Potager du Roy), recently restored, will be a center for agricultural research, as it was under the monarchy. A center for iconographic research may be created, perhaps in the museum devoted to all the glories of France.

The perfection of Versailles was made possible by the power flowing to the Bourbons from their absolutist concept of divine-right monarchy. This made for all manner of confident decisions, which sometimes destroyed masterpieces but almost invariably replaced them with things of equal splendor. Need we therefore mourn the Ambassadors' Staircase when its loss made possible the King's private apartment? Or the Grotto of Thetis, given that we can still admire its sculpture at the Baths of Apollo? The ceaseless quest for excellence kept Versailles modern, and it must guide whatever changes may occur over the next two decades, serving as a bulwark against sensation and banality. Without a sense of quality, Versailles would be neither alive nor even fragile, but merely lifeless and inert.

SELECTED BIBLIOGRAPHY

OLD TEXTS

DANGEAU (Marquis de). *Journal, [...]* éd. Soulié et Dussieux, 19 vols., 1854-1860, Paris.

FÉLIBIEN (A.). *Description du château de Versailles, de ses peintures et d'autres ouvrages faits pour le Roy,* 1696, Paris.

LOUIS XIV. *Manière de montrer les jardins de Versailles,* annoted by S. Hoog, 1982, Paris.

MONICART (J.-B.). *Versailles immortalisé,* 1720, Paris.

PRINCESSE PALATINE. *Lettres de Madame, duchesse d'Orléans,* éd. Amiel, 1981, Paris.

PRIMI VISCONTI (J.-B.). *Mémoires sur la cour de Louis XIV,* éd. Lemoine, 1908, Paris.

SAINT-MAURICE (Marquis de). *Lettres sur la cour de Louis XIV,* éd. Lemoine, 2 vols., 1911-1912, Paris.

SAINT-SIMON (Duc de). *Mémoires,* éd. Boilisle, 41 vols., 1879-1928, Paris.

SOURCHES (Marquis de). *Mémoires du marquis de Sourches sur le règne de Louis XIV,* Cosnac et Bertrand, 13 vols., 1882-1893, Paris.

VOLTAIRE. *Le siècle de Louis XIV,* Bibliothèque de La Pléiade, 1957, Paris.

PRINTED SOURCES

ENGERAND (F.). *Inventaire des tableaux du roy rédigé en 1709 et 1710 par Nicolas Bailly,* 1899, Paris.

GALLET (D.) et BAULEZ (C.). *Archives nationales. Versailles. Dessins d'architecture de la Direction générale des Bâtiments du roi,* t. I, 1983, Paris.

GUIFFREY (J.). *Comptes des bâtiments du Roi sous le règne de Louis XIV,* 5 vols., 1881-1901, Paris.

GENERAL

BLUCHE (F.). *Louis XIV,* 1986, Paris.

BLUCHE (F.). *Dictionnaire du Grand Siècle,* 1990, Paris.

HIMELFARB (H.). "Versailles, fonctions et légendes," in *Les lieux de mémoire,* II, *La Nation,* 1986, Paris.

MEYER (D.). *Quand les rois régnaient à Versailles,* 1982, Paris.

SOUCHAL (F.). *French sculptors of the 17th and 18th centuries. The reign of Louis XIV,* 4 vols., 1977-1993, Oxford and Paris.

CHÂTEAU HISTORY

NOLHAC (P. de). *Versailles et la cour de France,* 1925-1930, 10 vols., Paris.

VERLET (P.). *Versailles,* 1961. 1985, Paris.

MARIE (A.). *Naissance de Versailles,* 1968, Paris.

MARIE (A. et J.). *Mansart à Versailles,* 1972, Paris.

MARIE (A. et J.). *Versailles au temps de Louis XIV,* 1976, Imprimerie Nationale Éditions, Paris.

MARIE (A. et J.). *Versailles au temps de Louis XV,* 1984, Imprimerie Nationale Éditions, Paris.

CATALOGUES OF THE CHÂTEAU COLLECTIONS

BAULEZ (C.) et MEYER (D.). *Le mobilier du château de Versailles,* 1998, Dijon.

CONSTANS (C.). *Musée national du château de Versailles : les peintures,* 3 vols., 1995, Paris.

HOOG (S.). *Musée national du château de Versailles : les sculptures,* vol. I, 1993, Paris.

OPINION

APOSTOLIDÈS (J.-M.). *Le Roi-machine, spectacle et politique au temps de Louis XIV,* 1981, Paris.

BEAUSSANT (P.). *Les plaisirs de Versailles. Théâtre et musique,* 1996, Paris.

GUILLOU (E.). *Versailles, ou le palais du Soleil,* 1963, Paris.

MOINE (M.-C.). *Les fêtes à la cour du Roi-Soleil,* 1984, Paris.

NÉRAUDAU (J.-P.). *L'Olympe du Roi-Soleil. Mythologie et idéologie royale au Grand Siècle,* 1986, Paris.

SAULE (B.). *Versailles et les tables royales en Europe,* 1993, Paris.

THUILLIER (J.). *Charles Le Brun, 1619-1690, peintre et dessinateur,* 1963, Paris.

DETAILLED STUDIES

CONSTANS (C.). *La galerie des Batailles,* 1984, Paris and Beirut.

CONSTANS (C.). *Charles Le Brun (1619-1690). Le décor de l'escalier des Ambassadeurs,* 1990, Paris.

GAEHTGENS (T.-W.). *Versailles, de la résidence royale au musée historique,* 1984, Paris.

LABLAUDE (P.-A.). *Les jardins de Versailles,* 1995, Milan.

LEDOUX-LEBARD (D.). *Le Petit Trianon,* 1989, Paris.

LEDOUX-LEBARD (D.). *Le Grand Trianon, meubles et objets d'art,* 1975, Paris.

Le Repas chez Simon. Véronèse. Histoire et restauration d'un chef-d'œuvre, 1997, Paris. (Ouvrage collectif).

SCHNAPPER (A.). *Tableaux pour le Trianon de marbre,* 1967, Paris.

SALMON (X.). *Versailles : Les chasses exotiques de Louis XV,* 1995, Paris.

POPULAR WORKS

CONSTANS (C.). *Versailles, château de la France et orgueil des rois,* 1989, Paris.

SAULE (B.). *Versailles triomphant. Une journée de Louis XIV,* 1996, Paris.

Photo credits

All photographs by Jean MOUNICQ except:

© Château de Versailles, cl. Jean-Marc Manaï : pp. 19, 25, 26, 28-29, 30, 36, 37, 39, 49, 63, 69, 76, 77, 87, 88, 117, 135, 148, 149, 155, 156, 171, 220, 221, 225, 229, 232, 239, 242, 250-251.

© Réunion des Musées Nationaux : pp. 35, 48, 163 (Compiègne), 186 (Versailles and Trianon).

© Galerie Cailleux : p. 40.

© Artephot : pp. 112, 256.

© Photothèque des Musées de la Ville de Paris : pp. 114, 115.

© Frédéric Pitchal (Versailles) : pp. 45, 64, 86, 92, 132, 133, 144, 150, 160, 161, 165, 206-207, 212.

© Frédéric Pitchal (Archives Nationales) : pp. 108 et 109 (O^1 1792), 199 (O^1 1786).

APPENDICES:

© Bulloz/Bibliothèque de l'Institut : p. 265 (1).

© Bibliothèque Nationale : p. 267 (1).

© Stockholm, Nationalmuseum, Coll. Tessin-Hårleman : p. 268 (1).

© Frédéric Pitchal (Versailles) : pp. 269 (2), 272 (2).

© Frédéric Pitchal (Archives Nationales) : pp. 265 (2, 3 and 4. O^1 1768), p. 266 (1. O^1 1776 ; 2. O^1 1768 ; 3. O^1 1768 ; 4. O^1 1770), p. 267 (2 and 3. O^1 1772), p. 268 (2 and 3. O^1 1783), p. 269 (1, 3, 4 and 5. O^1 1783), p. 270 (1. O^1 1773 ; 2. O^1 1772 ; 3. O^1 1768 ; 4. O^1 1773 ; 5. O^1 1770), p. 271 (1. O^1 1768 ; 2, 3, 4 and 5. O^1 1773), p. 272 (1 and 3. . O^1 1887 ; 4. O^1 1777), p. 273 (5 and 6. O^1 1788 ; 7. O^1 1773 ; 8. O^1 1770 ; 9. O^1 1777).

The plans on pages 260-264 were produced by André Leroux.

ACKNOWLEDGMENTS

The authors would like to express their gratitude
to everyone who has helped in preparing
and producing this book.

At the Imprimerie Nationale, special thanks go to
Jean-Marc Dabadie, Director of Publications;
Lucile Theveneau, Editor;
Régine Gourmel, Production Manager;
Françoise Fiquet-Carmignac and Guy Le Roux,
for their careful proofreading.

At the Archives Nationales, further thanks go to
Jean Favier, Member of the Institut de France;
Nicole Felkay, head curator;
and Martine Constans, head curator.

Jean Mounicq would like to thank Jacqueline Gorne,
of the Arka Laboratory, for her control of color quality.

At the Vendome Press special thanks go to
Daniel Wheeler for his meticulous editing
and rewriting of the English translation.

Design and layout: Hélène Lévi
Cartography: André Leroux
Jacket design: Marc Walter

Published in the USA in 1998 by
The Vendome Press
1370 Avenue of the Americas
New York, NY 10019

Distributed in the USA and Canada by
Rizzoli International Publications
through St. Martin's Press
175 Fifth Avenue, New York, NY 10010

Library of Congress Cataloging-in-Publication Data
Babelon, Jean Pierre.
    Versailles : absolutism and harmony / Jean Pierre Babelon, Claire Constans.
    p.   cm.
    Includes bibliographical references.
    ISBN 0-86565-150-7
    1. Château de Versailles (Versailles, France)—Pictorial works.
    2. Louis XIV, King of France, 1638-1715—Art patronage.
    3. Versailles (France)—Buildings, structures, etc.—History.
    4. Gardens—France—Versailles—Pictorial works.   I. Constans, Claire. II. Title.
    DC801.V56B33 1998
    944'.366- -dc21
                                          98-21312
                                            CIP

Printed and bound in France

This book is printed in Garamond Book
on Consort Royal Silk 170 grams

Color separations by the Imprimerie Nationale

Printing completed in September 1998
on the presses of the Imprimerie Nationale
under the direction of its president, Jean-Luc Vialla